A

HISTORY

—— *of* ——

WATER

ALSO BY EDWARD WILSON-LEE

Shakespeare in Swahililand
The Catalogue of Shipwrecked Books

A

HISTORY

—— *of* ——

WATER

*Being an Account of
a Murder, an Epic
and Two Visions of
Global History*

EDWARD WILSON-LEE

**WILLIAM
COLLINS**

William Collins
An imprint of HarperCollins*Publishers*
1 London Bridge Street
London SE1 9GF

WilliamCollinsBooks.com

HarperCollins*Publishers*
Macken House, 39/40 Mayor Street Upper,
Dublin1, D01 C9W8, Ireland

First published in Great Britain in 2022 by William Collins

2

Maps by Martin Brown

A catalogue record for this book is
available from the British Library

ISBN 978-0-00-835822-8

Set in Minion Pro
Printed and bound in the UK using 100%
renewable electricity at CPI Group (UK) Ltd

MIX
Paper | Supporting
responsible forestry
FSC
www.fsc.org   FSC™ C007454

This book is produced from independently certified FSC™ paper
to ensure responsible forest management.

For more information visit: www.harpercollins.co.uk/green

For Gabriel and Ambrose
descifradores

TABLE OF CONTENTS

MAPS

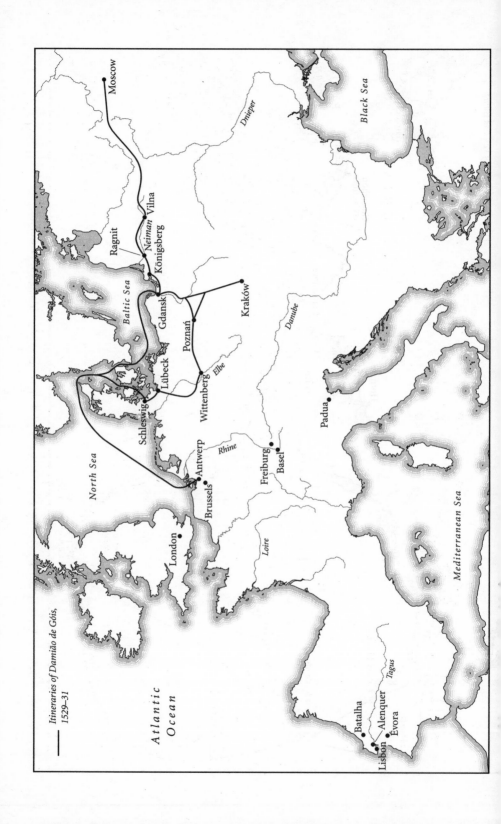

Itineraries of Damião de Góis,
1529–31

Moscow

Dnieper

Black Sea

Vilna
Neiman
Ragnit
Königsberg

Baltic Sea

Gdansk
Poznań
Kraków
Lübeck
Elbe
Schleswig
Wittenberg
Danube

Antwerp
Rhine
Freiburg
Padua
Brussels
Basel

London

Loire

North Sea

Atlantic
Ocean

Mediterranean Sea

Batalha
Tagus
Alenquer
Lisbon
Évora

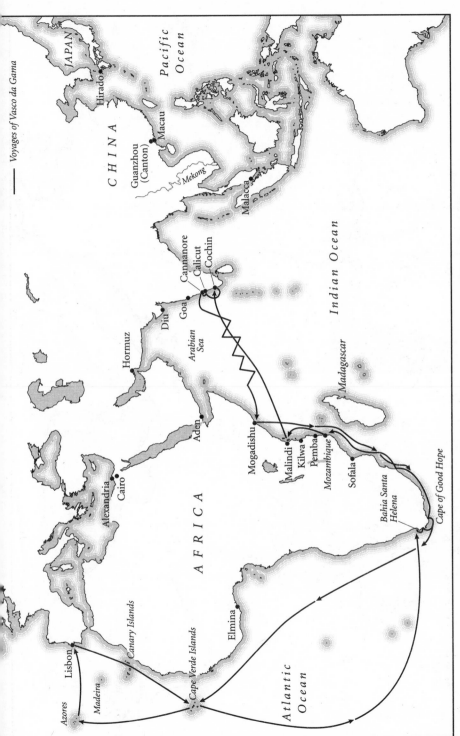

A map showing the route of Vasco da Gama's first voyage to India, as well as sites associated with Luís Vaz de Camões.

A NOTE ON QUOTATIONS AND
PORTUGUESE PRONUNCIATION

Following early modern practice, I have used italics in this text to represent direct quotations, the source for which can be found in the endnotes.

The tilde (ã, õ, etc.) found in many Portuguese words represents an 'n' that was once part of the word but which is no longer pronounced. The effect is that of someone beginning to pronounce an 'n' but then thinking better of it and carrying on, such that the name 'Damião' (equivalent to 'Damian') rhymes with 'meow'.

I returned, and saw under the sun, that the race is not to the swift, nor the battle to the strong, neither yet bread to the wise, nor yet riches to men of understanding, nor yet favour to the men of skill: but time and chance happeneth to them all.
ECCLESIASTES 9.11

When the ship parts from the quay
And feels again the space that opens
Between the ship and quay
A fresh pain comes over me – I don't know why,
A mist-bank of regret
Which shines in the sun of my reawakened pain
Like the first window on which the dawn breaks
And engulfs me like the memory of someone else
Who was mysteriously mine.
ÁLVARO DE CAMPOS, *Ode Marítima*

Some say that the soul is mixed in the whole universe. Perhaps that is why Thales thought that everything was full of gods.
ARISTOTLE, *On the Soul*, trans. Kirk & Raven

All mankind is of one author, and is one volume; when one man dies, one chapter is not torn out of the book, but translated into a better language; and every chapter must be so translated; God employs several translators; some pieces are translated by age, some by sickness, some by war, some by justice; but God's hand is in every translation, and his hand shall bind up all our scattered leaves again for that library where every book shall lie open to one another.
JOHN DONNE, *Devotions upon Emergent Occasions*

I

A Death in the Archive

It was in the last days of January 1574 that Damião de Góis began his slow transformation into paper. This ending would not, perhaps, have come as a particular surprise to a man who had spent his life among documents, as *Guarda-mor* in charge of the Portuguese royal archive. He was entered into the register of his parish church in the village of Alenquer, a half-day's journey from Lisbon, the sacristan's split-quill pen catching on the fibrous paper as he wrote that *on the thirtieth day of the month of January of the year 1574 Damião de Góis died and was buried in the chapel of this church.* The sacristan added further, underlining the words that note an unusually quick burial, that *in truth it was the same day and month and year as above.* It is fortunate that the register is so exact about the timings, as the tombstone Damião had commissioned for his own burial was wrong – gave a date, in fact, of more than a decade earlier. Many have looked for the body that was buried that day without success, and what remains of Damião de Góis is only paper: as well as the entry in the church register, he was folded into a letter that made its way to northern Europe with an account of his death, dispersed across Europe in unnumbered signed copies, found crumpled into a notebook that was discovered in the Lisbon archive some 200 years later. These documents may explain the sacristan's muted alarm, as a number of them suggest that the king's archivist was the victim of a most peculiar murder.

The pieces of Damião's death do not match up. One of the accounts suggests that he was stopping at an inn on the last night of his life, and that at the end of the evening he had sent his servants to bed, himself staying up next to the fire to ward off the midwinter cold and *reading a certain piece of paper.* Then something transpired in the illegible night. The report says that his body was found burned the next morning, though the description glances aside from the macabre scene to note that he was still clutching part of the same piece of paper he had been reading the night before, even if the rest of it had been consumed by the flames. The body is at the centre of the scene, holding all else around it in suspense with the newness of it being a mere object; yet it was the curious survival of the paper that caught the observer's attention, less fragile (it seems) than Damião's life. The report hesitates to say for sure what had taken place, when the shadows were dancing like moths at the edge of the fire, with the spit and pop of the wood, in the sough of the night's expanse. Instead, the testimony speculates that *this undoing came either from falling asleep or some incident that deprived him of his senses.* A slightly later anecdote also records his death by burns to his face and chest, head and arms, and suggests that his end significantly coincided with a day of *auto-da-fé* in Lisbon, the fires in which heretics were burned.[1]

A third report does not mention the fire at all, and in fact suggests that Damião's death took place at home. But it is also less cautious in its explanation of the events. While it allows for the possibility that the archivist may have died of *apoplexy* – a contemporary term for stroke or other sudden death – it proposes that he may rather have been killed by thieving servants, using the Latin term *suffocatus*, which can mean either strangled or drowned.

Clues regarding the events of that January night are scattered across archives in Lisbon, Antwerp, Rome, Venice and Goa, pieces of a man whose life was tied up with records. The archive Damião himself oversaw was barricaded inside a tower of Lisbon's hilltop Castelo de São Jorge, a site that had been Roman and then Arabic and then the stronghold of the Portuguese crown, though it had now largely been abandoned by the court, as the royal family preferred to live in the more modern riverside palace. Damião lived only a short distance from this Torre do Tombo – Tower of Records – in apartments that overlooked the Casa do Espírito Santo where residents of the castle attended church services. The building in which he lived no longer stands, having like much of Lisbon succumbed to the violent earthquake that shattered the city in 1755 and the series of fires and tidal waves that followed. But the tower itself remains, now empty but once the storehouse of Portugal's memory, a darkened chamber in which all the secrets of the kingdom were kept. To those unfamiliar with the archive, it might well have seemed no more than a farrago of mouldering papers; but this puzzle box, in which each document could spring a lock or lead to a dead end, offered enormous power to those who knew its technique. The legends of China and Vietnam, cultures that Europe was encountering for the first time during Damião's youth, are filled with archivists who can change a person's fate by cancelling half a line in the right ledger, and the Torre do Tombo was exactly the place where such witchcraft could occur.[2]

Damião had been exiled from his archive a short time before his death, though of course he would return to haunt the tower in the form of documents about his life. Some of these hold the rumours about him that were circulating in his final years, and which were a matter of scandal even to his near acquaintance. Among the charges were accusations that he had taken part in sacrilegious feasts on more than one occasion, had broken bread with the most dangerous men in Europe, that he had communed with them in his library even when they were absent or dead, and that all the while he had made a show of piety, to the mockery of the Church. Further rumours deepened the shadow in which he lived. These included a complaint that he had caused an image of Christ to be bathed in pig's fat and brine, perhaps even urinated upon, and that unsettling music had been heard coming from his apartments in the castle. The Inquisition, spurred on by an informant whose identity was unknown to Damião – at least to begin with – had also looked closely into his collection of art, which included paintings of strange and unheard-of things, pictures that forgot the difference between men and beasts and objects, so it was not clear where one began and the other ended.[3]

While every death happens to a single person and yet brings to an end a whole world that was theirs, a very few like Damião's also stretch out across much of the globe. If he ended his life in the archive, it was only after a youth that traversed much of Europe, including many corners rarely visited by those from the west, travels during which he showed the uncanny knack of finding himself present at the epicentre of the controversies of the age. Nor was the retreat to the archive an act of cutting himself off from the world, for the tower where he had served as *Guarda-mor* or Chief Keeper had long since ceased to be a local affair. Some of the most precious documents were older than the country itself and spoke of its foundation in 1139; but after the Portuguese carried the war against their former Arab masters across the straits of Gibraltar in 1415, documents began to flow back to the archive from the Maghreb. From that point on, and as the Portuguese ships pushed down along the coast of western Africa and into the Indian Ocean, the Torre do Tombo became an increasingly global repository of information. By the time that Damião began his work there, packets arrived daily from everywhere from Jesuit missions in Japan to trading factories in the *Terra da Santa Cruz* (colloquially known as 'Brazil' for its main product, a wood that produced red dye). In between there was a Portuguese presence throughout south Asia and the shores of Africa, in Macau, Siam, Malacca, Bengal, Coromandel, Gujarat, Persia, Hormuz, Ethiopia, the Swahili Coast, the *Isla San Lourenço* (Madagascar), Mozambique, the Cape, Benin and the Maghreb, as well as the Cape Verde, Canary, Madeira and Azores islands.

Portugal both initiated European traffic with most of these places and also remained for much of the sixteenth century the primary conduit between Europe and a greater part of the world. This meant that the Torre do Tombo was not only Portugal's paper memory of its own origins, but also served as the central clearing house for Europe's awareness of a world beyond itself – a *universal record*, as one contemporary account put it. This was knowledge that could only be transmitted and stored in written form, given the distances involved and the scale and variety of information. It was an archive in the fullest sense – drawing on the dual origins of the word as a place of safekeeping and a tool of power – but one that also teetered on the brink of anarchy, powerless to keep in order the world that was growing around it. Europe's ability to conceive of an earth that dwarfed in size and variety all it had until recently known was heavily dependent on what was sent to, retained within and released from the tower. For perhaps the first time in history, the shuffling of papers determined the shape of the world.[4]

While the age was witness to many marvellous encounters, in some ways it is stranger that, five centuries after traffic between Europe and the broader world commenced in earnest, the cultures of Africa and Asia and the New World are still largely unfamiliar to most Europeans. The opening of trade channels also brought a flood of information about the gods, heroes, lives and thoughts of people elsewhere, and for a brief moment it may have seemed as if all the world would flow together. We know that this did not happen: Victorian schoolchildren did not learn Chinese and Arabic, the stories of Rama and Sita were not in the mouths of the urchins of Munich, the politicians of Madrid did not model themselves after the queens of Madagascar. We live in the middle of a global marketplace, but our cultures remain startlingly parochial and fearful of the outside. That this is the case is not surprising to us, but perhaps it should be. What strange magic can make people unfamiliar to each other for so long? The history of this period is also the history of a moment when it might have been otherwise, when we might have become global but didn't, and presents us with a mystery as to why this is so. In the pages that follow, the contending impulses of curiosity and distrust will play out within the global lives and crossing paths of several figures who were there as the newly connected world was torn apart.[5]

Telling these stories requires an immersion in the archive itself, an understanding of its strange ways and its unusual practices. The later history of the Portuguese archives has contributed to the difficulties of navigating their holdings, for as well as being decimated by earthquake, fire and flood, they were pilfered shortly after Damião's time by the Spanish for their own archive at Simancas, and portions of those remaining in Lisbon were later moved to save them from Napoleon's approaching armies, while still others were taken to Brazil during the displacement of the Portuguese monarchy in the early nineteenth century. What hope is there, then, of shedding light on these questions surrounding the death of one old man some four centuries in the past – however intriguing they might be? The possible motives of servants for murdering him; whether a man can fall asleep into a fire without waking those asleep elsewhere in the house; whether he was burned, or strangled, or both; how a conflagration could burn a man but not the paper he was holding; the significance of one charred document among a whole world of papers. There is as much hope of discovering these things as of finding a single event in a universal record – and yet that is precisely what the archive is designed to do.[6]

Any hope of answering these questions lies through the puzzle box of the archive. This is not, however, a puzzle with only one solution; instead it presents myriad ways of proceeding, and leads to a different chamber depending on the choices made. If the chambers of the archive could be used as a fortress, they could also be used as a hiding place. Though archives were first constructed to safeguard the instruments of power and hide the secret workings of the state, the same archives can be reconfigured for other uses, as collections of the curious and the troubling, an ark for the voices of the accused, or a locker for crime scenes immaculately preserved down the course of centuries. Understanding the world in which Damião died on that January night requires opening up a lost history, one in whose shadow we are still living and in which a vast number are implicated.

II

Neither Fish nor Flesh

In the early months of 1554, Damião de Góis sat among his piles of paper and despaired. As if it were not enough that, as *Guarda-mor* of the Portuguese royal archive, he was expected to receive, sort and store a vast number of documents in confounding variety, tradition also assigned to the post the thankless and unending task of turning this maelstrom of papers into official chronicles of the realm. Damião's detailed researches revealed how many archivists had been defeated by this undertaking. It had begun well enough, when a distinguished predecessor had written histories of each reign from the founder king Afonso Henriques (1139) down to the capture of Ceuta (1415), Portugal's first overseas territory. Having reached that point in the mid-fifteenth century, a curse had settled upon the task that had not lifted since. Several attempts to continue the chronicles had failed to tie the myriad happenings together, producing in the end only accounts of isolated events; and even these few fragments had been borrowed by someone who took them to Italy and never brought them back. Attempts to reconstruct these lost volumes had proved fruitless. The task of covering the late fifteenth-century period considered by many to be Portugal's golden age, when its ships crept in stages down the coast of western Africa and opened routes to India and Brazil that were soon heavily travelled, had been an even greater curse to Damião's predecessors. It had consumed the life of one *Guarda-mor*, who had passed both the post and his incomplete chronicle to his son, who likewise died leaving the task unfinished. The next person assigned to work on the chronicle simply declined the honour, and when the fragmentary draft was handed on to Damião he found it in such disarray that he decided it would be easier to start again rather than fix the mess he inherited. He noted with some chagrin the opulent rings one of his predecessors had received as a bribe to write well of certain statesmen; the rings were long gone, but Damião still had to do the writing. Faced with the frustration of it all, he decided to begin with something else instead, something more manageable, something (he said) he could fit into the hours between his official duties – a description of the city of Lisbon, which spread out beneath the battlements of the Torre do Tombo.[1]

Damião's plan for his *Description of the City of Lisbon* was simple: moving upriver from where the Rio Tejo (or Tagus) flows into the ocean below Sintra, he would describe the northern shore as it passed the riverine fortress of the Torre de Belém and approached the city walls, and then follow the walls 7,000 paces around as they traced the knuckles of Lisbon's five hills, before reaching the river again on the eastern side of the city. At that point he would enter through the easternmost of the city's seventeen land-facing gates and describe the most notable of Lisbon's more than 22,000 buildings. This sensible plan, however, was brought up short almost at the beginning, when, at the mouth of the river, he paused to make an extended study of the sea caves and of the mermen who inhabited them. As a witness to the strange dignity of these marine people, he wrote down the account of a local fisherman who had met with one such creature when fishing off the Bárbaro Promontório, to the south of the estuary, remarking on how even to this day the man would give a delightful telling of the story to anyone who would listen. While the fisherman was taking his hook and line one day down past the Hermitage of Santa Maria, there suddenly leapt from the waves on to the rocks a merman or triton with beard and hair flowing and intertwined, and though his chest was strangely crumpled his face was well made and his features otherwise just like a man. In the fisherman's words, the two sat for some time in the sunshine inspecting each other cautiously, before the merman took fright at something and with an all-too-human yelp dived back beneath the salt waves.

Damião had also tracked down another fisherman's story, this time of a naked boy found eating raw the catch that was being kept fresh in a rock pool. When he was seen, he took flight laughing and also disappeared back under the water. These sea people had been encountered (Damião noted) as long ago as the Roman emperor Tiberius: reports had been sent to Rome from this distant outpost of the empire of a triton or merman who was spotted blowing on his shell, in a cave where the waves are sucked in and clash to roar exploding out. Damião had a magpie-like fascination for the strange, for the vast and astonishing realms that might lie beneath the mirror-surface of the water. In the bowels of the archive Damião had even found a contract three centuries old which reserved to the kings of Portugal the right to tax anyone who caught one of these citizens of the sea.[2]

Having satisfied his curiosity in this respect, Damião finally moved on towards the city, reaching the walls at the Old Palace of Santos-o-Velho, and starting from there the first climb of the swooping city.

Attempting to give the lay of the land to his readers, Damião suggested that, from the opposite bank of the Tejo, Lisbon would appear to have the shape of a fish's swim bladder: the bottom of the oval tracing a long smooth line along the riverbank, while along the scalloped top a great building crested each hill – São Roque, Santa Ana, the castle of São Jorge from which Damião wrote, and Nossa Senhora da Graça. When the ocean clouds sailed up the

Overleaf: *Map of Lisbon*, possibly based on Damião's description, by Braun and Hogenberg, first published in *Civitates Orbis Terrarum*, Vol. V (1598).

Tejo unchecked, the rain unspooled like grey chains from the skies onto these hills, turning the streets into channels as it washed down their slopes, and causing one Dutch visitor of the time to make a particular note of how hard it was to walk on the slick cobbles in a Lisbon downpour.[3]

After tracing the outline of the capital, Damião began to fill it in, putting in pride of place the two great charitable institutions of the city, the Church of the Misericórdia and the Hospital of Todos-os-Santos, which between them provided 24,000 *ducados* to the poor each year, gave beds to the sick and needy, and even put some money in their pockets when they were well enough to leave. Along with these he described the public granary, established by a benevolent crown to make sure the city never went hungry, and the many public fountains that gave spring water to the citizens of Lisbon. Damião paused to record tasting notes for the different fountains: though the waters emerge slightly warm and cloudy, they soon settle into a clear and refreshing drink. The fountains continued to be referred to by the Arabic term *chafariz*, and each was distinguished by a name: the *chafariz* of the king, for horses, and so on. These gushed out of the hillsides down onto Lisbon's beating heart: the quays on the river frontage, great open spaces where the world could gather, framed by the symbols of Portugal's sudden power: the royal Paço da Ribeira (River Palace) with its new tower from which the kings could watch the fleets arriving from across the world, the armoury, and the great customs houses built to receive the goods from northern Africa, western Africa and the east – the Ceuta House, the Mina House and the India House.

Lisbon had always traded on its position as halfway between the rest of the world. The taking of the city from its Muslim residents in 1147 had only been possible because a fleet of Crusaders, on their way from northern Europe to the Holy Land, had stopped in the Tejo estuary to restock, and Lisbon remained a regular way station for pilgrims shipping to Jerusalem. (We owe most of our knowledge of the siege to the writings of an English clerk named

Osbert, whose account was pilfered from a priory during the Reformation and ended up in a Cambridge college library.) There were even suggestions in classical sources that the very name of the city – *Olisipo* in Latin – was a corruption of 'Ulysses' (the Latin for Odysseus), and was so named because the silver-tongued and wandering Greek had founded the town on his meandering return from Troy, suggestions to which Damião was romantically partial. Lisbon and its vast river estuary had always provided an ideal midpoint where the north and south could mingle, a convenient place for ships to meet between the great markets of northern Europe, where England and Germany were served by the ports of Antwerp and Amsterdam, and the great markets of the Mediterranean, where goods coming from Alexandria and Istanbul passed through Venice and Genoa. This continental trade passed through Lisbon's New Custom House (Alfandega Nova) and spilled outside into the square, where the local raw materials could be mixed with imports to line the city. Damião listed the traders who filled the square every day: confectioners, fruitsellers, butchers, bakers, candymakers, and weavers. Chief among them though were the fishmongers, whose trade was so great that they had to rent a basket in order to sell there at the prince's ransom of 2,000 *ducados* a year.[4]

The thriving trade with other European ports, however, had been eclipsed during the course of the fifteenth century as goods began to flow in with the Portuguese ships returning from Africa and eventually from Persia, India and beyond. It was to process this trade that the Houses of Ceuta, Mina and India were built, and the fact that they flanked the royal River Palace marked a development of singular importance. While most other European monarchies remained stubbornly attached to royal and noble traditions, in which status depended on owning land and leading the men who worked it, the Portuguese crown had taken an early interest in the possibilities of trade, financing exploratory voyages and reserving for themselves royal monopolies in the most important products. If even the greatest of them, the very King Manuel whose chronicle Damião was supposed to be writing, was sneered at as a *grocer king* by the disdainful royals of the north, the shame was likely assuaged by the extraordinary profits swiftly accruing from these ventures. Damião had even responded to these sneers with a detailed inventory of all the things that passed through the harbour of Lisbon. Beginning with western Africa, goods from which were received at the Mina House, he noted gold, cotton and ebony, cow and goat skins, rice and 'grains of paradise', or malagueta – a citrusy red peppercorn that was less popular with Europeans than black pepper as it did not stand up well to cooking. The best sugar was brought from Brazil, along with the Brazil-wood that became synonymous with its place of origin. From India and China there was silk, ginger, nutmeg and the flowers of the same plant, camphor, cinnamon, tamarind, rhubarb and 'myrobalan' (prunes). The houses of the city were panelled with Sarmatian wood from the Black Sea, and pearls and *guayacán* bark flowed through Seville from the Americas. These remnants of plant and animal life, sprung up from the soil far away before being harvested, handled and preserved for shipping, are in many cases unfamiliar to us now, though they were to play a strange and central part in Damião's life.[5]

Not all goods arrived in Lisbon as raw material, to be transformed and finished for European tastes. Also on Damião's list are cloaks and headdresses made of bird feathers by the peoples of Brazil and the Canary Islands, palm-fibre cloths woven into arresting garments in western Africa, gold and silver vessels made in India and China, as well as Chinese porcelain, which he believed to be made from powdered seashells and was supposed to have been buried underground for eighty to a hundred years to age. It is perhaps no surprise that this wondrous fabrication made from strange life and deep time could sell at fifty, sixty or even a hundred *ducados* apiece, though there were also cheaper varieties which were making chinaware an everyday thing in wealthier households. Damião was later to recall with wonder the bark cloths sent from the kingdom of Kongo shortly after he arrived at court, which could hardly be told from silk unless you were right up close. Growing up as a page in the king's wardrobe, Damião had been given charge of some of the most unusual pieces that arrived from around the world, such as the immense felt turban sent from Shah Ismail of Persia. Perhaps the greatest treasures were the ivories that arrived from Benin and Sierra Leone, vessels and sculptures so artfully made that Damião pauses in his inventory to remark upon them. These masterpieces of western African art, a few dozen of which still survive scattered through the museums of the world, are almost unbearably eloquent in the witness they bear to these initial encounters. From the sides of these salt-cellars and 'oliphants' – hunting horns made from elephant tusks – peer the faces of the Portuguese as they were seen by the artists of Benin: bulging eyes, spade-like beards, beak noses, and attached to their screaming horses like some kind of hybrid beast. Their bodies are obscured by chainmail, brocaded cloth, ruffs, helmets and necklaces, a strange animal carrying about with it the collected matter of the world.[6]

Many things that arrived on Lisbon's docks were still living. Carried along in the ships with the spices and worked materials, and noted in Damião's careful inventory, were also parrots, macaques and sable cats. During his youth in the city there had also been five or six elephants and a rhinoceros. He was later to dwell at great length on these animals in his chronicles, filling both columns of six pages with several thousand words about the intelligence of elephants. The longest description is reserved for an event that took place in 1515 in Ribeira Square, across from the Mina and India Houses, when a specially constructed arena was built to test an idea inherited from classical antiquity – namely, that the rhinoceros and the elephant were inveterate enemies. They were brought together in the ring, and the rhino, straining at its chain, pushed forward to smell the elephant, stirring up the dust and hay with urgent breaths from its nostrils. The elephant was faced away from it but turned towards the rhinoceros as it approached, alarm blasting from its trunk in what the audience took to be a sign it was about to attack. But as the rhinoceros drew close to the elephant's belly, the elephant bolted in alarm, bending the close-set bars of the metal gate and escaping along the embankment towards the river houses, leaving behind the mahout who had been riding on its back, stunned and lucky not to have been brained during the escape. From there it took the Caminho dos Estaus inland, making such havoc as a battalion in retreat. The elephant was returning to its home, its paddock near the Old Palace of Estaus, and seemed to know the way.[7]

What is remarkable about Damião's detailed account of that day is his attempt to read meaning into the noises and actions of the elephant, imagining its motives as he would those of a person – the proud defiance of a warrior, the desire for home in a moment of terror. He was to come across many more strange characters in the archive, when he should have been chronicling the glories of the Portuguese crown, and in his encounters he often exercised this same characteristic impulse, a reflexive desire to widen the boundaries of personhood. It was, however, an impulse that was countered in the period by a powerful movement in the other direction, a drive to restrict the number of those who deserved that humane treatment owed to creatures of one's own nature. Damião's unusual ability to imagine sea people and elephants as persons, understandable in the same terms he would understand himself, makes it all the more sorrowful that his inventory should pass in just a few words over one part of the traffic seen at the docks in Lisbon – slaves. One foreign visitor commented that there were so many black people on the streets of Portuguese cities that they resembled chessboards, as many black figures as white; and

Opposite: 'Rhinoceros', by Albrecht Dürer, a posthumous portrait of the rhinoceros Damião saw in Lisbon in 1515.

RHINOCERVS

while there were freemen, the majority were slaves. Damião's list records that every year there came from Nigeria 10,000–12,000 slaves, in addition to those who came from Mauretania, India and Brazil. He notes that they would fetch ten, twenty, forty and fifty gold *ducados* apiece, but with no more emotion than when speaking of the Chinese porcelain which fetched the same prices. Indeed, there is little distinction made between this and the other kind of 'black gold' on which the Portuguese fortune was built – pepper, the trade in which was reserved to the king. Two thousand tons of pepper a year, bringing in over a million *ducados*; 12,000 souls, bringing in slightly less than half of that. A visitor of the period remarked that *when one of them is a girl and she is carrying a baby from abroad that baby belongs now to the master who bought her and not to its father*, and that the men were made to run races along the dock to show their fitness, but Damião is silent on this. His reticence is even more striking in that, as his life will attest, he was one of the few who saw Europe's expanding horizons as a wonderful broadening of the meaning of humanity, a view which set him in perilous opposition to those who felt every difference as a threat. While there is no evidence to suggest that Damião owned any slaves himself, he lived like most others of his age in a tragic labyrinth, where even a capacious moral imagination is coupled with blindness to the inhumanity near at hand.[8]

Among the manifold horrors of slavery, perhaps not the least was the silence to which these people were condemned. The vast majority of them arrived with no knowledge of Portuguese, much less any literacy, and of course the system of slavery sought to change this as little as possible, in part by sustaining a belief that slaves had no capacity for learning. If the Dutch humanist Nicholas Clenardus, arriving in the 1530s to spread techniques of Humanist learning in Portugal, acquired two 'Ethiopian' slaves and taught them Latin, this was only to demonstrate his miraculous powers of instruction by training those believed to be unteachable. It was, however, far from the case that everyone arriving from beyond

Christian Europe came as a slave, and among Damião's earliest memories, found scattered within his writings, are records of the world he met in Lisbon itself, besides all those he would meet in his travels abroad: Brahmins, Armenians, a Chinese interpreter, Moroccans, a merchant from Hormuz they called 'Cojebequi' (Khwaja Beg), the homesick heir to the Kongolese throne, an Ethiopian priest. Only a few years after he had arrived at the royal court as a page, Damião had been present near the elephant stables when a Brazil-wood merchant presented to the king three men who had come with the ships returning across the Atlantic. The sight of these Tupinambá men brought the things of their world to life: they were wearing the same feather garments which were found for sale in the India House, and their lips, noses and ears were hung with jewels and pendants made of bone and an amber-like tree gum, a majestic regalia that can be seen in the *Adoration of the Magi* of the same period by Grão Vasco, whose Tupinambá 'King Balthazar' provides the first European portrait of a South American. Each of the men Damião saw had a bow made of the same Brazil-wood, and arrows made of cane, fletched with feathers and tipped with fishbone, weapons of which they were masters but which, according to a new myth being told among the Tupinambá and Guaraní peoples, was the relic of a fatal choice: when given their pick of all weapons by the gods they had chosen wooden over iron arms for their lightness, leaving to the Europeans the engines of their misery. The king spoke to them through their interpreters and asked for a demonstration of their skill, and with seeming ease they took aim at certain pieces of cork floating down the river, no more than a palm's breadth, and struck their targets each in turn without missing once. The Tupinambá seem to have been less impressed with Europeans: they struggled to understand why some men (or 'halves', as they called them) were destitute while other 'halves' had an excess, and why grown men would lower themselves to the service of princely children. Almost exactly a year after his encounter with the Tupinambá, and in the same spot, Damião also witnessed the reception of an ambassador from Ethiopia, a man named Matthew who came with letters in Arabic and in Persian, and a holy relic in a golden box. These letters, and many like them, were taken as a matter of course to the Torre do Tombo, infiltrating the royal archive with otherworldly voices, voices that lay dormant until the right listeners came along.[9]

It was not only foreign visitors whose voices were finding their way into the written record for the first time. The spread of Humanism had expanded the number of those who could read and write, and uncoupled these skills from religious vocations, releasing the literate to make their way in the world. For many this was a mixed blessing, as the growing social importance of literacy did not necessarily immediately transform into enough skilled employment for these educated men. Alongside the great variety of occupations Damião recorded in his description of Lisbon, perhaps the most intriguing are the men sitting at desks out in the middle of the Pelourinho Velho (Old Pillory Square). For all the strangeness of their setting up office in the street, these men look no different to notaries or clerks – only they have no official position. Instead, they win their bread simply by listening to the detailed accounts given them by their clients, and producing written versions of these for those who cannot do so themselves, writing (in Damião's extensive list) business correspondence, love letters, prayers, speeches of praise and blame, funeral addresses, begging notes, petitions, poems, idle musings and every manner of thing that can be written down, each given its own proper style by the scribe. The writings produced by these down-and-out men of letters, both for others and for themselves, made up what was in effect a parallel universe to the world of official documents and decrees, an archive of public life that revealed a Lisbon far messier than guides like Damião's would care to record.[10]

Some of the most detailed and debauched accounts of Lisbon's demi-monde came from the pen of a young man who until very recently had been incarcerated in the notorious Tronco prison, one of the dark places of the city, which was near the Hospital of the Todos-os-Santos on Rossio Square, but which Damião omitted to mention in his glowing portrait of the Portuguese capital. The author of these letters was highly educated, deeply cynical and missing an eye, and he would one day be the national poet of Portugal.

III

House of Smoke

I n his epic poem about Vasco da Gama's sea voyage to India – the
Lusiads, or 'Song of the Portuguese', who traced their descent
from the mythical figure Lusus – Luís Vaz de Camões wrote about
captivity like one who knew it well. He said it was like

> The light reflected from a mirror
> of polished metal or bright crystal,
> rays of light caught up
> and sent elsewhere,
> which being controlled by the hand
> of a bored young man stuck inside
> go across walls and roofs,
> trembling and unquiet.

Camões was in jail many times in his life, so we can't be certain
that he was thinking of his time in Lisbon's Tronco prison when he
wrote these lines. But they certainly capture much of what must
have been his experience during his months of incarceration in
1552 and 1553: the view from the windows of the Tronco, in a
depression between two of Lisbon's hills, which would have
presented terrace upon terrace of houses for his thoughts to dart
between; the restless, nervous uncertainty of his current predica-
ment.[1]

Camões had been arrested for a street brawl that had taken place on the Feast of Corpus Christi, 16 June 1552, one of three men accused of roughing up a certain courtier named Borges in the street. Whether or not the finger pointed at the right man that time, this kind of thing wasn't exactly out of character: a second warrant was also issued for his part in another assault just eight nights later, this time as one of eighteen who beat up another well-to-do gentleman. Camões had written to a friend in the country, to warn him that the friend's name was near the top of the wanted list, though the chief culprit in this case was an unidentified 'philosopher' called João de Melo. The letter doesn't admit that Camões was involved, but it doesn't deny it either, and doesn't seem too bothered by it anyway. All in all, the letter gives the impression of a hardened lawbreaker – if they were rounding up the usual suspects, it was probably because they were more than usually suspicious.[2]

This letter, and one sent a few months before to the same anonymous friend, are a guide to the underbelly of the city, a city that took up the same space as Damião's merchant-metropolis but had a very different feel. This was a city of idle young layabouts, tricked out in the latest fashions and looking for love or trouble, easy prey for the procuresses who strung them along and promised them a meeting any day now with the woman they'd been eyeing: just a little more time, just a few more expenses that couldn't be avoided – you can't be cheap in a game like this! You could spot these types from a distance: leaning on their swords, a hat drawn down to hide the eyes, short capes, long legs, and a certain swagger in their step, a certain hunch in their way of holding themselves. This sort would have a bit of gold on their scabbard to catch the light, a book of the love-poet Boscán tucked in their sleeve to show the depths of their menacing silence. The women – at least in Camões' way of seeing it – were every bit as much part of the game. The mistresses of this craft always had a husband who wasn't there – off in the Cape Verde islands, maybe, or maybe dead somewhere – and my, were

26

they pious, always taking themselves off to the Dominicans or the Jesuits to confess, gorgeous as Helen of Troy but decked out in mourning weeds, stroking their rosaries. They make sure nonetheless to sway their hips as they go, and he *knows* that under those drab dresses they are wearing the most alluring garments that can be bought. These women, Camões says, cannot be won with fine words and a certain style, but only with golden *cruzados*, and the way to them lies not through some madam but through the very monks, friars and priests who help them to pray that their husband doesn't go showing back up anytime soon. The confessional box, says Camões, gives them plenty of leisure to get through all sorts of business.[3]

This fool's game wasn't for cynics like Camões and his correspondent-confidant, who preferred to have the mercenary side of love dealt with out in the open. The main thrust of the poet's letters is to give his friend the latest on the Lisbon prostitutes, whom he feels sure that the man is missing during his exile in the country. *Some would say*, he writes, *that as with these women there is nothing but paying and getting on with it, there can be no misunderstandings.* Not Camões, though: he thinks that in many ways they're just as bad – all wide-eyed innocence and milky skin, as slick as mermaids because they never go outside. But *boy, beware the snake in that grass.* Some say that they fleece their pimps as much as their customers, though Camões thinks the pimps are doing just fine themselves.

The world that Camões sketches in these letters is savage and merciless, at times unbearably so. He jokes with his correspondent about the town's assassins, whom he riddlingly says are paid at a certain *treasury* in *marmalade pastilles and jugs of cold water* – apparently a thieves' cant whose meaning has been obscured by time. Camões also reports that the prostitute favoured by his friend, one Maria Caldeira, has been killed by her husband, and that her companion, Beatriz da Mota, joined her soon afterwards. Another, named Antonia Bras, had fallen into a dispute with some

Spaniards and was dragged off to their ship in the harbour and beaten. Her supposed protector and pimp did nothing, which at least meant she could send him packing. These forlorn women bore upon them the violence of the world, and even so (he said) were the best singers and dancers that the city had to offer, so poised and pitch-perfect that the king's court could show nothing better, foremothers of the fado singers of the recording age, whose voices rest in the painful place between ululation and melody. For all his heartlessness in the letter, the young Camões (in his mid-twenties now) may not have been as tough as his talk suggests: he reveals at the end of the second letter, in the days before he went to prison, that he was hung up on the same Antonia Bras who had survived the Spanish attack. It seems that she had been playing with this boy, making bets with him with her body as a prize if he won. Presumably it was an old trick to use on lovestruck youngsters who had no money now but might do later. He lost the bet, saying she had deceived him, and now he was feeling it painfully and dreaming up ways to make her his before too long.

There is little doubt that these women always saw a lot of violence, but this summer seems to have been worse than most, and a group of them banded together to set up a house for themselves where they could live and work in safety. It was, Camões said, a real-life modern-day Tower of Babel, groaning under the weight of so many languages spoken there – at any given hour you would find Muslims, Jews, Castilians, men from León, friars, priests, married men and bachelors, young and old. The same João de Melo who led the attack on St John's night had given it another name – 'the Batting Cage', a joke that's hard to figure out and probably better left alone, though it seems to have something to do with there being three women who liked to dole out pain (including Antonia Bras) and one willing to take it. Camões had his own name for it, which could be roughly given as 'the Dungeon' – because as a John you were sure to get done one way or another. This temporary sanctuary Camões calls a *pagoda*, a temple that surpasses the wildest dreams of the Epicureans, curiously using the Malay word which would serve the Portuguese as a catch-all term for places of worship in India and further east. Camões had not at that point actually seen such a *pagoda* with his own eyes, but it wouldn't be too long before he did.[4]

It should be no surprise that Camões mentions Moors and Jews among the customers at the Tower of Babel. Although they were all now Christians by name, there were still a great many people whose fathers and mothers were born into Jewish and Muslim families, and who were widely suspected of paying only lip service to their new religion. The entire district stretching between where Damião worked in the castle and where Camões sat in prison was taken up by the Mouraria, the neighbourhood which had been left to the Muslims after the conquest of the city in 1147 and which had remained largely theirs ever since, though there were Christian residents as well, including Camões' parents. The existence of these converts was a precarious one, and recent decades had seen a number of reversals in a once fairly tolerant approach. The Portuguese king had at first opened his doors to all the Jews who were banished from Spain after the last Islamic kingdom, Granada, fell in 1492. Portugal soon caved to pressure from Spain, though, whose Catholic monarchs Ferdinand and Isabella were bent on an apocalyptic cleansing of the peninsula that would usher in (they thought) a universal Christian empire under Spanish command. The Jews were given two choices – to depart as a people without shelter or shepherd (as Damião put it), or to stay and convert, while the Muslims were to be expelled en masse. Some at the Portuguese court argued against this, if only (to be sure) because they feared that the Jews would take their knowledge of guns and explosives – not to mention the money they were believed to be hoarding – over to the Muslim enemy, and that Muslim kingdoms would retaliate by giving the same treatment to the Christians who lived in Egypt and Syria and elsewhere. Those Jews who chose (or were forced) to convert and stay did not see an end to the matter, and they remained at the mercy of the *Cristãos Velhos* (Old Christians), easy scapegoats for whatever problem might arise. Many children were separated from their departing families, and were later referred to by a name which recalled the dismal beaches on which they watched their parents disappear: *os d'area*, 'those of the sand'.[5]

That did not mean that these New Christians lived at a distance – as their presence in the Tower of Babel suggests – or even that it was a simple matter to tell them apart. The ruffian and wit João de Melo named by Camões has never been identified for certain – the name is not uncommon – but one intriguing candidate is a man of that name who was living in Camões' neighbourhood of Mouraria in those years. He had been given the name 'João' (or, rather, 'Giovanni') at birth in Genoa, but at the age of four had been captured by a Turkish ship and taken to Istanbul, where he had been circumcised and given the new name 'Mastafar'. He grew up as the slave of a sea captain by the name of 'Sinan the Jew', who took him to Mecca and on to Jeddah, where he shipped for Calicut to serve the king (or zamorin) for a year, after which he went to Chaliyam which was held by the Christians. It was there that he declared himself a Christian and was baptised again, with the same name he had before, and with the commander of the nearby fort at Cannanore (one Ruy de Melo) standing as his godfather and giving him his new surname. Mastafar or João knocked about after that as a shiphand from there to Cochin (Kochi) and then Goa, moving from one Indian port to another until eventually he boarded a fleet bound for Portugal. We know all this because at some point during his time in India he was drawn back to Islam, and was pulled in by the Inquisition a few years after the events of Camões' letter, after he and a few others had bungled an attempt to flee to northern Africa in the middle of the night and defect to the Moors. The Inquisitors left a detailed account of the man they called Genoese by birth but *a Turk by nation*. It seems that he had fallen in with certain other baptised Muslims in the Mouraria, and one of their number had taken it upon himself to teach them snatches of Arabic from the Qur'an and lead the rest in their reconversion. It is pitifully obvious that none of them were very clear on what the practices of Islam were, other than a way to set themselves apart from a city that already held them at arm's length. In their meetings they performed a bizarre hybrid ritual, each being in turn presented with a piece of bread by the ringleader, but saying *bismillah* afterwards to make clear that this was not the Christian Mass but rather was meant for the other God. It may not have been this man of the world who was Camões' companion – it isn't clear why he would call this João de Melo a 'philosopher', though he'd seen his share of beliefs – but the point still stands that this underworld was every bit as global and diverse as the market wares on Lisbon's docks.[6]

However varied and tolerant the company was at the Tower of Babel, much of Portuguese culture was still oriented by a hatred of the Muslim enemy. The very same vagabond sort who got into fights on the streets of Lisbon were also sent off, by tradition, to cut their teeth fighting Muslims in northern Africa, as Camões himself had been in his early twenties. His garrison at Ceuta, the first foothold gained by the Portuguese across the Straits of Gibraltar, had been the staging post for the Muslim invasion of Iberia in 711, and was held to be the last line of defence against another such attempt, though by the time Camões was stationed there the Portuguese also controlled large stretches of coastline in the western Maghreb. After a century and a half of Portuguese presence, life in the Maghreb had settled into a routine of attacks and counter-attacks against the local magnates, each an opportunity for those without fortune to give a taste of their quality. Camões would soon have learned, however, that the simple narrative this heroism required, of a pitched battle between the forces of light and dark, was harder to see from up close. In truth, the armed expeditions mounted by the Portuguese often amounted to little more than cattle raids, even if the soldiers sometimes lost their lives in harming their enemies, like hailstones that melt away after destroying the crops.

Portuguese efforts were by now directed less at the defence of the homeland against threatened invasion than at the securing of Atlantic sea ports used as relay points for western African trade. And while at the beginning of the century the Portuguese still at least had a clear enemy – the Wattasid sultans of Fez – this dynasty had since then faced a Muslim challenge itself, in part because its rulers were seen as too cosmopolitan and decadent, as epitomised by Sultan Mohammed 'al-Burtuqali' (the Portuguese), who had spent seven years as a hostage in Portugal and spoke the language. Their challengers, the Banu Saadi who headed up a group of clans from the southern Moroccan hinterlands of mountain and desert, were inspired by Sufi mystics and *marabutin* (holy men) who denounced the impure state of the faith in the north, too reliant on things for which they saw no basis in the foundations of Islam – sumptuous prayer mats and beads, and a religious life characterised by frenzied periods of self-denial and ecstatic excess. These innovations, they felt, had made the Wattasids unfit to face the challenge presented by the Portuguese invaders – just as in Europe at the same time, as we shall see, there were those who felt that the luxuriant global marketplace was sapping the ability of Christian nations to withstand the encroachment of Islam. The Portuguese, then, faced at least two different Muslim enemies in Morocco, and on top of this much of the land that they claimed outside of the port cities was actually controlled by so-called *Mouros de Paz*, the 'peaceful moors' who accepted Portuguese sovereignty but remained largely their own masters in everyday life.[7]

The traces that remain of Camões' time in Ceuta, and indeed his entire life before his arrest and imprisonment in 1552, are vague and uncertain – a letter believed to be written during his time there, reams of poetry which may refer in veiled ways to the experiences of his young life – and obscured by later mythmaking. It is not even known for certain where he was born – perhaps in Lisbon or its environs – though it seems that he lived part of his young life in the university town of Coimbra. These were tumultuous years in that place. What had until recently been the centre of Portugal's connection to European intellectual life was now contested by the fervour of the Jesuits, whose Portuguese chapter had been founded there in the early 1540s by one of the original companions of Ignatius Loyola, a man named Simão Rodrigues. The foreign professors who had been recruited from across Europe were imprisoned, their cosmopolitan and decadent teaching suspected of spreading heresy. This turning tide had reached its height in the summer of 1545, when Simão Rodrigues had pushed the Jesuit novices to run amok, coursing through the city streets in the mouth of the night to ring bells and shout into the darkness about the hell that awaited those in mortal sin. The novices intentionally dressed in rags and invited humiliation from their fellow students, which served as proof of their distance from this fallen and corrupted world. One even carried a human skull to a university lecture, despite the revulsion it provoked in him, and left it on the desk for the full two hours as a reminder of the death that was coming for all.[8]

Camões had not been recruited by the morbid antics of the Jesuits, who were sending increasing numbers of talented fresh recruits on overseas missions to expand the faith. Instead, he followed the same path as many young men who fought to join the elite using the meagre opportunities and resources at hand. It has even been suggested, though with little evidence, that he may have worked for a while under Damião at the Torre do Tombo, which would at least explain the ways in which his writings overlap with those of Damião. What we do know is that Camões found himself in the orbit of a few noble families, to whom he dedicated a profusion of verses. The relationships behind them remain obscure, in part because the fashion of the time was for courtly verses that presented themselves as the anguished laments of a disdained lover, even if the real wish was to display the eloquence of the poet in hopes of employment, or at the very least something to tide him over. Having failed to make his mark in this way, Camões traded

33

Opposite: Portrait of Luís de Camões later in life by Fernao Gomes, likely
c.1573–5.

his pen for a sword and went abroad to serve in northern Africa,
though that brought him no greater luck. In fact, the period in
Ceuta seems to have made things even more hopeless. The right
eye that is missing in all surviving likenesses of him was probably
lost there, though the circumstances are unclear.

Whatever they were, his wound did not bring with it a consoling
reputation for valour; instead he was taunted for his disfigurement
as a *devil* and an *eyeless face*, unfit for the amorous games of polite
society. Whatever youthful bravado he may once have had can be
seen evaporating in the only letter thought to be from Ceuta: *there
is no avenging spirit*, he writes, *that takes more souls from their
bodies than this damned thing called honour*. There were perhaps
not many steps from this disillusionment to becoming the
debauched author of the letters from Lisbon, for whom all the
grapes of life have soured.[9]

It was at this low moment, when Camões had turned his back
on the pursuit of glory abroad, that the force of events was to take
over and carry him along regardless. On 5 March 1553, some eight
months after the warrant for his arrest, Camões was issued a
pardon, the man Borges having dropped the charges against him.
This was not, however, a triumphant exoneration. Camões was
ordered to pay a fine of 4,000 *reais*, and was bound over to serve
the Portuguese king in India for a minimum of three years. He had
in fact signed up for the India fleet three years before, when
the India House dockets show that one Luís de Camões, esquire,
twenty-five years old, son of Simão Vaz de Camões and Anna de
Saa, was to sail on the *São Pedro*; but it seems that this was just
another urbane vagabond's trick, to take the king's shilling and
then desert before the ships had even left Lisbon. This time,
however, there was no backing out. Since the early days of
Portugal's exploration, the fleet had been stocked with *degredados*

– degraded or exiled men, convicts who could be marooned in unfamiliar lands, to win their freedom by bringing back useful intelligence or to die trying. While it is not clear that Camões was one of these degraded men – his claim to be a gentleman may have saved him from that – his exile amounted in the end to the same thing: a banishment that would only be lifted when he brought back something that would merit a reprieve. On Palm Sunday 1553, three weeks after his release from the Tronco prison, Lisbon closed its doors to Camões and sent him out, a prisoner of the wide world. As was traditional, the fleet left from the Torre de Belém, the river fort downstream from the city, built as a safeguard for the harbour and a monument to maritime life, a stone warship scuttled in the estuary and carved with all the trappings of navigation – stone ropes, stone portholes, stone barnacles, for all the world like a castle built to trick the sea into thinking it belonged there.[10]

IV

A Hole in the Wall, a Cavity
in the Stairs

I f the Torre do Tombo was the central chamber into which the information of the world flowed, you wouldn't know it by the look of the place. Unlike the archive of the Serene Republic of Venice, which employed a highly trained staff of eighty in a series of increasingly secret chambers, the Lisbon archive was an altogether more spartan affair. Two floors in a squat tower of the Castelo de São Jorge, sparsely furnished: two wooden tables and two chairs, to which a few decades before had been added some sacks of old wool to blunt the discomfort of the hard seats. When Damião had taken up the post of *Guarda-mor* in 1549, it had cost him some effort even to get hold of the keys to the tower, and when he did finally gain entrance, he found it in complete disarray. This perhaps was not surprising to a resident of the castle like Damião, who also noted at this time that the roof of the Casa do Espírito Santo chapel was leaking and likely to cave in if not fixed. The grandiose references by some to the Torre do Tombo as a 'library' were little more than wishful thinking. Some of the most important charters, it is true, were being gathered under Damião's direction into exquisite parchment manuscripts, where the property rights of the realm were enshrined among the delicate pen drawings, curlicued thickets filled with birds looking half ready to sing.

But while these volumes of *Leitura Nova* (New Reading) were housed in sturdy wooden closets, the truly overwhelming mass

Opposite: Working with documents at the end of the fifteenth century: an image of the translator Jean Miélot, secretary to the Duke of Burgundy.

had resisted such neat arrangements. These documents could not be bound together into books because they were wilfully dissimilar: many had wax seals attached, others were the wrong shape, and some weren't even made of paper or parchment. The loose items were kept instead in *gavetas* (drawers) and *arcas* – a term for trunks or chests derived from 'ark', like the one that held the Tables of Mosaic Law – in which the writings of the world sat in strange profusion. Among the earliest documents in the Torre do Tombo was a record of the size and weight of a particularly large sturgeon that was presented to the king in the thirteenth century by the head of the local Jewish community. There were letters from the Ottoman sultan Suleiman the Magnificent, whose *tughra* (signature) curled out in magnificent gilding along the lines of Arabic calligraphy, like a squid dipped in gold; palm-leaf letters from the kingdom of the Battak in Sumatra; a copy of the Japanese alphabet, sent back by the Jesuits upon their arrival there; letters from the zamorins of Malabar and the kings of Kongo. And though the archive was mostly meant to store legal charters, letters, treaties and other documents to bolster the crown's position as arbiter of all disputes, the people writing these documents often failed to keep out the chaotic fullness of the world, with its stories and its marvels and expressions of feeling. Even the bureaucratic tomes of the *Leitura Nova* couldn't prevent the oddity of the world from creeping into them, especially in the gorgeous *Livro das Ilhas* (Book of the Islands) in which Damião had begun to record overseas ventures. In it Damião noted an edict from 1461 that prevented private citizens from trading in pepper, civet cats and unicorns.[1]

Of this mad variety how could one even begin to make sense? One way was to try to sketch an outline of the world as it was then known to Europe, to serve as a framework in which the infinite details could sit. There were among the state papers some fledgling attempts to map the world in words: the first fragmentary Portuguese accounts of the globe drawn up by those who had seen something of it, and who attempted to update and correct the accounts of medieval travellers such as Marco Polo and Niccolò de' Conti. Among these was the *Esmeraldo de Situ Orbis* by Duarte Pacheco Pereira, a celebrated veteran of the Portuguese campaigns in India who had later also served as the captain of the main Portuguese fort in western Africa, at São Jorge da Mina, as well as defeating the French pirate Mondragon when he was terrorising the seas off Finisterre. In the intervals of his bravado, he had begun a cosmographical account of the world, beginning from northern Africa and following the coast down and around and across to India, though his account never got further than the Cape. The passages he did complete are a strange mixture of dry observation and feverish nightmare, detailing commerce with the people below the 'Sahara' – the Arabic word for 'desert' – but also obsessing about the creatures of the region. Among these were snakes that left the River Niger up near Timbuktu and grew as they went, measuring almost a mile in length by the time they reached the ocean. But along the way, Pereira notes, their soft flesh is incessantly pecked at by birds, so that when they come to the delta they are no more than skeletons that dissolve into the coastal shallows. Pereira's writings are witness to his struggle to shape what he was seeing across the salt roads into an understanding of the world with some consistency; his shipboard experiences even persuaded him to subscribe to the belief of Thales, the first Greek philosopher, that the earth had a liquid core, and that all the earth's crust covered this water like a shell.[2]

Taking up where Pereira left off, the *Book of Duarte Barbosa* provided a guide from Mozambique along the periphery of eastern Africa, the Arabian peninsula, Persia and Gujarat, down the

Opposite: The title page of the *Livro das Ilhas*, a volume of the *Leitura Nova* dealing with Portuguese possessions overseas.

Liuro
das Ilhas

Malabar coast and up past Coromandel to Bengal and beyond. Barbosa had lived for many years as a factor for the Portuguese in Cochin, where it was claimed he knew the local language of Malayalam even better than native speakers, and Damião came to consider his writings about Asia as the most trustworthy guide for those (like Camões) who were setting off for the east. But it is also clear that Barbosa was wholly reliant on merchants' reports for information about points east of India, and beyond the places he knew first-hand in western India his writings become increasingly sketchy, often relating little more than the goods that could be acquired from the regions towards China. Fuller information about the Far East could be gleaned from the *Suma Oriental* (Complete Guide to the East) by Tomé Pires, which like the *Esmeraldo* and Barbosa's book had been presented to King Manuel when Damião was a young page at court. But though Pires had spent an extended period in China, the *Suma* was written before he even got there, using information gleaned from traders in the busy port of Malacca, which had served from 1511 as the centre of Portuguese operations in southeast Asia.

These books provided some starting points for the chronicle Damião was beginning to write, which would cover the years of Portugal's first encounters with the wider world, but there was no chance of pressing the authors for further information on points of doubt. Duarte Pacheco Pereira had ended his days in poverty and captivity, being brought back from western Africa in chains under mysterious circumstances that Damião was at a loss to explain. Barbosa had settled in India, into a life of domestic obscurity. And Tomé Pires, having finally made it in person to the regions of China about which he had written so extensively, was arrested shortly afterwards, following the arrogant grandstanding of an inexperienced Portuguese commander. Pires seems to have died after a few years in a Cantonese prison, though there were several curious and unexplained reports of Pires being sighted again in the east many years after he was believed to be dead.[3]

For all their fragmentary nature and reliance on reports that had passed through many hands or were even the product of fantasy, these guides were closely guarded secrets, providing as they did the most recent European witnesses to Africa and Asia and so conferring upon the Portuguese a considerable advantage in the race to extend trade networks and empires across the world. Yet as Damião began to gather documents for his chronicle covering the reign of Manuel, sorting the history of Portugal's southward advance into various packets and drawers and following the route Camões was taking south and west along the Carreira da Índia (Route to the Indies), he would find right there in the tower archive other accounts of this world, direct testimonies from the inhabitants of these regions.

Among these he took particular interest in the letters of a Moorish soldier named Yahya ben Tafuf, upon whose story Damião became fixated. This is what Damião pieced together from the documents to hand: ben Tafuf came from Safi, a town on the Atlantic coast of Morocco, and at an early age he had become involved in a coup against the ruling family, coming to the aid of his best friend Hali, whose life was in danger after he was caught in a love tryst with the ruler's daughter. The two friends decided to strike first, and took command of Safi, agreeing to share all aspects of power equally. In order to survive the plots against them by partisans of the former ruler, they had turned for help to the commander of the nearest Portuguese garrison, who agreed to send a ship and men to help them in return for one small concession – a strong building on the waterfront to serve as a trading factory for Portuguese merchants. As soon as peace was restored, however, the Portuguese set about undermining ben Tafuf and Hali, sowing discord between them. Among other things, the Portuguese commander had suborned the services of a Jewish doctor who treated both friends for a sickness that was sweeping the town, getting him to plant notes in their bedrooms suggesting each was plotting against the other. The two friends refused to be corrupted against one another, and when the Portuguese demanded that one of them take sole command, they strongly insisted on each other's right to the office. At the same time, the Portuguese were slowly pushing forward the conversion of their factory into a fortress, smuggling artillery into the building to stand behind gun holes that pointed *back towards* the city, gun holes that had been loosely bricked over to hide their purpose. The Portuguese continued to play local factions off against each other until everything was in readiness, and then finding a suitable pretext – a slap one of their men had received from a local merchant – they started a brawl that gave them the excuse to break open the gun ports, fire upon the furious citizenry and take the town.[4]

It is possible that some of this story had been told personally to Damião by Yahya ben Tafuf, who had lived in Lisbon for two periods during Damião's youth, after accepting the loss of his town and agreeing to serve the Portuguese as a commander of local forces in the Maghreb. But the archivist was not content to rely on word of mouth, however trustworthy the source, and he set about collecting evidence from inside the tower and out to deepen his understanding of this dramatic moment in the nation's history. He had access, of course, to dozens of letters from the Portuguese commander who had taken Safi, and from the local factors and merchants; but the attractions of the story took him further than this. His search in the archive also turned up a large number of letters from ben Tafuf himself, written on cotton paper which today is browned, delicate and veined as the wing of a moth, and through which the ink has bled in such a way that every Arabic phrase entangles with the one behind it. Damião also made a detailed comparison of the Portuguese version with Arabic accounts, including that of the Arabic writer al-Hasan ibn Muhammad al-Wazzan al-Fasi, who had lived in Italy and published a history of his continent under the name 'Leo Africanus'. This was painstaking work, and Damião remarked on the immense difficulty of establishing an exact chronology of events, given not only the use of both Christian and Islamic calendars in various documents, but also that the field captains often gave a day and month but no year on reports which they could be sure would reach Lisbon in a matter of days or weeks. Later suggestions that Damião could himself read Arabic were probably a partial misunderstanding: a large number of the archive's Arabic manuscripts were actually in the Portuguese language, so-called *aljamia* documents composed by translators who could speak Portuguese but could only write their translations down in Arabic characters, and it is possible that Damião was among those who could read Arabic script without speaking the language.[5]

Whatever the case, this minor episode in Portuguese history which Damião had gone to great lengths to flesh out also created a problem. For starters, the hero of the story was not Portuguese – in fact, ben Tafuf's letters revealed that he was as loyal to the Portuguese as he had been to his boyhood friend Hali, only to be repaid by suspicion and ingratitude from the newcomers, of which he continually complained to the Portuguese king. In one magnificent act of disdain, ben Tafuf had with a small band of men taken Marrakesh – the jewel of the Maghreb – for Portugal, simply to demonstrate how ridiculous the rumours were that he could not be trusted. But worse than this personal betrayal of ben Tafuf, the episode in Safi began to reveal a pattern, which Damião was to find repeated across the world: of how the Portuguese won the trust of peoples they encountered, professing that their sole wish was to trade on terms that were fair and beneficial to all, only to lie in wait for a local division which could be exploited to turn their influence as merchants into political power – all the while protesting innocently that this was a necessary step to preserve trading interests. If one were to choose a symbol for the global empires that European nations were beginning to build, one could do worse than the fortress with its guns trained upon the marketplace.

This attempt to find local sources to place alongside Portuguese accounts was not always a simple matter, as Damião was to find (for instance) when writing about the Azores, first settled by the Portuguese in the early fifteenth century, at the very outset of the period which his chronicle was to cover. The volcanic, mid-Atlantic archipelago was uninhabited by humans when the Portuguese arrived, and they named it after the immense populations of goshawks (*açores*) that lived there, which Damião noted were more powerful but slower than the familiar Irish goshawks. Though the Portuguese prided themselves on the profits they had made from the island, turning its abundant wheat crop into *pasteles* that were shipped to Amsterdam and London, Damião also noted the lamentable decline in the goshawk population since the arrival of human settlers.

It seemed, however, that the birds were not the only witnesses to the island's history before the arrival of the Portuguese, and in ordering the documents about the Azores Damião once again moved quickly on from celebrating the Portuguese discovery to delve into the mysterious revelations that the islands had brought forth. At Corvo on the northernmost point of the archipelago, the Portuguese had come across evidence that they were apparently not the first humans to land there. On the top of the island's highest peak they had discovered a statue of a man on a skeletal horse, bareheaded and dressed in a short cape, erected by some people unknown and long-since disappeared. The man's left hand was resting on the horse's mane, while his right hand was extended, with its fingers clenched, *other than the one that in Latin is called the index*, which pointed to the west. Hearing a report of this marvellous statue, carved by unknown masons from a single megalithic slab, King Manuel had sent his personal draughtsman, one Duarte d'Armas, to draw it from life. This only increased the monarch's fascination, and he then commissioned a man from Porto, who had travelled widely in France and Italy where he had learned all the newest engineering techniques, to travel to the distant peak and build equipment to transport this antiquity down the mountain for shipping to Portugal. This was when disaster struck. The man reported that, on his arrival, he had found the statue destroyed by a great storm that had thrashed the island, a story that Damião wholly rejected, attributing the tragedy instead to the engineer's criminally poor workmanship. The engineer had brought back with him a few of the remaining fragments of this great treasure: the heads of the horse and the man, a leg, and the finger that pointed westward across the ocean. These relics had been displayed for a time in the wardrobe of the king, where Damião himself had served as a page. In the time since his childhood at the court, however, these pieces had disappeared, and he had been unable to trace their whereabouts.[6]

This was not entirely the end of the story. Visiting the site in 1529, the clerk of the king's chancery – who had been granted rights to the island – had heard local rumours that there was an inscription on the rock where the statue had stood, but that it was difficult to read, not only because it was worn by time, but also because it was carved into the cliff face below the statue, and so could be reached only with great difficulty. Undaunted by this, the clerk mounted an expedition and several men were lowered down on ropes to where the inscription was, with wax to take an impression of the letters. When the wax impressions were retrieved, however, attempts to decipher them had failed. Not only were the letters badly eroded by age and the Atlantic weather, but they were also clearly not in the Latin alphabet, which was the only one known to those on the expedition.

The riddle of this horseman on the Azores remains unsolved to this day. Commentators in the seventeenth and eighteenth centuries believed that the statue might have been erected by Phoenicians or Carthaginians, whom antiquarians insisted must have reached the Americas before the moderns. More sceptical modern accounts suggest that the whole thing was a figment of the imagination: a volcanic feature in which observers saw what they wanted to see, or a false memory, derived from the horseman found on medieval maps warning sailors not to pass beyond the safety of the east

Atlantic coast. Damião, who after all had seen the fragments of this thing, was not in doubt – was it not the case, he wrote, that ancient authorities traced Egyptian history back 13,000 years before his lifetime? Who was to say what had come and gone and been forgotten in that time? The classical cosmographers Herodotus and Pomponius Mela (he noted) attested that during the course of Egyptian history even the sun had changed course four times, and during two periods had set where it now rose. Damião had his own favoured explanation for the statue and its undecipherable inscription. There were many such things, he said, spread across Norway, the land of the Goths, Sweden and Iceland, whose people long before the coming of Christianity were seafarers of extraordinary talent, and left records of their feats carved into the living rock, sculptures of immense size like this one. There were, further, men who could read their almost-forgotten writing, like Johannes Magnus, the Bishop of Uppsala in Sweden, whom Damião had come to know during his youthful travels in the Baltic. It would be a simple matter, Damião says, to send someone to the Azores capable of solving this mystery, if only kings were as eager to discover the world as to profit from it.[7]

The sole thing of which we can be sure, Damião says – paraphrasing Solomon, the supposed author of the Book of Ecclesiastes which he had translated decades before – is that there is no thing that was not before: *there is nothing new under the sun*, and even the sun itself had changed direction many times. That all these things run together in Damião's mind – Norsemen, ancient navigations of the world, the shifting course of the sun – is perhaps no surprise, since he had encountered them at the same time, during a particularly tumultuous period more than twenty years before.

V

The India House

To arrive at Antwerp in the 1520s, as Damião had, was to enter into something strangely new. While the newly rebuilt river fort, the s'Heeren Steen, was reminiscent of Lisbon's own Torre de Belém, the city itself was like a cathedral precinct of trade, where opulent buildings stood as monuments to the power of merchants. The soaring tracery that lined the Grote Markt, the Gothic cloisters built to house the Handelsbeurs (New Exchange), the cathedral-like guildhalls, all made the arriving goods into something like a pilgrimage of wealth. Halfway along the thoroughfare that split the semicircular city in two, Damião had spent his twenties as the secretary to the Portuguese India House, not far from the Sint Jacobskerk. This should have been Antwerp's second church but its outsize tower, still growing across the street from Damião's residence, was threatening to dwarf the steeple of the city's cathedral. The Jacobskerk was an ancient way station along the pilgrims' route to Santiago de Compostela in Galicia, a reminder that traffic between the Netherlands and the Iberian peninsula was nothing new; but, as its tower suggested, the flow was now much stronger in the other direction, especially since Spain and Flanders were united in the Habsburg empire of Charles V. Damião was just one of the thousands who emigrated to Antwerp every year in the 1520s, and who had swollen this little port on the Scheldt estuary to one of the largest cities in Europe. Though the marketplaces, walls and surrounding fields were familiar features of a late medieval town, they did little to mask this new thing that Antwerp had become: a place where nothing was produced and everything was for sale – a truly global city.[1]

The secretary of the Portuguese India House at Antwerp was required to be a jack of all trades. Shortly after arriving in the early summer of 1523, Damião was signing for cargoes of Portuguese sugar that had shipped directly from Madeira, not bothering to stop at Lisbon on their way to the refineries in Flanders – thirty-six chests on board the *Reis Tres Magos*, 251 on the *Concecão*, their contents formed into loaves and sorted into different grades, from the purest white, through honey-sugar, to muscovado and *açúcar d'espuma*, made from the dregs of the syrup vats. These would be boiled down and crystallised again in Antwerp, resulting in granules of more concentrated sweetness than had ever before been tasted. But this was just the icing for the cake, and Damião listed among the other goods shipped north from Spain and Portugal to Flanders oil, wax, honey, rice, saffron, raisins, dried figs and plums, almonds, pine nuts, chestnuts, olives, purslane, conserve of whale and spermaceti oil, soap, purple dye, vermilion and cochineal, jasper, alabaster, coral and jet.

On top of this, there were of course the racks of spices coming through Lisbon from the east, which if anything were more popular in northern Europe, where the strong flavours made up for the blandness of the Lenten diet and covered the taste of food and drink turned rancid with age at the end of winter. The young Ignatius Loyola, future founder of the Jesuit order, who during these years was a student in Paris but often visited the Spanish and Portuguese merchants in Antwerp to beg for alms, was horrified by how the locals used spices to turn the Lenten fast into a feast. The traditional season of deprivation, when the faithful lived abstemiously and nurtured their hunger for the resurrection of life and of the Saviour at Easter, was being replaced by a year-round orgy of global flavours. Pickled eels were heavily spiced with pepper and saffron, and wine that had dulled with age was filtered three times through a mixture of cinnamon, ginger, cloves, mastic and Ethiopian cumin to refresh its flavour. One might even say that the seasons were disappearing with the advent of global trade, with many more people having access to exotic fare during months when once winter stores would have had to suffice. From Antwerp the wealthy houses of England, France and Germany were supplied with fragments of the world, making each dish and every piece of furniture a strange collage of flavours and textures from across the globe. Ships going south from Antwerp were loaded with German guns and grain from eastern Europe, grain produced in such abundance and so cheaply that not only Antwerp but Portugal and Italy also had given up trying to feed themselves and regularly lived off Polish wheat. The nationalism that was to unfold across sixteenth-century Europe was in part a virulent reaction to the increasing dependence on global trade and the cosmopolitan flavour of daily life.[2]

Sugar was not the only thing brought to its most luxuriant finished form in Antwerp. The wealth swiftly accruing from countless small commissions on trade also called forth artisans offering the unthought-of exquisite, which Damião went out into the city to acquire for the powerful back in Lisbon. The new exchange at the Handelsbeurs provided a covered space for trade of unfamiliar opulence, and provided a model for the shopping malls that sprang up across Europe in the Renaissance. In his years in Antwerp, Damião bought a statue of St Sebastian carved from coral for the king, on a pedestal of chalcedony; manuscripts of Dutch and Spanish history for the young Infante Ferdinand; a Book of Hours for the queen by the unrivalled Simon of Bruges, to be finished by another Dutch artist back in Portugal; a gown made from golden cloth, sent from the king of Portugal to the king of Spain on the occasion of João III's admission to the Order of the Golden Fleece, a Habsburg fraternity sworn to ally themselves against the Turk. These artisans were in great demand, and Damião had to write to the Infante Ferdinand on more than one occasion to apologise that the tapestries he had ordered from the famous workshops of Flanders were not yet ready, and the weavers were not to be rushed. Swiftly emerging as an elite faction among these makers were the painters, whose names were widely known and who had to be courted rather than just commissioned by the great. Dürer had been a guest at the India House a few years before Damião arrived, leaving drawings of the same roofscapes that the young secretary later saw from his windows, as well as of some of the other residents of the India House, and receiving in return an armful of the world's marvels, from sugar cane and coral to coconuts and silk.[3]

Among Dürer's drawings from the India House is a silverpoint drawing of a western African woman named Katherina, who was almost exactly the same age as Damião and who was the 'girl' of his employer, the factor João Brandão. It is not clear whether she was one of the slaves who gave Antwerp the second largest black population in Europe after Lisbon itself, or one of the much smaller number of free Africans recorded in the northern city. The headdress she is wearing may include a carrying-ring, a loop of fibre to help her balance loads on the top of her head. This was a practice that many African women brought with them, with Brandão himself noting that the lowliest of these back home in Lisbon carried the excrement away from chamber pots in this manner. While Dürer's portraits are always miracles of perfect surface, hinting at the interior of the silent subject precisely by hiding it, Katherina's averted eyes are a particular masterpiece, both giving away nothing about this woman and gesturing towards the immensity she brings with her – a single human bearing a memory of elsewhere and the world's tragic depth. Like other western African women of the period, she would not only have suffered degradation herself but also been forced into silent witness of the

Opposite: Portrait of Katherina, who lived like Damião at the Portuguese India House in Antwerp, by Albrecht Dürer (1521).

Opposite: Portrait of Damião de Góis, by Albrecht Dürer or one of his followers, 1520s.

humiliation of their men – brothers, fathers, lovers – broken down and deprived of all dignity. The only surviving image of Damião was also drawn in this period, either by Dürer himself or one of his followers who was less in demand.[4]

The young secretary was a quick study and had soon acquired both his own taste for extraordinary artworks and the means to acquire them, means that could not have come either from his modest inheritance or his salary and were probably the result of canny trading on the side, which was entirely expected among agents of the crown. Visitors to his rooms in Lisbon castle remembered particularly the many paintings, which were sought out by the great and the good of the city and which must have taken up much of the space in his lodgings. His taste in art, however, had taken a different turn after sitting for that early portrait. If Dürer's paintings and drawings captured without error the light as it fell upon the objects of his world, these still moments of time did nothing to show the crowded and jostling confusion in which Damião lived his days. There was, however, an artist whose style caught Damião's eye and induced him to spend startling sums on three paintings, one of them alone setting him back 200 *cruzados* – almost as much as the pieces he was buying on behalf of the royal family. This prized picture was not a portrait but rather a scene that defied explanation. A man kneels in prayer outside a ruined chapel; in front of him is another man who has no body, is merely a head set upon bare legs. Behind the back of the kneeling man a table of drinkers carries on: one with a pig's face and an owl perched above his snout, a woman made apparently of stone, and a cowled figure who has the eyes and cheeks of a bird, but a bird whose beak has transformed into a sackbut or oboe. In the background a city is burning, and there is a house on a hill that is entered through the spread legs of a giant person bending over; in the sky various frogs and people ride airships through the blue, machines that are themselves made from birds and fish and ropes and planking. In the foreground a wading bird wearing a funnel for a hat ice-skates across a pond to deliver a letter, and a man who is partly a tuber rides a saddled mouse past another creature which is made up of animal hindquarters and a jug. At the front of the scene, a monkey slowly rows an armoured fish across the water, guiding it past a horned mouse with his spoon-oar.

This triptych of the Temptation of St Anthony was one of three works Damião would eventually own by Hieronymus Bosch, and he was to remember even in the blinding pains of his Inquisition trial that paintings by Bosch were worth these beggaring prices because their originality, invention and perfection were unparalleled, taking care to specify that these were works by the hand of the master himself and not some imitator. One of Damião's closest friends from his early life was to leave a description of him among his paintings, when he came upon Damião prostrate and in tears at the power of what he saw. Though the St Anthony that belonged to Damião is generally agreed to be the one still on show today in Lisbon, it is less certain what became of his other two Bosch paintings: one of them portrayed the crowning of Christ with thorns, and may be the same that now hangs in London's National Gallery after spending many years in Rome; the other, clearly a pair with the St Anthony, depicted the sufferings of Job, and it may have eventually found its way back to Bruges, near where Damião made his purchases. Bosch had died a few years before Damião's arrival in Antwerp, and though his star was rising, especially among Spanish royals who were displaying his works in Brussels and sending them south to their royal collection, there was little clarity as to what his unsettling visions meant. Many claim to have deciphered their elements, as relating to alchemical mysteries or the doctrines of certain secret religious brotherhoods, though there is no reason to believe that Damião was an initiate to any of these occult truths. Rather, when put together with the other paintings he owned – by Quentin Matsys, for instance, another master of disorientation – Damião's obsession with Bosch seems very much of a piece with his interest in mermen and the emotions of elephants. For while the legends of St Anthony and Job are both examples of human endurance, of how these two men were exposed to the unthinkable, the treatment of these stories by Bosch is not a study in horror: many of the elements of Bosch's surreal dreamscapes are intriguing, hilarious or even endearing, and is hard to imagine that Damião did not see in them a master laying himself open to all the wonders of this many-splendoured world.[5]

While the young secretary had emptied his pockets for art, paintings were not the thing that most captivated him during his years in Antwerp. A poem in praise of him during these early years, as an open-handed young man who was quick to laugh, makes special mention of his love of music, and the music of one man above all – Josquin des Prez, the undisputed master of polyphony. Josquin, like Bosch, had died recently, and little was known about his life; but also like Bosch, and Michelangelo, he was quickly recognised as someone with an ability to see in the world what was not visible to other people, an ability that would later be called genius. Into the hollow spaces of Josquin's biography stories soon began to creep, to give him a life that matched the power of his work: that he worked not by dull theory but by a second sense, which allowed him to construct music of unparalleled complexity and to modify it almost without thought, as another man might run his hand through his hair; that he was prized by kings above their wealth, but did not sell himself to the highest bidder; that he wore his brilliance so lightly as to compose masterpieces to serve as practical jokes, as when a new motet set to the words 'Remember O Lord thy servant' was sung before the French king in order to remind him to pay Josquin what he had bloody well promised.[6]

What exactly Josquin did was hard to put into words, though few would say his reputation was undeserved. He certainly did not invent polyphony – composers had for centuries before his time been departing from the single musical strains of plainchant and simple harmonisations to weave in third and fourth parts that swooped around each other, then tearing apart, only to end up in chilling alignment, as if the notes were hunting each other across the intervals. This made of the human voice something new and strange, something like a church organ, as suggested by the Portuguese term for polyphony, *canto de órgano* (organ-song).

Josquin's fluid trickery was of a different order, however, and this master of counterpoint clearly entranced the secretary of the India House, who was later to publish poems in praise of Josquin and his mentor Ockhegem, celebrating the manner in which their *liquid and subtle art wound its way around the rocks of sacred buildings*, as well as writing and publishing his own polyphonic compositions. In this music's conciliation of jarring opposites there was something nearly miraculous, unexpected resolution in a world apparently racked by confusion. The Portuguese were to use polyphony's strange magic around the world to suggest the wondrous nature of Christianity: as early as 1504 it was being taught in the Kongo, and from the 1540s in Goa as well. Not everyone was comfortable with this, or rather not everyone enjoyed the discomfort it stirred within them, and some Church authorities had set themselves against polyphony, complaining that it obscured the words that were supposedly being elevated in song and that it smuggled bodily pleasure into the place of worship (both in the involuntary shudders it provoked and the young boys needed to extend the harmonies through higher octaves). One of the neighbours who was later to inform on Damião reported to the Inquisitors that he had heard coming from Damião's apartment in the castle singing unlike any he was used to, and the words of which he could not understand.[7]

Goods flowed in, goods flowed out, and the current stirred Antwerp to new heights of invention; but the course was not smooth and one thing made the difference between those who profited and those who lost – information. As well as mastering the shipping routes and ocean currents, the merchants also had to navigate the shifting alliances between political powers, which might make the difference between a smooth passage and a cargo lost to enemy ships or state-sanctioned privateers. So as well as being a clerk of the ledger and an art buyer for the Portuguese nobility, Damião found himself in those years at the India House playing the role of intelligencer, writing back to Lisbon with information he had gleaned from the marketplace about troop movements in northern Italy or the Duke of Gelders' changing allegiances, tremors often felt first and most strongly in how they affected trade. Damião had been given a rough and ready introduction to the fickleness of international relations on his way to Antwerp in 1523, when his fleet from Lisbon had been confronted in the Channel by French and English ships sent against the Emperor (and his ally Portugal). Damião had been lucky enough that the captain of the fleet was a veteran of naval battles in the Indian Ocean and so was able to run this blockade without significant incident; but a few months later he wouldn't have needed the luck, as the English king Henry had switched sides and was now allied with the Emperor against France. Before five years were out, Damião was in London in person, probably to extricate a Portuguese merchant whose ship had been wrecked on the English coast and whose goods were stranded in the shipping courts. And the information that could be picked up in Antwerp was not just local. Travellers from across the world washed up in this great port, and Damião gathered many of his first-hand accounts of Indian affairs from his neighbour on the Kipdorp, one Rutgerte, who was a veteran of the wars in Goa and Malacca.[8]

By small increments Damião moved in just a few years from serving as secretary of the India House to leading embassies himself to foreign courts. His first brief was in 1529, when he went in search of King Sigismund of Poland and caught up with him at Vilnius in his province of Lithuania. His purpose was further to cement a friendship between these trading powers which had begun during Damião's youth, though he also noted a potential opening for Portuguese goods as sugar was entirely unknown in these parts, the only sweetener in use being honey. It was on his return through Gdansk (Danzig) that he first met Johannes and Olaus Magnus, the exiled heads of the Swedish Church, and the men who introduced Damião to those Nordic cultures he felt he had recognised in the giant horseman of the Azores, and which were to become a curious obsession for him. The Magnus brothers had been stranded abroad when their king, Gustav Vasa, had been seduced by the cause of Protestant Reform, and they set up in Gdansk across the water from their homeland, waiting and hoping for a reversal. Driven by their nostalgia for home, they began to compile the first great encyclopaedic accounts of Scandinavian history and culture. Olaus was drawing up the most detailed map of the region ever seen, and at the same time writing down everything he could learn or remember about it, comparing the sources available but dismissing most as having no basis in personal observation.

In the end, his compendium would record everything from the danger of being decapitated by ice during skating races to the immense snow forts built by Norse children, as well as the penalties for those who deserted during snowball fights (snow down the back) and those who stooped to the use of ice or grit-balls (ducking in the freezing water). The aesthetics of the frozen was among the main claims that Olaus was to make for his beloved homeland, and he dedicated lengthy passages of his writing to naming the different kinds of icicle and describing the pattern of ice as it grows along the windowpanes, as well as the way in which nature stamps upon the soft and tiny bodies of snowflakes artistry beyond human capacities, though an artistry that had been taken as a model by the peoples of the north. The priest in Olaus is even able to justify his fascination with ice by a quotation from Psalm 147, which marvels at the cold of the Lord, who *sends snow like wool and scatters hoarfrost like ashes*. Perhaps the most lyrical passages of Olaus'

Description of the Northern Peoples are reserved for his memory of the light in his homeland, where (he noted) on the longest day of the year, even the smallest writing can be read at midnight without the need for a candle. He recorded also the local practice of watching solar eclipses reflected in a bucket of tar, and that the Northern Lights were widely believed to be a reflection from the iridescent bellies of plump herring as they made their way through autumnal waters. The obsession of the Magnus brothers with noting the minutiae of daily life in unfamiliar places was to serve as a model for Damião's own extraordinary surveys of the world.[9]

Gdansk would have felt very familiar to Damião after Antwerp, as a city built by northern merchants on a semicircular island carved out of a river estuary, and organised around similar institutions of trade. Goods were bought down the Vistula from eastern and central Europe, and across the Baltic from Lithuania and Scandinavia, before being sent on to Antwerp for redistribution across the world. At the heart of the city was a marketplace dominated by a cathedral (also dedicated to Our Lady) and the centre of civic governance, the Artus Court, so named because its founders aspired to build a new Camelot with Arthur's court at its centre. The Marienkirche was even stocked with Flemish art, most strikingly Hans Memling's immense *Last Judgement*, a masterpiece that had been commissioned by the Medici agent in Bruges but waylaid en route by a Gdansk privateer. Damião would doubtless have known the church well, as he was to become friends with its Catholic minister, Jan Dantyszek or 'Johannes Dantiscus'; their correspondence would over the course of decades connect Damião to the most revolutionary ideas of the age – perhaps of any age. What may have surprised Damião most, however, was that his friend Dantiscus was in the curious position of having to share his Church with a heretic.

Overleaf: A section of the *Carta Marina* of Olaus Magnus, the first detailed map of Scandinavia and a record of Scandinavian culture.

As at Antwerp, the ideas of the Reformation had spread quickly among the merchant elite of Gdansk, who were perhaps understandably attracted to the Protestant vision of a world without a cumbersome aristocracy of saints, and where grace was attested by honest and steadfast labour. The early Reformation, with its series of arguments about who (if anyone) had authority in the Church and how (if at all) the faithful could interact with God, was proving explosively divisive across northern Europe. The group of six knightly brotherhoods which oversaw the life of Gdansk from Artus Court, however, had freedoms from the Polish crown of which the city fathers of Antwerp could only dream, and so had responded to the arrival of Protestantism with a novel solution: the main church of the city would have both a Catholic and a Protestant minister, and it would play host to both kinds of services.[10]

Damião was to become fast friends with Olaus and Johannes Magnus, and his meeting with them was to begin a lifelong fascination with these northern places, most especially those parts of Lapland which had not yet been fully converted to Christianity. If he had not already sensed this on his journey through Lithuania, Olaus must have brought home to Damião just how close the northern borders of the Christian world were. It was less than a century and a half since Lithuania had formally converted to Christianity, and Olaus felt that the old beliefs recorded by the Polish historian Matthew of Miechów – in the sacredness of fire and forests and the animal gods that lived in them – lingered just beneath the surface. The Sámi (or Lapps, as they were commonly known) in the far north of Johannes Magnus' bishopric knew nothing at all of the Christian God, and two years after meeting Olaus, Damião was to dedicate part of his first published work to advocating for the cause of this distant and little-known people. He did not, of course, argue that they should be left to their pagan beliefs – that would have been tantamount to heresy – but he did forcefully condemn the way in which the Swedish nobility wrote them off as barbarians precisely to justify the continuing pillage of their land. Following his friend Olaus Magnus, Damião's pamphlet on the Lapps expressed a hope for the conversion of these peoples to Christianity while lamenting that knowledge of their culture was in danger of disappearing.

Olaus was insistent that just because this heritage was not recorded in the same kinds of books found further south did not mean that it was not also a form of knowledge: perhaps the northern peoples had written down their stories in runes on staves and rocks and sung them in oral histories, but didn't cultures more ancient than the Romans do the same? Hadn't the Medes and Persians woven their stories into garments, the Chaldeans used leaves as a writing surface, and still others had used an alphabet of nails to make books of wood? In the northerners' runes, believed to be invented by giants and still in use by folk-astronomers whom Olaus had met near Uppsala, the history of these peoples was written on the living rock in characters the thickness of a man's finger, and often accompanied by great stone monuments. Weren't these records worth saving from oblivion, worth making space for in books and archives? The world recorded by the Magnus brothers, right on the doorstep of Western Christendom, was after all brimming with unthinkable things: a world where foreign gods were simply absorbed into existing beliefs when they arrived, while others were expelled if their habits were deemed unsuitable. The Norsemen were even known to go to war against their own gods, and the relationship was imagined as one in which the gods had responsibilities as well as powers. This, Olaus was to write, was not so distant from Christianity as we might be tempted to think, noting that the Tower of Babel had been built in the hopes that the combined forces of mankind could withstand the tyrannical power of the heavens.[11]

Damião had been able to offer the Magnus brothers something in return, and had promised, when he was back in Antwerp, to send them details of the Ethiopian culture that he encountered during his youth at the Portuguese court. He had only been twelve years old when Matthew, the emissary of Eleni the Queen Mother of Abyssinia, had arrived in Lisbon, and though he remembered the ambassador's appearance and the boy his own age who had accompanied him, his recollection of what had transpired was understandably vague and incomplete. To supplement his own memories, then, Damião obtained a copy of the letters that Matthew had brought with him from Ethiopia, and translated them into Latin for publication alongside his pamphlet on the Lapps that he would dedicate to Johannes Magnus.

This curious mingling of Ethiopian and Lappish cultures, which was the first work on either available to European audiences, was the earliest evidence of Damião's uncommon appetite for other ways of seeing and for the counterpoint they provided to what he and his readers knew. But if Damião's pamphlet was to be his introduction to a broader stage – it was quickly reprinted in Antwerp and in London – it was not without problems. The arrival of Matthew in Lisbon in 1514 had been the answer to King Manuel's prayers: Europeans had for centuries dreamed about finding Prester John, the legendary king who reigned somewhere in the east over a fabulously wealthy and powerful Christian kingdom, and who would join forces with Europe to surround Islam and bring about a universal Christian empire. It certainly may have seemed at first that the Christian empire of Ethiopia was this promised land for which they had long been hoping. Matthew's letters, which were believed to be in the ancient biblical language of Chaldean, spoke about an alliance against the Muslims, and his reports on Ethiopian Christianity confirmed that this faraway land shared the religious convictions of Europe – at least in some respects.

The success of Damião's pamphlet had been in part down to anti-Protestant triumphalism, providing something that loyal Catholics could wave at the Reformers as evidence of the antiquity of Church traditions, which survived intact in the parallel universe of Ethiopia: even the distant Ethiopians, they crowed, showed more reverence for this inheritance than the schismatic Reformers. This was, however, only part of the truth, and as much as Damião tried to focus on what the Ethiopians shared with his European readership, it was impossible to prevent the unsettling strangeness of this otherworld from creeping in.[12]

The Ethiopian Christians practised circumcision and avoided pork – the marks by which Europeans recognised Jews and Muslims – and were baptised every year rather than just once, but these differences were shrugged off as mere custom rather than any matter of faith. They allowed their priests to get married, something that had been banned in the Roman Church for centuries. Fasting also played a much more central role in religious life than it did in the Church of Rome. Most unsettling, perhaps, was the treatment of criminals, heretics and lapsed priests in the Abyssinian kingdom, who were given smaller and smaller portions of food until they perished in an act of ritual starvation, after which they were considered absolved and buried in the church with all due ceremony and sorrow. This was, after all, a more literal sense of 'excommunication' – which in its original sense was a casting out of the condemned from the shared table – though it also showed a worrying divergence from European understandings of the scriptures. These differences were perhaps inevitable, given that the Ethiopian Church had been out of contact with Rome for a thousand years and had followed more closely the path of the Eastern Orthodox Church; but it was nevertheless a disappointment for all those who had hoped to find a miraculous and unproblematic ally in Ethiopia.

Those who wished to would be able to live in denial for a little longer, however, because a ready scapegoat for this disappointment was found in the person of the ambassador Matthew himself. For starters, Matthew was not actually Ethiopian – something his sallow skin might have given away – but rather an Armenian, a member of that extraordinary stateless nation who had in the east (like the Jews in the west) made themselves a great force by providing the links that tied the world together. Damião remained faithful to his youthful acquaintance, and argued that Queen Eleni had sent Matthew rather than an Abyssinian nobleman precisely because of the qualities that made him the perfect go-between – not least his fluency in Arabic and Persian, which had allowed him to make his way through Muslim Aden to the Portuguese station at Goa, disguising himself as a merchant and (in Damião's lovely phrase) *making himself ever among the turkes a turk*. But rumours had begun to circulate soon after he had arrived in Goa that he was not an ambassador at all, but rather an interloper who had kidnapped the Abyssinians that accompanied him. This had justified the vile treatment Matthew had received on his way from Goa to Lisbon, of which he had complained bitterly on arrival in Portugal, and also gave those who wished to dismiss his account of Ethiopia just the ammunition they needed. The rather more complicated truth – that Matthew was indeed an emissary, but merely from one of two warring factions at the Ethiopian court – would eventually come out (with some help from Damião himself), but in the meantime Damião's attempt to introduce Europe to Ethiopian culture was on shaky ground. Before long he would have an Ethiopian source that it was harder to dismiss, and with it the opportunity to fall foul of the Portuguese religious authorities for the first time. For the moment, however, Damião was free to immerse himself in a world that held in suspension the Ethiopians and the Lapps, Hieronymus Bosch and vocal polyphony – new wonders that kept Europe spinning, with as yet no sense of where things would fall.[13]

VI

The Degraded

C amões' journey to India began poorly and got steadily worse. Before the fleet had even left Lisbon the *São Antonio* caught fire while being loaded, reducing the convoy to four ships – the *Santa Maria da Barca*, the *Santa Maria do Loreto*, the *Conceiçao* and the flagship *São Bento*. These four then set out on the standard Carreira da Índia, the route pioneered by Vasco da Gama in 1497 that finally allowed the Portuguese to break through the doldrums of navigation in the eastern Atlantic. For the better part of a century, the obsession with circumnavigating Africa had made painfully slow progress: though numerous ancient historians told of Greek, Phoenician and even Egyptian voyages which had made it from Gibraltar right round to the Red Sea, their methods and routes had not survived, and the Portuguese made only incremental progress as they headed south. As they went, they left *padrãos* – stone crosses brought along from Portugal, proclaiming their 'discovery' of these lands in Latin, Portuguese and Arabic – in modern Angola in 1483, at Cape Cross (Namibia) in 1486 and at the Cape of Good Hope itself in 1488. These monuments may have been inspired by the Libyan Berber habit of erecting pillars inscribed in the local script to stake claims to land, and the Portuguese use of Arabic makes clear whom they felt might have contested their claim. The cross left at the mouth of the Congo River in 1485 read:

In the year bjMbjclxxxb (6685) of the creation of the world, and
of Christ llllclxxxb (1485), illustrious King D. João II of Portugal
did direct this land to be discovered, and this padrão to be set up
by Diogo Cão, an esquire of his household.

Yet whatever the truth of the classical stories with which the
Portuguese were obsessed, none of them had hinted at the counter-
intuitive trick that would turn sailing around Africa from the stuff
of heroic legend into a regular, if never quite mundane, event. The
agonising slowness of coasting along while supplies quickly dimin-
ished in the throbbing heat could be bypassed by standing off far
enough into the Atlantic to catch the southern currents that slung
ships towards the Cape – so far off into the Atlantic, in fact, that
ships headed for India would soon stumble upon Brazil.[1]

For Camões as for da Gama, though, this shortcut was not without its problems, sending ships and sailors out into unpredictable
waters. The 1553 fleet was separated early in the voyage, with each
ship left to fend for itself in the struggle to save the lives and
cargoes on board. This was Camões' first experience of sailing in
the open ocean, and he was to pause at this point in the *Lusiads*, in
his retelling of da Gama's Atlantic passage, to mock those who had
only book knowledge of these *black storms, dark nights, and thun-
der that shakes the world*. It is easy to doubt from the comfort of a
library, but he has seen himself (he writes) the *living lights which
sailors think divine, in the time of storm and wind and black tempest
and sad moaning*. Camões' autobiographical sections – like this
memory of the static electricity known as St Elmo's Fire – are rarely
precise about the when and where of his experiences, though it is
often clear that telling da Gama's story triggers his own memories
of the same places. He continues his tirade against those *wise in
letters* with a description of a water spout, that *sublime miracle and
cause of true astonishment, of seeing the sea-clouds suck up the
ocean through a great straw: I saw it clearly lift, like a steam and thin
smoke in the air, whipped about by the wind … it grew bit by bit*

until it was as thick as a mainmast, here thinner, there thicker, suck-
ing in the water in great gulps, breaking against the waves, as above
it a cloud grew fat on this great body of water ... like a leech drinking
with fierce thirst the blood of cattle. Living with the ever-present
fear of shipwreck would knot the guts of most people, and perhaps
it was even worse for Camões, for whom shipwreck was a family
tradition: his own father had died shortly after his ship had gone
down off the coast of India, a catastrophe that had determined the
early life of the poet and thrown him upon the charity of his relations.[2]

During his seventeen-year absence from Europe, Camões was
to transform the unmemorable verse of his youth into a powerful
and original voice, one that was never more alive than when writing of the ocean. The naturalist Alexander von Humboldt was to
call him a *great sea-painter*, whose writing is unsurpassed in its
representations of the water world, the *never ceasing mutual rela-*
tions between the air and sea, and Herman Melville was to say that
Camões' poem was *the epic of the sea*. But his most striking writing
was often also a tell, bluster to cover an uncomfortable truth, when
the realities of seafaring life were less heroic than the story
required. This was certainly the case at this point in da Gama's
story, where the south Atlantic storms weathered by the Portuguese
fleet did not end in some triumph, but rather brought da Gama's
ships back to the Western Cape – faster than the earlier coasting
voyages, to be sure, but no further along than Bartolomeu Dias
had reached a decade before. Worse than that, their first meeting
with the people of the region had been a complete disaster.
Anchoring at a bay they named Santa Helena, a landing party
encountered two men fumigating a beehive, and captured one of
them for interrogation, though when attempts at communication
failed, they released the man the next day with clothes and other
presents. This overture clearly worked, as the following day a depu-
tation from the nearby village arrived and invited a Portuguese
party to follow them home. But the man volunteered for this task,

71

Fernão Veloso, lost his nerve somewhere between the roasted sea lion he was served and the sense of complete estrangement from what he knew. Returning to the ships, he broke into a run, escaping from hosts who didn't know they were his captors, and provoking a skirmish during which Vasco da Gama was wounded in the thigh. The first contact on the da Gama voyage was a moment of neither wonder nor heroism, but rather a foolish misunderstanding of which it was hard to make great poetry.[3]

The ships of the dispersed fleet carrying Camões eventually rounded the Cape, arriving separately on the island of Mozambique, which from the time of da Gama on had established itself as the main Portuguese station in the southern Indian Ocean. It would have quickly become obvious to Camões, as it had to da Gama half a century before, that there was going to be another problem in framing the early voyages to India as a triumph for Christendom and for Portugal. While the Spanish explorers of the western Atlantic could announce the discovery of an unknown land, a New World which Spanish technologies would allow them to conquer, the people da Gama encountered soon after rounding the Cape were already part of an oceanic network covering much of the globe, one in which the Portuguese hardly cut an impressive figure. While the presence of silk clothing and the growing fluency in Arabic assured da Gama that they were on the right track for India, this soon gave way to a flood of global cultures which made it clear that the Portuguese were entering an immense and well-established trading community. The merchants of Sofala had a longstanding commerce with the Indian kingdom of Gujarat, whose dyed cloths they unravelled and wove anew for local tastes, though they were also partial to Turkish fashions. Further up the coast at Kilwa they traded golden jewellery to the island of Madagascar, and across the water from Madagascar the sultans of Gedi were fond of tricking out their mosques and palaces in Chinese porcelain and Venetian glass. The Portuguese were told in eastern Africa that there were people to the east who were, like them, *the colour of the sun*, though they did not yet recognise this as a memory of the Chinese ships that had regularly visited the area earlier in the century. Though this route had fallen into abeyance, the Chinese had not long before cherished Malindi as the source of the giraffes sent to the Yongle Emperor at Nanjing: its graceful walk confirmed that the giraffe was a *qilin*, a celestial beast so careful to avoid hurting anything that it scarcely trod upon the grass under its feet. And everywhere the Portuguese found Arabic already established as the language of commerce: they continued to erect *padrãos* announcing their claims to these lands, but it was clear that there was little new or surprising that they could offer this world.[4]

This was not to say that eastern Africa had yielded many of its secrets to those from outside. While Arab and Indian traders had been using the monsoon winds for centuries to visit these coasts, exchanging cloth and finished goods for ivory and slaves, their activities were largely confined to the ports, and the inland regions remained almost wholly unknown to outsiders, who had none of the tools required to navigate this terrain. If Camões had not already discovered it in Duarte Barbosa's guide to the Indian Ocean, he would have heard at Mozambique of the kingdom of the Monomotapa (ruler of the Mutapa), who had governed the coast until the arrival of the Portuguese: it was said that the kingdom was an astounding 800 leagues in circuit, not including the tributary kingdoms from which gold poured in constantly. The king lived in seclusion at the city of Zimbaoche, heard but never seen as processions laden with tribute passed under his window, and was defended by an army of some 5,000 or 6,000 female warriors. To show allegiance to this king each household was required once a year to extinguish the fires in their hearths and receive fire anew from the king's torchbearer, or be crushed as rebels. The local civilisation was also reported to be of very great antiquity: Damião was to note down references to a palace in the Butua kingdom, where the masonry was so finely wrought as to need no mortar, and where the entrance bore an inscription so old that no one any longer understood the language. However open-minded he may have been, Damião (like most cosmographers) reflexively assessed the worth of other cultures in terms derived from his own. European travellers of the fifteenth and sixteenth centuries often saw agriculture, literacy and dressed-stone buildings as the surest signs of a civilised people; the Arabic cosmographer Ibn Khaldun, on the other hand, thought that nomadic life and scarcity made for superior people, as well-fed city-dwellers were *dull in mind and coarse in body.*[5]

The terror that these unknown African hinterlands held for the Portuguese was made clear by a story that was trickling into the ports of Mozambique at the very time that Camões was passing through the region. At the centre of the tale was the homeward-bound India fleet of the previous year, which had left from Cochin early in 1552 bearing what was reputed to be the richest cargo yet to make the return journey – only 12,000 *arrobas* of pepper (about 176 tonnes), as the wars raging against the Ottomans in the Arabian Sea were making trade very slow, but also an estimated 100,000 *cruzados* in gold and gemstones. Against the advice of his pilot, the captain Manuel de Sousa Sepúlveda had led the small fleet – a galleon and a *nao* – close to the Eastern Cape to get a better look at the land, only to be caught in a squall that eventually destroyed their rudders, masts and sails. Camões was later to write of the storms around the Cape that, in the midst of them, *the machine of this world seemed to be undoing itself in torment.* De Sousa's fleet had eventually managed to land 500 men – as well as his wife Leonor, his children and the treasure – on a beach in what is now the Transkei district of the Eastern Cape, but the initial plan to build a small craft which could sail back and raise the alarm had to be abandoned when the storm left no timbers larger than a man's arm. After spending a few days in a fort made out of barrels and chests, they had set off to walk overland to the nearest Portuguese presence at the Rio Tembe in southern Mozambique, a distance of 600 miles along the coast, but almost twice that given the inland detours they had to make. The party was made up of 180 Portuguese and 300 slaves, some of whom were carrying de Sousa's wife and children in litters.[6]

While the rice salvaged from the ships lasted nearly a month when supplemented with bush fruit and seafood gathered on the beach, they found no people with whom to trade, and desperation began to settle in. One of the first to be lost was a child of de Sousa's by a mistress (probably an Indian woman), whose bearer stopped to rest and wait for the rear of the column, but was missed in the bush as night was falling. A panicked de Sousa offered 500 *cruzados* – more than twice what Damião had paid for a Hieronymus Bosch masterpiece – to any man who would go back and look for them, but no one would take even this much to face the predators that routinely picked off stragglers from the group, which included lions and 'tigers' (as the Portuguese called the striped and as-yet-unidentified hyena). This was only the start of the night-marish inflation that was to set in: water was soon passing hands at ten *cruzados* a pint, and any man willing to head off into the bush to fill a cauldron from a stream could earn himself 100 *cruzados*. They were now entirely reliant on scavenging, and a roaring trade in scraps emerged: fifteen *cruzados* would buy you a dried snakeskin which you could crush and mix with water – another ten *cruzados* – for a meal that would cost twenty-five times what you could live on for a month in Goa.

After more than three months the party unexpectedly met an elderly chieftain of the Tsonga people who introduced himself, rather surprisingly, as Garcia de Sá. He had been given this name as an honorific by two Portuguese traders whom he had assisted, and he offered to accommodate them all in the two villages of which he was head. He also begged them not to continue heading north across the river, as the kingdom beyond was dangerous to outsiders. But de Sousa's judgement was beginning to turn, and he suspected that the headman only wanted to detain them to further his own political ambitions; de Sousa insisted that they be given transport across the river, not realising that this was itself one of the branches of the river they had been looking for, which would have led them down to the coast. They managed to reach the next branch of the river, but by all reports Manuel de Sousa had now lost his mind, drawing his sword on the local boatmen they had hired, convinced that they were plotting against him. The baffled boatmen jumped into the river and swam away, and on the far shore the Portuguese were received at a village where they were offered food and shelter, but only if they agreed to split into smaller contingents and surrender the arms which made the locals too afraid to approach them with supplies. Despite the pleading of his wife and officers, de Sousa agreed, and the story went that after this they were robbed and stripped and sent out into the bush, where de Sousa's wife, in shame at her nakedness, had buried herself to her waist and refused to move any further. De Sousa tried frenziedly to find food for his wife and children, but to no avail. They died and de Sousa himself wandered off into the bush never to be seen again. Of the 500 who had landed on the Cape, twenty-five managed to make it to Mozambique – fourteen slaves, eight Portuguese, and three female attendants of Dona Leonor de Sousa – where the captain and pilot of the second ship soon filed a detailed record of their misadventures. Soon the story was circulating in Goa, from the mouths of the survivors and in a cheap pamphlet that was one of the first things printed in India, and Camões would fold it into his *Lusiads* to illustrate the dangers that the Portuguese adventurers had faced in their journeys to the east. It would in time become one of the most famous seafaring stories of the period, the subject of several plays, an epic poem, and retellings in many different languages.[7]

Not all the reports of this episode match up. Camões' telling of the story did not detail the crazed way in which gold passed between the starving members of the convoy, reducing this great wealth to worthless dross when compared to the basic needs of the flesh. None of the printed accounts mentioned the money that changed hands shortly before Manuel de Sousa disappeared from the story, which meant that the pilot (whom the survivors' report wholly exonerated of the shipwreck) found his way back to Mozambique at least 1,000 *cruzados* richer. And a curious sequel to the story tells how the second-in-command on the expedition, one Pantaleão de Sá, arrived in Mozambique somewhat later than the rest, having wandered in the bush *until he came upon a great palace.* There, he said, he was told that the king lay dying of a wound that would not heal, and as his last roll of the dice Pantaleão had announced that he was a medical man who would cure the king of his illness if they would only feed him. Having no actual medical knowledge with which to back up his boast, he told how he concocted a poultice by urinating in the dirt and making a paste of the resulting mud, which was taken and applied to the king's wound. The end of the report bears all the marks of being told by a consummate storyteller: how Pantaleão waited patiently for the certain death that was coming first for the king and then for him, only to be surrounded by a jubilant throng a few days later who announced that the king was miraculously healed before bearing Pantaleão to an altar where they worshipped him as a god. The grateful king, the story would have it, had begged him to stay and rule over half his kingdom, but Pantaleão nobly declined out of a wish to see his own people again, and so was packed off loaded down with gold and gemstones. No one, it seems, thought to question Pantaleão's piss-taking story, to connect it to the Arthurian legend of the Fisher King to which it bears certain similarities, nor to connect the wealth he had acquired with the treasure which had supposedly been stolen from de Sousa by the merciless peoples of the Mozambican hinterland. The episode was instructive for Camões in at least one regard: it was clear that when you brought a story back from the great unknown, there was little chance of it being checked or contradicted, leaving the teller a free hand to shape it as circumstances required. Or, as one writer of the period put it, *great journeys make for great lies.*[8]

Those determined to turn the Portuguese India voyages into the stuff of legend found ready aid in one of the discoveries – or rather rediscoveries – made in the southern hemisphere. The sighting of a constellation that had been known to the ancients, the Argo Navis recorded by Ptolemy as late as the second century but not witnessed by Europeans since, was all the confirmation some needed that Europeans were renewing the legendary voyage of Jason and his crew, which included the poet Orpheus and the demigod Hercules, aboard a ship named the Argo which was later immortalised by being turned into the constellation. The prize the Argonauts were seeking – the Golden Fleece that hung from a branch in the kingdom of Colchis – promised to confer upon its owner not only great wealth but also soldiers that grew from ground sown with dragon's teeth, a miraculous ally not unlike the one the Portuguese were seeking. The poet Virgil had even foretold a time in which the sea would tempt men to try the legendary voyages again, *and another* Argo *will carry the chosen heroes, and there will be another war, when great Achilles will be sent again to Troy*. Naturally enough, perhaps, the Portuguese saw themselves in this prophecy, though there was some disagreement about whether the ship in Argo Navis pointed east towards India or west towards the Spanish conquests in the Americas. The Order of the Golden Fleece, which had been founded in Burgundy as a brotherhood of crusading knights, took on a new life as the symbol of European expansion into the world; Damião had even been present in Brussels when Charles V made King Manuel a member of the order, and had acquired a golden vestment for the fraternity's chapel. The classical account of Jason's voyage, the *Argonautica* by Apollonius of Rhodes – culled, it is believed, from the great Library of Alexandria by its librarian-author in the third century BC – became wildly popular following the voyages of the 1490s, and was

Opposite: *Jason Returning with the Golden Fleece* by Ugo da Carpi (1480–1532).

studied by scholars across Europe, including in Portuguese universities, for the clues it might hold regarding ancient navigation. Even Damião was reading it, though he was mainly interested in the mermen that the Argonauts supposedly encountered in Africa.[9]

Once Vasco da Gama had connected with the Arabian Sea network at Mozambique, it was only a matter of the Portuguese working their way up the eastern African coast until they found a pilot willing to guide them across to India. They eventually secured at Malindi the services of a Gujarati pilot named Malemocanaqua, and after an uneventful passage of twenty-three days arrived at Calicut (Kozhikode) on the Malabar coast. This was the first experience for the Portuguese of the shuttling monsoon winds, which during half the year brought ships quickly down from India to eastern Africa, before reversing and pushing the same traffic back to the Malabar coast, though the Portuguese were slow to accept the pointlessness of sailing against these winds. On 17 May 1498 they hove into sight of Calicut, though it was hard at first to recognise it through the rain, as heavy (as one Tamil poet has it) as metal chains unspooling from the sky. When the sky cleared, however, it seemed that their prayers had been answered: though the locals had some difficulty at first understanding the Maghrebi Arabic spoken by the Portuguese translators, a man was quickly located in the merchants' quarter who not only understood the interpreters but even spoke Castilian Spanish, being himself from Tunis and having had many dealings with Portuguese merchants in Oran. This man, Ibn Tayyib (or 'Monçaide' to the Portuguese), congratulated them on reaching the richest port in the world, and offered to act as go-between with the local zamorin (ruler) whose palace was some fifteen miles inland at Patane. The Portuguese even learned that there were local Christian communities, which served as confirmation that the Apostle Thomas really had reached India and spread the Gospel in this strange land, and that Asia was (as the Portuguese wilfully believed) entirely divided between their Muslim enemies and longed-for Christian allies.[10]

An audience with the zamorin was quickly arranged and da Gama, in his excitement, agreed to leave his ship, abandoning the rule he had observed so far in the journey of always remaining on board. The Portuguese officers were carried in palanquins with which the exhausted foot soldiers struggled to keep up, and the group paused for refreshment at Capotati, before proceeding upstream in leaf-covered boats to a religious house where their host suggested they stop and give thanks for the success of their voyage. Damião, in his meticulous reconstruction of these events, remarks how it was clear to the Portuguese contingent that this was a place of great importance, a site of pilgrimage among the devout, and apparently Christian: there were bells above the entrance, just like the campanile of a church, and even a pillar like a steeple with a rooster at the top; and though the holy men who met them were naked from the waist up, they were draped in scarves like priestly stoles and blessed the visitors just as they would have been at home, by sprinkling them with water from a hyssop branch and anointing them with sandalwood. They were led into a building the size of a large convent, through rooms with many painted images on the walls – astounding, to be sure, though perhaps no more so than the scenes of supernatural things in the altarpieces of Memling and Bosch – into an inner sanctum, where the silhouette of a statue could just be made out in the darkness. The Portuguese were allowed this far but no further. Gesturing towards the statue and saying *Maria! Maria!* their hosts all prostrated themselves with their hands out in front of them before rising to their feet in prayer, and the Portuguese followed suit, falling to their knees and worshipping the Blessed Mother in ecstatic fellowship.[11]

The dawning realisation that the Portuguese had mistakenly fallen into worship of a foreign idol was in time to become a matter of embarrassment and not a little concern. There were those who saw in the existence of an Indian Trinity – Brahma, Vishnu, and Shiva, who were suggestively known as the 'Trimurti' – confirmation that the ideas of Christianity were universal and so could only have been arrived at by revelation, rather than chance. The similarities did not end there: the Indian creator god Brahma was (like the Christian Jehovah) a somewhat absent figure, to whom religious buildings were rarely dedicated; instead they often prominently featured statues of mother figures, just as Europe's cathedrals were overwhelmingly dedicated to the Virgin Mary. Of central importance to both faiths is a holy feast – the Mass of Christian worship, and the charitable *prasad* given out as a good deed – and to this day churches in India have signposts to clear up the confusion that the Holy Body of the Saviour is not a free lunch. Tomé Pires reported a widespread belief that the Trimurti proved the Indians were once Christians, whose faith had merely been corrupted by the presence of Islam. For others, however, the symmetries were deeply alarming, a suggestion that there was nothing unique or privileged about the Christian revelation that lay at the heart of European culture, and by extension nothing that required Europeans' presence in the non-Christian world. Many concluded that it was all a diabolic trap to lure Christians into heresy by dangling in front of them idols with the comforting allure of familiarity. In his rewriting of the scene in the temple at Calicut, Camões was to avoid the awkward similarities entirely, instead suggesting that the shrine was immediately recognised as a deviant and heretical place to which the Portuguese reacted with horror: *There were the gods, their likenesses carved in wood and stone, cold but in postures and appearance as if the devil himself had made them: they saw abominable things made up like a chimera of various bits; the Portuguese were astonished by these inhuman gods.* One of the gods had horns, and another had two different faces; a third had arms that were split so that limbs stuck out like tentacles; and yet another stared at them from the head of a dog.[12]

The shock that Camões wrote into the minds of Vasco da Gama and his crew was, in fact, rather artificial. Sculptures and images that blended the animal and the human were also a common feature of Christian churches: angels had birds' wings, Moses was often given horns (as he had been in Michelangelo's greatest sculpture at San Pietro in Vincoli in Rome), the four evangelists were represented by beasts – sometimes with bull, eagle, lion and angel faces all staring out from the same human head – and there was even a tradition of portraying St Christopher with the head of a dog (St Christopher Cynocephalus), as in the great church of San Millán in Segovia. And while some reacted to the encounter with Indian gods by roundly denying the similarities to Christian art, for others it was irrefutable proof that the icons in European churches were dangerous, foreign intrusions that must be swept away in order to cleanse the faith and return it to its original purity. This sentiment is perhaps best captured by the Protestant English commentator who drew the following lesson from da Gama's experience in Calicut: *How neare a consanguinitie is in all kinds of Idolatry? How easie a passage from the worship of ye know not what, to the worship of the devil himself?* Not long after da Gama arrived back from India, Europe was to be torn apart by a religious conflict in which the central matters of contention were precisely those things in which the eastern faiths provided startling echoes of Christian practice: idols, abstinence and fasting.[13]

VII

Between the Cup and the Lip

No one could remember years later whether it was a Friday or a Saturday on which Damião hosted at his rooms in the castle a very unusual dinner. In fact, even the year was a matter of some disagreement: 1557, probably, right about the time he turned from the sorting of papers to begin writing his chronicles, but it might have been 1556 or 1558. The many testimonies are in agreement about other elements of the scene. Damião himself was present, of course, and apparently in good spirits, as was his wife Joanna, and their daughter Catarina, who was eight or perhaps nine years old. They were hosting several family members, including Damião's nephew, his nephew's wife and their daughter Briolanja, who was pregnant at the time. There may have been other guests, as Damião often put up people from the northern parts in which he had spent his youth; during much of 1555 and 1556 Leonhard Thurneysser zum Thurn had been living with them, and Damião had been helping him to compile an exhaustive study of Portuguese plants, animals and peoples (which included mermen, likely at Damião's prompting). What is certain, though, is that oranges were in season.[1]

It appears that the food was already on the table and the servants dismissed when the pregnant Briolanja, queasy at the thought of the fish which had been prepared, took herself off in search of some orange juice, presumably hoping that the sharp liquid would settle her stomach. Damião had strong views about fruit, noting the best orchards around the city in his guide to Lisbon and writing also in his chronicles about the fruit trees that could be found in the Azores and Malacca and Mozambique; he even wondered whether it might not have been this that tempted the mermen on to land near Sintra, which after all had the most wonderful fruit of every kind that could grow in that part of the world. Damião had caught up with Briolanja and it had been decided that perhaps as well as the orange juice she might like some nice salty pork instead of the fish that had been prepared, a good combination to settle a lurching stomach. This was perhaps a little bit naughty, as meat and dairy products were forbidden on fast days, but not exceptionally so, as these days made up almost a third of the year and exceptions could be made for infirmity, and it was widely accepted that childbearing created in women an appetite for strong foods. Briolanja had even spoken to her confessor of these appetites.[2]

Damião (who was by all accounts very solicitous of the enjoyment of those around him) had some choice cuts fetched, some *linguiça* sausage and some *posto* like pancetta and some *presunto* ham made from the loin, or was it perhaps the *entrecosto*. They needn't worry that people outside the dinner party would be any the wiser, as he did not have to send out for these things, because he had a pantry or a storeroom that was crammed to overflowing with provisions, at the end of his apartments where his rooms backed on to the Casa do Espírito Santo, the chapel set aside in the castle for its residents. The pantry was tiled and had barrels in the middle of it and was looked after by another daughter of his, an illegitimate daughter named Maria. The contents of this larder stuck in the minds of many at the castle – there was wheat and barley and oil and wine, there was bacon and cured meats and sacks of wheat and sardines and jars of pickled and brined fish from Flanders, tastes that Damião had brought back with him (along with his Dutch wife) and which he continued to crave despite the plentiful fresh seafood of the Lisbon docks. Finding room for it all was in fact something of a problem, so the provisions spilled out from the storeroom into a gallery that looked down on to the chapel itself. This balcony, like a box at the theatre, was supposed to allow the privileged resident to attend services from a comfortable perch without the trouble of leaving home and mingling with others, but no one had seen Damião use it for that, which was perhaps not surprising given that the balcony was crammed full of provisions overflowing from the storeroom. Worse than this, though, there were complaints that droppings from the stores had fallen through the cracks between the planks of the gallery into the chapel below, fat and vinegar and brine dripping from the meat and fish down into the chapel and mixing with dustings of flour from the sacks, and the man sent to clear it up thought at first that it was maybe urine, which was understandable given the strange smell, thinking perhaps that someone had been caught short and gone there or had not been caught short and gone there anyway. The Master of the King's Works had been informed and someone had been sent to complain to Damião and the situation had improved, but not before several days had passed and some had noted that the king's archivist was slow to react to this very concerning turn of events.[3]

When the salted pork had been fetched and brought to table Briolanja ate some of it, because she was after all unwell, and it was possible that Damião's wife Joanna was also feeling unwell and also ate some. But Damião was clearly in a playful mood, and Briolanja remembered him saying that it was a pity that she should eat alone, and so ate some sausage and there was shoulder of pork as well which he ate, or maybe it was even the case that he had eaten first and said that she might as well join them as they were all doing it, though Briolanja's husband remembered that he was only doing it to make her feel more comfortable and was it possible he had a licence to do so. If Damião did have some kind of condition which exempted him from the rules of fasting it was not in evidence that day, and Briolanja had been shocked by his behaviour, though

87

perhaps not that shocked, as her father had always said that Damião *no more believed in God than this wall does*, no more than a stone or a stick, and anyway he never trusted Damião, who wanted to send his children back to Flanders to be brought up there. Someone must have mentioned something or raised an eyebrow at least because Damião had responded to the doubters that *nothing which entered the mouth could damn the spirit*, or perhaps it was *what went into your mouth did not dirty the soul*. This was not the only time he had said this, though his daughter Catarina thought that he meant it about simply eating more or less and not about what it was precisely that you ate.

Damião was later to say that he had come across this phrase as part of a drinking game at the University of Louvain, where he had gone to study after almost a decade of serving as a secretary and emissary at the Antwerp India House. There was a culture of inebriation among the scholars at Louvain, and when they challenged one another to take more drink than necessary – an outlawed German ritual known as *Zutrinken* – they egged their companions on by saying this, *that nothing entering a man from outside can condemn him*, and it was clear (Damião insisted) that the joke wasn't an affront to the church's authority because the people making it were all Catholic theologians. Indeed, you kind of had to be a theologian to get the joke, because you had to know that it came from the Gospels and was said by Jesus, and that the rest of the verse made clear that only *that which came from inside a man which could defile him* (Mark 7.15) – a challenge to the drinker to hold his liquor and not bring shame on himself by throwing it all back up.

Damião was arriving at university rather late in life, and while he never quite managed the fluency in Latin and Greek achieved by those who had started young, he had certainly seen his fair share of drinking; but if Louvain was the first time he had played that particular game, it was certainly not the first time that drinking had brought him within spitting distance of heresy. Before leaving the Portuguese foreign service he had spent two years in intensive travel on behalf of the crown, for the most part returning to the same northeastern areas of Europe as his first embassy, seeing Johannes and Olaus Magnus again in Poland, and also going to Denmark and Prussia and perhaps some other places. The mixture of indulgence and controversy during these travels even led Damião to coin his own phrase, calling the peoples he encountered *philosophers of the belly*. It was while leaving Denmark in the Lenten season on the way to Poland that he had accepted an invitation to visit one of the Danish royal councillors in Schleswig, and in the full flush of drinking the man had sent for a chalice formerly used for the Mass and filled it with white wine in order to drink the next pledge from it, saying to Damião that *his ancestors had long been duped* into believing such things were sacred. Whatever heat was in Damião's head, there was no doubt that this was indeed an affront to the Church. He was afterwards to claim that when he begged the man not to behave in such a manner it only encouraged his host, and setting the glorious, intoxicating cup in front of Damião the councillor had lifted his hands in a mockery of the consecration and called on God to perform a miracle and turn the white wine into blood. The party seems to have broken up after this, when the host called Damião superstitious for not being goaded into drinking, and *if that is not everything that happened*, Damião would later say, *let fire come from the sky and consume me.*[4]

For all the atmosphere of bonhomie, both Damião and the Danish councillor knew that this was a deadly serious matter, that Damião was being invited to switch sides in a battle that was raging across Europe. At the centre of the theological debates of the Reformation was the question of what part man's physical actions played in his salvation, with the Reformers moving towards the belief that all the lesser observances of religious life were as nothing compared to the simple and utter submission to God's will – faith. Though there were many areas of disagreement, none perhaps lodged itself more in daily life than the matter of food –

whether, that is, Christians should pay any mind to the Church's prohibitions against eating certain foods on fast days, or whether these rules were contrary to the spirit of Christianity and of little concern to God. By the time of the Reformation there was a complex dietary calendar that orchestrated digestion across Christian Europe: during the forty days of Lent, no one was supposed to eat meat or dairy products, which were also prohibited on all Fridays and Saturdays and a number of other days scattered throughout the year. These regulations had profound effects on every culture, from prompting the invention of substitutes (like milk and cheese made from almonds, which were popular in Flanders) to shaping agricultural and fishery labour. Protestant England hesitated to ban Catholic fish days for fear that the fisheries would collapse and take with them the supply of sailors and ships that could be pressed into service in times of war. As a result the government simply decided instead to continue the tradition but deny its religious meaning, inviting Englishmen to buy fish for the health of their country rather than the health of their souls.

The battle over dietary laws had come to a dramatic crescendo in the Swiss city of Basel in 1522, in an incident that started as a food fight and ended up threatening the career of the most famous man in Europe. It seems that a certain doctor, inspired by the atmosphere of rebellion sweeping Europe, had decided to hold a grand banquet during Lent, inviting his guests to eat pork and to throw their eggshells out of the window in derision at the benighted citizens who persisted in their foolish superstitions. The city government took a low view of this behaviour, and roundly punished the doctor for his impertinence. At this point Erasmus, the famously brilliant humanist scholar at the height of his influence as the first celebrity of the print age, weighed in with a response that pleased neither side. On the one hand, he deplored the behaviour of the banqueters, whose heedless zealotry was a bane upon society and a harm to good religion. It was always those who claimed righteousness, he observed, who behaved in the most intoxicated and debauched manner. On the other hand, he also deplored the punishment of these transgressions, as they were against rules that had no basis in scripture and were largely a tool for bending people to the will of the enforcer. He quoted the central text in the debate, from the Gospel of Mark – *That which goes into the mouth does not defile a man* – and backed it up with another from St Paul, who had said that *The kingdom of God is not food and drink*. While Erasmus admitted that the early Christians had fasted – had even adopted a form of veganism – this was more about distracting themselves from bodily appetites than about following a series of arcane rules. Nowadays, he pointed out, the rules on what to eat do nothing to encourage restraint: quite the contrary – the kitchens are never busier than on fish days, and everyone prefers sturgeon, trout and moray to smoked mutton or pork; foods permitted on fast days, such as tortoise, snails and snakes, are far richer than beef or mutton and also provoke more lust. (Erasmus himself had been given a licence by the Pope allowing him to eat meat on fast days, though it was always claimed that this was for health reasons.) *What is the point of abstaining from mutton if you stretch your belly with herbs, dates, figs and raisins, truffles, artichokes, and onions, that inflame the sexual organs with lecherousness more than young chickens do?* The only point of these rules, Erasmus suggests, is the opportunity they afford for the melodramatic performance of indignant piety: *nowadays there are dinners everywhere, and no one goes into the tragic mode. But if someone has tasted flesh, everyone cries, 'O heaven, O earth, O seas of Neptune'; the status of the church totters, heresies flood in!* Erasmus' brilliant and piercing satire managed both to enrage the Protestants, who attacked him in print, and to convince many Catholics that his allegiances clearly lay with the other side.[5]

Damião may not have had that last drink in Schleswig, but over the coming days he certainly felt a hangover from that night, his actions taking on the lopsidedness of imbalance. He wrote to a number of people giving his own account of the evening, among them the king of Portugal, clearly anxious about other reports reaching him first. But that did not mean that he had kept his nose clean from that time forward. On the road from Denmark to Poland he had decided to make another stop, this time at Wittenberg. One of his friends in Gdansk was fond of saying that *who had seen neither Wittenberg nor Rome had seen nothing* – though of course, unlike Rome, there was only one thing to see in Wittenberg, and it seems that not long after Damião arrived on Palm Sunday 1531 his host asked him if he wouldn't care to see Luther preaching that afternoon. The scenes that followed were clearly etched in Damião's memory, as many people reported in near-identical terms his descriptions of them. Perhaps the encounter was so striking because Damião had expected more pomp to surround the monk who had broken Western Christendom, and instead Luther arrived with only his chief lieutenant Philip Melanchthon, the diminutive Polish scholar Melanchthon on foot and bareheaded, leading his mule and singing hymns as they went. If Damião recognised this as a re-enactment of Christ's own entry into Jerusalem on Palm Sunday as his fateful hour approached, he never said so. Damião claimed that of the sermon itself he understood not a word, as he spoke no German and could only understand the bits of the Bible quoted in Latin; but that merely meant he had less to distract him from noticing the power of Luther's words upon the congregation.[6]

As suggested by the staged entrance that so captivated Damião, Luther was in all respects a master of the drama. In the previous day's sermon he had led the audience, their appetites keen from a month of Lenten fasting, into the Gospel of John, to those passages that discuss the miracle of the loaves and fishes, where Christ had fed a great multitude with only a few meagre provisions. To the Jews gathered by the Sea of Galilee, Jesus had (Luther preached) performed his miracle of loaves and fishes to make clear that they should not strive after physical food but only after the food of the spirit, that *he* was himself the bread of life, and that only through eating him could salvation be gained. This was not, Luther pronounced, like saying that Wittenberg beer was thirst quenching and that Annenberg beer was thirst quenching as well; it was instead saying that only Wittenberg beer could quench the thirst. He scoffed at those in the Church of Rome who preached, sang, *howled* these words in their churches, but still pretended that other things could lead to salvation – building chapels, going on pilgrimages, praying to saints. *This*, he proclaimed, *is comparable to a drowsy and babbling drunk, who does not know what he is saying in his stupor.* Of course the rest of the Bible, with its specific pronouncements on various parts of human life, also need to be consulted at times; but these (Luther said) are like the parsley that is scattered on the meat sliced from the roast, the roast that is the main part of Christian life, the lettuce and the parsley that serve as garnishes to the roast.[7]

Luther continued to play upon the gastric juices of those around him the following day, when Damião was granted an audience with the great man at his own house. Luther's table in the Black Cloister, the former Augustinian monastery that he had been given by Wittenberg's city fathers, was the setting for many scenes in which Luther's ideas were impressed upon the listener, as much through the staging as through what was said. Though Damião would occasionally be vague about the other details in the years to come, he would remember clearly that they ate apples and hazelnuts, and that it was Luther's wife, the former nun Katharina von Bora, who brought them to the table. The house was a pattern of domestic bliss, entered through a doorway that Luther had given his wife as a birthday present and opening on to a garden where they planted melons and gourds and pumpkins, and Katharina set the tone in the household, worrying over the harvest of mulberries. There was nothing accidental about the fact that Damião was served only frugal things that were still close at hand in early April in the middle of the German lands – the only things, that is, that were local and fresh and needed no recourse to spices.

While Luther was himself a critic of the autocratic dietary regulations of the Church, this certainly did not mean that fasting played no part in his idea of piety; rather, his followers were expected to demonstrate even greater feats of self-denial, and Lent remained part of the Reformist calendar even though other fasts were ridiculed. Since the early days of the Reformation, Luther's followers had railed against the flooding of Germany with saffron, cinnamon and other strange spices, while men replaced the woollen garments of their grandfathers with silk, and many Protestant writers lamented the German obsession with pepper. *Though this country bring forth that which is necessary for life*, one of Luther's acolytes had written, *yet, as though nature had utterly forsaken them, they run to strange things, fetching their garments, their meats and medicines from Hercules' Pillars, from the island of Taprobana, from the river of Ganges, and from places farther off than this.* Luther himself called the great trade fair at Frankfurt the golden sinkhole through which all the wealth of Germany was drained away, and argued that while cattle, wool, grain, butter and milk were bought and sold by the early Christians, *foreign trade, which brings from Calcutta and India and such places wares like costly silks, articles of gold, and spices – which minister only to ostentation but serve no useful purpose, and which drain away the money of the land and people – would not be permitted if we had proper government and princes.* Meals served in the Luther household could be heavy – he was fond of roasted meat and beer – but they were never exotic, and Katharina kept any hint of profligacy from the door, even hiding one of their pewter plates which Luther was wanting to send someone as a present, a gesture that she considered a needless extravagance. There was a clear parallel in Luther's mind between the way in which simple German appetites had been corrupted by foreign delicacies and the way that the meat of

94

Christianity was being lost among the many garnishes that had been added to it. The faithful, he felt, should return to a simpler life, which was also a more local life, detached from the web of foreign practices, pilgrimages and spices by which the soul was all too easily ensnared. For all Luther's conviction that belief in Christ was the key to salvation, there was a code of behaviour every bit as strict to be observed in this new sect, and central to this was a strong allegiance to the local over the global, honest German fare over nasty, spicy, foreign food. Before leaving Wittenberg Damião also visited Melanchthon's house several times and was similarly impressed by what he saw: his wife was to be found at her spindle, dressed in an old sackcloth dress, the very picture of holy poverty.[8]

Luther was not alone in responding to global trade by zealously promoting the local over the foreign. Across the world and at the same time, religious movements that favoured asceticism and internal spirituality over external, material shows of piety were gaining ground: the European Protestants shared much in this regard with the Sufi *marabutin* of northern Africa and the Sikh gurus of northwestern India. There has been a curious reticence, when writing the histories of these movements, to consider them as responses to the same experience of instability caused by expanding markets and power bases, despite the fact that they often (like Luther) explicitly identified the encroaching forces of global markets and politics as one of their great enemies. Instead, these religious movements have tended to be treated as emerging specifically from the internal tensions and contexts of Christianity, Islam, or Indian religiosity. The very determination to see these movements as local phenomena, however, is a testament to the powerful impulse from which they derive: our resistance to thinking about these movements globally is of a piece with their own resistance to outside political influence or the increasing reliance

Overleaf: Martin Luther as the seated poor man (Lazarus), looking on at the feasting Pope (Dives), from an engraving by Hanns Lautensack (1556).

on foreign markets. To admit that these movements were responses to the same tremors and fissures of globalisation would be to concede not only that they were reacting to material circumstances rather than revelations of the spirit or leaps of understanding, but also that none of them had privileged knowledge of the situation, and indeed might require knowledge of the rest of the world to understand what was happening in each part of it. The appearance of events at a local level might be deeply misleading; only when viewed globally would patterns emerge. Resistance to this disorientation may have been sufficiently strong in turn to make attractive any narrative that offered to preserve appearances, reassuring believers that the course of history really could be understood as a part of their own local, personal and spiritual battle.[9]

All of this, however, was often thought through and fought out in covert ways, over dinner tables and the questions of which foods should be eaten at them and which languages spoken, just as Damião's story is curiously tied up with what he was eating and with whom. The roots of his troubles, however, were to lie not so much in the white wine of Schleswig or the fruit and nuts in Wittenberg, or even with the orange juice and salted pork in Lisbon, but in another meal, in Padua, where he was later sent by none other than Erasmus himself, to whose house he had gone after leaving the University of Louvain, around about the time when body parts started mysteriously disappearing from the environs of that university. Before either of those things, though, Damião was to go on the last and most eccentric embassy of his career, moving against a plot to short-circuit the world economy and destroy both Portugal and the Ottoman Empire at one fell swoop. But that is getting ahead of things.

Back in 1557 or so, in his apartment in the castle in Lisbon, Damião and his guests finished their pork and then also ate the fish that had been prepared as well, covering up the evidence of their other, impious feast from the prying eyes of the servants. It is likely that Damião never gave the meal a second thought, until fifteen years later it reappeared at the centre of his trial by the Inquisition, from whose archive the detailed accounts in this chapter have been taken. Then his table became a snare for him, and that which should have been for his welfare became a trap.

VIII

Cooking the World

The first thing noticed by Portuguese arrivals in India was the smell. At sunset the air on the Malabar coast was full of the scent of *mogory* and *champa*, Arabian jasmine and magnolia. According to local tradition, the magnolia tree was once a woman who fell in love with the sun but who burned herself alive when the sun moved on. From her ashes the tree was born, a tree whose flowers abhor sunlight and do not appear in its presence. The importance of fragrance in the east was a matter of astonishment to many Europeans: not only did the great kings of Vijayanagara expend 5,000 *pardaus* a year on scent, but Indians were known to leave off eating to enjoy aromas alone; their houses were full of flowers, and blossoms were given as alms to the poor who also spent their last coins on perfume, leaving themselves nothing with which to buy food. This powerful attraction to smell seemed to lend credibility to the ancient stories, which Camões often repeated, that there were people on the banks of the Ganges who lived off the odour of flowers alone. The locals were also much given to washing, and while the Muslims in India washed at least every three days, those following Indian practices (referred to as 'gentiles' by the Portuguese) bathed themselves at the beginning of each day, and tied this cleanliness to godliness. In Camões' words,

the inhabitants live bathed in the Ganges
and they are certain that even if steeped in sin
this water will wash them clean and pure.

Europeans, by contrast, stank: as one early modern Mughal chronicle put it, the Portuguese *wear very fine clothes, but they are often very dirty and pimply.* There was no habit of washing among Europeans, and they must have been highly conscious of this, as those settling in India tended quickly to fall in line with local ways. You could tell a recent arrival by the fact that they still put their lips to the cup when they drank, rather than following Indian custom and pouring into their mouth from above, and newcomers were mocked for their clumsy behaviour.[1]

By the 1550s the final port of call on the Carreira da Índia was not Calicut, where da Gama had arrived in 1498, but Goa. Even during that first voyage it had become clear that the Portuguese had a very weak hand to play in the region, with little to offer that was new or better, and considerable competition from well-established Muslim merchants who were not in the least ignorant of Portuguese intentions. The existing trade routes, which took spices from Gujarat and the Malabar coast via the Red Sea across to Cairo and up to Alexandria, also connected the same merchants to a wider Islamic world, and early Portuguese records of India are filled with encounters with Muslim Spaniards and northern Africans, as well as Italians, Poles and Slavs who had passed through Istanbul on their way to the east. This not only meant that Indian rulers were put on their guard against the Portuguese almost as soon as they arrived, but also that the technologies relied upon elsewhere to demonstrate European might could be readily acquired, either from the Turks or directly from Christian Europe itself. The Portuguese in Calicut fell back upon their well-rehearsed tactic of establishing a trading post that quietly transformed itself into a strategic fortification, but within five years of da Gama's arrival the zamorin had engineers from Milan and Venice working for him to counter the Portuguese firepower. Near Damião's rooms in Lisbon castle there was a gigantic 'basilisk' cannon with an Arabic inscription, which had been brought home from a campaign at Diu in Gujarat, and even the king of Mombasa had salvaged a ship's gun from a sunken vessel to use against the Portuguese. And it was not only European military technology that was easily acquired in the east, but cultural knowledge as well: a ship captured by the Portuguese in 1509 was found to contain a great number of European books, in Latin, Italian, German, Slavic and French, as well as in Spanish, and even a few in Portuguese. The title that King Manuel had assumed upon da Gama's return to Portugal – *Lord of the navigation, conquest and commerce of Ethiopia, Arabia, Persia and India* – was less a reality than an aspiration, and a faintly preposterous one at that.[2]

The fragmentary nature of the Indian political landscape, however, had lent itself perfectly to the Portuguese practice of playing one local power off against another, fluidly switching allegiances between different kingdoms and even between different factions within each kingdom, and exploiting the instability this created. When establishing a base in Calicut proved difficult, they simply hauled anchor and settled instead at its rival Cochin further up the coast, offering to tilt the balance between the kingdoms by increasing trade through one port and blockading it at the other. The Portuguese proceeded in a similar fashion with the other minor kingdoms of the Malabar coast – Cannanore, Cranganore, and Coulam – and eventually set their sights on Goa, a province of the much mightier Muslim Adil Shahs of Bijapur. Here the Portuguese exploited tensions between the non-Muslim citizens of Goa and the Muslim ruling class, capturing the town by force and then offering concessions that removed any appetite for returning to its old masters – tax cuts, a transfer of lands and offices from Muslims to gentiles, and the free practice of local traditions and beliefs, all confirmed by a Brahmin delegation to Lisbon. Though Goa produced very little of its own, like Antwerp, and was largely supplied by staples from Gujarat in the north, its geographical position made it the perfect centre for Portuguese operations in India: situated on an easily defensible estuary, it was midway between the trading centres of Gujarat and Ceylon, and sat directly in front of a pass that led through the Western Ghats. The Ghats manage to be at once both astonishingly steep and covered with almost impenetrable vegetation, separating the cosmopolitan Malabar coast from the very different world of the Deccan plateau beyond, which makes up much of southern India. Though the Portuguese had no hopes of advancing into central India, the pass did allow them to supply the great Vijayanagara kings of the Deccan with the Arabian stallions that gave them military control over the plateau, and make both a profit and a useful ally against the Muslim provinces to the north.[3]

It was at this *Goa Dourada* – 'Golden Goa' – that Camões arrived, landing at the Mandovi gate after sailing up the river for which it was named, a silky brown inlet leading between islands that rise up in precipitous green. Walking inland from the quay the palace of the former Shahs was on the left, the exquisite dark pilasters of its basalt gateway providing a first introduction to Indian masonry, a craftsmanship that seemed to Europeans to defy natural explanation. Here, as elsewhere, European factors mixed their business with the acquisition of art. As early as 1515, an agent for the Medici had written from Goa to his patron, Duke Giuliano, describing an *ancient temple, called a pagoda, made with miraculous skill, having antique statues in a certain black stone worked to the greatest perfection*, and offering to acquire some of these antiquities to join the portrait Giuliano had just commissioned from Raphael. On the right of the road up from the quay stretched the far dowdier and more stolid European churches, including the Franciscan chapel and the Church of Santa Catarina, built over the gate through which the Portuguese assault had finally broken on St Catherine's Day in 1510; and up a hill straight ahead, beyond a final gate named Bachareis, was the College of São Paulo, which had recently been taken over by the Jesuits. Right through the middle of the town went the Rua Direita, the 'straight road' that was the main artery of Goa, along which all its highly complex life was arranged.[4]

If Camões had ever hoped that India would give him a fresh start, a place in which he could use his talents to remake himself, these illusions were quickly stripped from him as he discovered the factionalism and rot of Goa, a town he was to describe as *the graveyard of the honourable poor*. Though the vast majority of the town's residents were still Indian – 3,000 Portuguese, as against 10,000 Indians inside the walls and another 50,000 outside – power was exercised in the town by a small clique of *casados*, those Portuguese who had been given offices and generous grants of land to encourage them to marry Indian women and settle there permanently. The intention behind this policy had been to create a population loyal to the *Reino* (the 'Kingdom' – Portugal), but this had been a complete failure, and instead the *casados* focused their energies on local power struggles and on expanding their share of trade within Asia, which was not subject to the same crown monopolies. Shortly before Camões arrived, the breach with the *Reino* had been made clear when the *casado* community had refused to provide help for a military expedition mounted by the governor.[5]

The governor and other officials on temporary appointments from Portugal could, however, draw on the support of the much larger community of visiting *soldados*, those who like Camões were billeted in Goa during military tours of the east. The town was awash with these vagabond types during the monsoon season, when the weather made military expeditions impossible, and during these unpaid furloughs they crammed the Rua Direita, ten to a house. A fifteenth-century Russian traveller to India had remarked of the monsoon that *for four months there is but rain and dirt*. With no money, and no means of earning any, the *soldados* were obliged to throw in their lot with one of the Portuguese nobles resident in the town, who would build and feed private armies for use when the campaigning season started again. Perhaps unsurprisingly, this period of downpour and indigence descended relentlessly into violence. Camões had left the underbelly of Lisbon only to find himself somewhere much worse, with little pretence that the marauding gangs were subject to any kind of law. He was to write of Goa as *this Babylon, to which were sent all the bad things of creation ... this labyrinth where virtue goes with all its wisdom and power to beg at the door of cowardice and depravity, this dark chaos of confusion, where are the cursed things of nature only.* He was often to return to this idea, of Goa as the damned city of Babylon, to which he was exiled from Lisbon as the Jews had been exiled from Zion.[6]

The feeling of estrangement can only have been increased by the local culture, which most Europeans found utterly bewildering. The early hopes of the Portuguese – that the Malabari Indians would swarm to Christianity given the lavish rewards offered to converts and *casados* – were largely disappointed. While the Brahmins showed polite interest in the Church and the Christian idols, and said that there was little distance between their beliefs and those of the Portuguese, they often met suggestions that they give up their own practices in favour of these others with bemusement. When the Portuguese attempted to force the king of Cochin to convert, using his debts as leverage, his response was that his particular piece of Malabar was put there by *Our Lord Beneath the Mountains*, and though he was grateful for Portuguese help, his people would continue to observe their own traditions – a bitter pill for the Portuguese to swallow, especially as this meant that he was choosing the monkey god Hanuman over their own Lord and Saviour. The king of Tanur had been open to the idea of conversion in private, in exchange for Portuguese military aid, with the proviso that he could also still perform the traditional rites and wear the symbols of his old beliefs – for form's sake, of course, so as not to scandalise his subjects. The suggestion that Christianity simply be absorbed into existing religious beliefs – as Olaus Magnus' Norsemen had done – was ridiculous to most Portuguese, a complete failure to understand that their jealous God would brook no rivals. And it was not only in matters of religion that the Malabaris and Portuguese failed to see eye to eye. In one striking episode, the king of Cochin agreed to award Duarte Pacheco Pereira – the author of an early account of India and hero of a recent battle – with a coat of arms for his bravery. The grant, recorded at length by Damião in a transcription of the local Malayalam language, gave to Pereira a red shield, surrounded by a border of white with blue waves, and in the centre five gold crowns, eight castles of green wood inside eight ships, and seven flags, as well as a silver and gold helmet with a castle inside it and a flag on top. Evidently the ruler of Cochin, confused by the request that he reward a war hero with a picture, had filled the picture with many things in order to make up for the fact that it was, after all, just a picture. In response to a request from Pereira, the king quickly conceded that he was free to mix these arms with the existing arms of his family, or not, and generally do with said picture as he saw fit.[7]

The Portuguese reacted to these frustrations with a series of measures designed to make life more and more difficult for the unconverted in the regions they controlled. This began with an interdiction against the building of new temples in the *Estado*, as the Portuguese domain in India was known, and then moved on to ban any repairs to old temples, attempts to bring converts back to traditional beliefs and finally non-Christian preaching of any kind. If the Medici agent was offering to acquire Indian antiquities for his patron, this was because many great works of art were lying around, discarded when the stone was stolen to build churches – the sculptures abandoned *because* (the agent said) *the Portuguese do not hold them in any esteem*. The promise made on the conquest of Goa, to let the gentile and Jewish communities follow their own traditions, was withdrawn, and taxes were raised on gentiles while making conditions very favourable for converts. Non-Christians were barred from holding state offices, and orphaned gentiles were turned over to the religious orders to be brought up as Christians, reinstating many of the Muslim policies the Portuguese had posed as saviours in removing. The pressure on non-Christians had intensified with the arrival of the Jesuits in the early 1540s, the Goan chapter being led by one of the same fervent acolytes that Camões would have encountered at university in Coimbra. By the time Camões came to Goa, only the Indians who had converted to Christianity were allowed to live within the confines of the city, with the much larger unconverted population living outside.[8]

For all the efforts of the Portuguese to make Goa an enclave of Christianity, the town was not all *casados* and *soldados*, and there were resilient elements of the highly cosmopolitan world of southern India. Among the eclectic residents of the city were the thirteen blind kings of Hormuz, victims of a policy that regularly deposed rulers who proved inconvenient, depriving them of sight as that disqualified them from rule under Islamic law. The region had also long played host to droves of Persian intellectuals, who were often prized additions to the courts of Deccan princes, and a few of whom could be found in Goa itself. There were also refugees from religious persecution in Europe, including one who probably acted as a guide to Camões, judging from the verses the poet wrote in his honour. This was the Jewish-Portuguese doctor Garcia de Orta, who had trained at the universities of Alcalá and Salamanca before leaving the Iberian peninsula, one of the many New Christians who fled as attitudes hardened towards even those who had converted and the Inquisition gained power. In India he had made himself indispensable by synthesising European and Arabic medicine with Indian traditions, and had been called upon to treat Muslim kings in the interior as well as Portuguese viceroys and dignitaries. During Camões' time in India, Garcia de Orta was compiling an encyclopaedia of medicinal plants, bringing together knowledge from all the cultures that met in southern India, as well as the names of these plants in Greek, Latin, Arabic, Gujarati, Castilian, Portuguese and the local language Konkani, often finding links between them which would soon lead some to suspect the existence of an Indo-European language that linked these distant cultures.[9]

Orta was a wellspring of information about local customs, including (for instance) the use and physical effects of *bhang* (cannabis), which was acquired for him from the market by his Indian servant Antónia. Though Orta insisted that he had never tried the stuff himself, he considered it his duty to gather knowledge of its effects from those who had, including his servants, who reported that it made them very averse to work and rather inclined to eat. It also caused laughter and made people seem as if they were taken out of themselves, transported above all cares. *Bhang* was, in fact, only one of many drugs that Europeans were to encounter in the east, a wholly new discovery for a culture that had almost no tradition of consuming narcotics for pleasure. From the very first voyages the Portuguese had been struck by the chewing of *paan*, a package of areca nuts inside betel leaf with rose water, whose attractions as a stimulant they were slow to understand.

Orta also introduced Portuguese visitors to the wonders of Indian food. While early visitors considered the local cuisine to be inedible by Europeans owing to the amount of pepper used, Orta had a wide knowledge of the region's dishes. He had, for instance, discovered the secret ingredient which accounted for the delicious taste of many Indian dishes, an ingredient unthinkable to many Europeans, as it was the gum they called *assa foetida* – 'stinking mastic' – but which was the most widely used spice in India, even purchased by the poor to go with their bread and onions. Much of this information seems to have come from the servant Antónia, who is constantly mentioned in his work as having gathered the samples for Orta, though she is never credited as a source of knowledge alongside the Greek and Arabic authorities. Orta also

Opposite: A Portuguese man and unmarried Indian Christian women, from the *Codex Casanatense*, contemporary with Camões arrival in India.

saw fit to record that she made a delicious starfruit pastry and jam that were popular with visitors.[10]

Camões' black moods were not, or at least not entirely, down to the tensions of living as a stranger in an occupied territory. In part his hatred of Goa seems to have come from the fact that he had no better luck with women in India than he had in Lisbon. In a letter written about a year after he arrived, he complained to a friend back home that the few Portuguese women in town were too old and that the Indian women were wholly immune to his charms. His attempts to seduce them with a few lines from the poets Petrarch and Boscán had, it seems, fallen on deaf ears, and their matter-of-fact responses seemed to him shockingly coarse, wholly unlike the sophisticated dalliances to which he was accustomed. This may well have been because the local women were interested only in arrangements that led to marriage, which would bring with them the security and status of a *casado* wife, or it may have been because it was the habit of local women to dull their senses with a heavy dose of *bhang* when they had to deal with Portuguese men.[11]

The disdain he expressed to his friend, however, was mere bravado, as suggested by a sonnet written during this time about a *black love*, a *captive who has captured him* and whose dark hair – black, as the *Ramayana* has it, as the raven's wing – was all his thought.

> In the field there are no flowers
> In the sky there are no stars
> That are beautiful to me
> As she is, my love;
> Nothing is like her face,
> the quiet of her eyes,
> which are black and tired –
> but not of killing me.

We know little about this woman, other than that she was called Bárbara – allowing Camões to riddle poetically about the fact that, though foreign, she was not *barbara* (a barbarian) – and thus was probably an Indian convert, rather than a literal 'captive' as the poem describes her. Perhaps it was Bárbara who was immune to Camões' poetic flirtations.

Camões' periods of indolence in Goa were interrupted by service on the Portuguese ships on their expansive patrols, for it was not only in India that the Portuguese had infiltrated and occupied port towns. In a much wider and more ambitious game they had played Sofala off against Kilwa, Malindi against Mombasa, and within twenty years they had built forts around the entire rim of the western Indian Ocean, creating a giant net to prevent Muslim traders from leaving the Red Sea and so destroy the longstanding trade route through Cairo and Alexandria. The desired effect was achieved, with the trade flowing through the Levant to Venice collapsing by two-thirds and almost nine-tenths of the pepper supply disappearing from that route in a matter of years. The major anchors of the net were at Cape Guardafui on the Horn of Africa, at Hormuz and at Diu, with further stations occasionally being held in Oman, and at Socotra and Aden. The maintenance of these anchoring points, and the patrolling of the waters that connected them, was the main task of those who, like Camões, were bound over to serve in the India fleets.[12]

There was little that was heroic about daily life at this work. Camões was to write from near Guardafui about the days being *sad, painful, harsh and lonely, full of work and dolour and rage*, the shrill heat and thick air leaving him trapped with desperate thoughts of his own failures. He would later describe shipboard plagues, *which made the gums swell and polluted the air*, and how bravery in this world was *teaching your face to appear assured and light-hearted while a bullet takes the leg or arm of a friend*. The ports on this beat were understandably hostile, given that the early Portuguese attempts to force themselves upon these places

diplomatically had quickly given way to brutal acts of violence –
as in the Horn, where the town of Baraawe had been burned to
the ground when it did not cooperate, the locals watching (as
Damião noted) from a nearby palm grove *as the city that was rich
and affluent was destroyed and massacred in an instant*. Some
local magnates did what they could to undermine the Portuguese,
as when the Sheikh of Qalhat in Oman sent sacks full of cowshit
and street sweepings out to the fleet instead of food, though the
fact that his town was burned in reprisal showed the high price
of defiance.

Even in the places that cooperated, provisions were hard to
come by: the island of Hormuz, where Camões spent the winter of
1555, was extremely arid, and supplying it from the mainland was
so difficult that merchants there had a page carry a silver keg of
water in front of them wherever they went as a mark of their great
status and of the luxury they could afford. One contemporary
painting by an Indian artist shows the Portuguese at Hormuz
taking their meal in the cool of a water tank. A Portuguese guide
to the region said that the winds of the Red Sea were so hot that no
dead thing went rotten there, instead being dried into a powder – a
macabre observation, though perhaps less so at the time, given
that Middle Eastern corpse powder (known as *mummia* or
'mummy') was widely in demand throughout Europe as a medicine. While in some verses Camões wrote with affection about
shipboard life, of swapping stories during the endless indolence,
the lion's share of the days were black, hot and desperate.

> Next to a sterile, dry, fierce mountain,
> misshapen, naked, useless and barren,
> abhorred by nature in all things –
> where never a bird flies or a beast sleeps
> or a river flows or a spring appears,
> where no green branch rustles ...
> Here, in this remote, harsh and bitter

part of the world, I wished my brief life
was even briefer, my life that has been
broken and strewn across the world.

These lines and others like them leave little doubt of the disillusionment Camões felt as a tiny and insignificant part of this huge inglorious machine.[13]

The Portuguese strategy in the Indian Ocean had, if anything, been a victim of its own early and overwhelming success. The evaporation of the spice trade that had flowed through Alexandria to Cairo contributed directly to the fall of the Mamluk Sultanate in Egypt, ending the bizarre arrangement by which for hundreds of years the nominal leaders of Islam were selected from among slaves, at least some of whom had started life as Christians. As late as 1503 the Mamluk sultan had threatened Western Christendom, proclaiming himself the true heir to Alexander the Great in a letter that Damião transcribed in full into his chronicle. Announcing himself as *God's shadow on the land*, and deploring the treatment of Muslims by Christians in Iberia as in the east, the sultan threatened in retribution to destroy Christian sites, including Jerusalem, *so that no stone will remain upon another stone, and the stones themselves shall be ground to paste.* The confrontation culminated at Diu in 1509 when, after suffering an initial defeat at the hands of a combined Gujarati–Mamluk navy, the Portuguese routed the enemy fleet and set the dominoes in the eastern Mediterranean toppling. While undermining the economic foundations of Islam had been among the main goals of European exploration for several hundred years, this triumph was actually a disaster in disguise, because it contributed directly to the ascendance of a much more powerful opponent in the form of the Ottoman Empire, and it was the Portuguese weakening of the Mamluk Sultanate that gave the Ottomans the final piece they needed to implement their ambitions on a global scale.[14]

The conquest of Egypt by the Turks in 1517, and its transformation into a province of the Ottoman Empire, not only transferred the control of the Indian Ocean trade to Istanbul, but also made the Turks protectors of the holy cities of Mecca and Medina as well as transferring to them the Caliphate, the spiritual leadership of Islam. In place of a decadent and poorly organised enemy, the Portuguese now faced a vast and sprawling empire with far greater sophistication, resources and ambition, as well as control of a secondary shipping lane leading through the Persian Gulf, an area that Camões patrolled in 1554. The Ottoman intelligence and cartographical networks were equal to anything the Europeans could claim, as suggested by the map of Piri Reis that integrated American geographical findings as early as 1513, and by the fact that the only surviving Portuguese map from the period is to be found not in Lisbon but in Istanbul. While Ottoman ships did not have the deep-ocean capabilities of the Portuguese craft, they had, by the time Camões arrived, found an edge, with their corsair captain Sefer Reis luring one Portuguese vessel after another into the shallow and sheltered coastal waters where the oared Turkish ships were more manoeuvrable. And a project was underway to resurrect an ancient canal from the Red Sea to the Nile, allowing sea traffic to sail directly from the Mediterranean into the Indian Ocean. If Portugal and Spain had envisaged their explorations leading to global and even universal empires that recreated the glories of Rome, they soon discovered that they were far from alone: similar ambitions were part of the cultures of the Mongols, the Chinese, the Mughals, the south Indians and of course the Ottomans. The Ottomans saw themselves as taking up the legacy of Alexander the Great, and one of the many titles that their sultans accorded themselves was *Qayser-i-Rum* – 'King of the Romans'.[15]

In an attempt to adjust to this new reality, the Portuguese had been forced to invent a new form of global politics. The miraculous ally that they had once sought in Prester John, legendary Christian king of the east, had proved to be an illusion; if the

Ethiopian monarchs were indeed the basis for the myth of the priest-king, they were no match for the Ottomans, as amply demonstrated when Portuguese–Ethiopian armies were routed by Ottoman-supported forces in the 1530s and 40s. When an alternative offered itself in the form of Shah Ismail of Persia, the Portuguese believed their good luck, even managing to convince themselves in their desperation that the Shia, who did not recognise the Sunni Islamic Caliphate and had ambitions of their own, weren't really Muslims as such and so were entirely acceptable as an ally against the Sunni Ottomans. Ismail was, after all, descended from the Christian emperors of Trebizond on his mother's side, and these were people who spoke the same language, as suggested by an immense drunken feast in 1515 at which Shah Ismail hosted Portuguese emissaries, which Damião recorded with the precision he reserved for matters of the stomach, to show how *humanely* the Persians lived. The Portuguese had travelled more than 1,000 miles inland from Hormuz to find the Persian monarch, and caught up with him south of Tabriz, where his city of 35,000 tents sat in the shadow of the snow-capped Sahand volcano.[16]

They found him in a pavilion much like the ones made famous by Persian artists, heavy with brocade and gold thread, thick with carpets and centred around a tank in which he liked to watch trout swim. He was being attended by the ambassadors of Lores (in Armenia) and Georgia, two of the fourteen Christian kingdoms that were his vassals, and he was wearing the immense twelve-fold Shia turban, the same as the one that this expedition brought back to Lisbon and which Damião looked after in his role as a page. During a feast that lasted from ten in the morning until late at night, the Portuguese were continually pressed to drain cups of the fine Shiraz wine by Ismail, who himself kept pace, drinking from an enormous jewelled goblet that could hold half a *canada*, equivalent to a pint and a half of wine. When the Portuguese emissary suggested that it must have been watered down, Ismail sent it over to confirm that it was full strength, and the ambassador had to drink the whole lot down as a forfeit, which he did in three long gulps. By contrast, the Shah joked that the Portuguese wine with which he had been presented was barely distinguishable from honey or butter. In the heat of their drink, when the governor of the local province declared tearfully that his love for the guests was so great that he considered himself a *firangi* (a 'Frank', or western Christian foreigner) and would go and live with them, the ambassador asked Shah Ismail for his friendship. Shah Ismail's sobering response was that it was not the behaviour of friends to steal from each other, as the Portuguese had done in taking his province of Hormuz, and that while his own mind was focused on the defeat of the Turk and the capture of Mecca, he would – as a favour to them – ask the Shah of Bijapur (a longstanding client of the Persians) to leave them in peace. The ambassadors were sent back to Hormuz with letters of extraordinary eloquence and beauty, greeting the Portuguese king *whose greatness is like a fragrant rose* and his general in India *who is great in our favour like the breaking of day or the fragrance of musk* – but without the desired alliance.[17]

It was in this ocean, this cauldron of contending ambitions, that Camões spent his first years in the east, and from which he would have to find the materials for the epic poem that was not only his passport back to the promised land but would make him (according to the German poet Friedrich Schlegel) the most beloved poet since Homer. The daily life on board a patrol ship must not have given opportunity for composing much more than the dark lyrics in which he lamented his outcast state. But for good or for bad, Camões was soon back in prison, with plenty of time to think and plot and write.

IX

Summertime, 7037

Portugal was not alone in seeing Persia as the solution to its problems. At about the same time as the Portuguese embassy to Ismail, a Genoese merchant named Paolo Centurione was headed north to Moscow on an outrageous quest, hoping to save the fortunes of his homeland by rerouting the spice trade north from India through central Asia and Russia. If, in undercutting the trade that flowed through Cairo and Alexandria, the Portuguese had managed to topple the Mamluk Sultanate in Egypt, they had also undermined the economic foundations of Venice and Genoa, which for centuries had brought eastern wares from Alexandria to the markets of Europe, and the Italian merchants were furious. The complete Portuguese control of the spice market, Centurione complained in a pamphlet written by the Italian humanist Paolo Giovio, allowed them to charge *more grievous and intolerable prices than was ever heard of before*, and for shoddy produce at that, with the freshness of their spices *corrupted by the infection of the sump and the other filthiness of the ships, as well as long storage in Lisbon, so that their natural savour, taste and quality vanishes and drifts away*. Centurione proposed to beat the Portuguese at their own game, pioneering a new route for spices up the Indus to where they could be transferred by a short voyage over the Paropamisus to the Oxus, and so down into the Caspian Sea where they could head from Astrakhan up the Volga to Moscow and so on to the Baltic, circumventing entirely the need either to deal with the Ottoman-controlled Levant or to rely on the Portuguese routes around Africa.[1]

That Centurione's plan was unworkable – not least because Russia did not control the region north of the Caspian and could not even trade there itself – was not remotely obvious to western Europeans, given their very limited knowledge of central Eurasian politics and geography. Giovio had produced a map – the only surviving copy of which has newly been rediscovered in Venice – showing the proposed route, and it was plausible enough to alarm the Portuguese, who knew that their ability to control land traffic in the east was very limited indeed. Damião may well have seen further evidence that this route was possible when he visited the great library of Konrad Peutinger in Augsburg, where the greatest treasure was the *Tabula Peutingeriana*, believed to be the only surviving map of the Roman road network.

This twenty-foot-long map, which lays the whole world out in a straight line as it would have been seen from these roads, shows various routes through central Asia that might compete with the ocean path. Damião was to publish a response to this Italian attack on the Portuguese handling of spices, rejecting entirely the suggestion that they were elevating prices and selling stale wares. On the contrary, he wrote, he himself had smelled the fires in which the Portuguese burned old spices when he was a boy, and besides, the Portuguese spent more than their profits on spreading Christianity and fighting against the Turk – a sly dig at the Venetians and Genoese, who traded directly with Alexandria and Beirut and so shored up the finances of Islam. But it was not enough for the Portuguese to win the publicity war, and Damião was to travel east from Poland at the end of his diplomatic career, around about the Russian year 7037.[2]

Opposite: Section of the *Tabula Peutingeriana*, the only surviving copy of the Roman road map, showing India and the area east of the Caspian Sea.

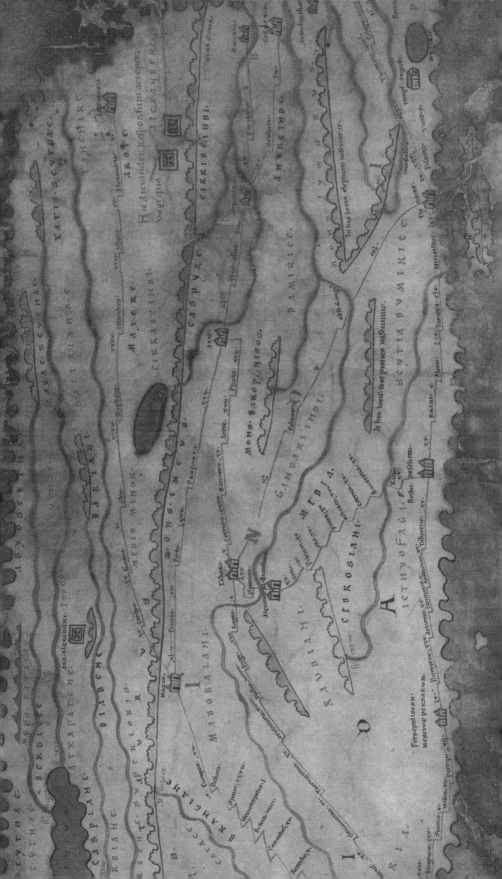

The reason for Damião's travels in this region is something of a mystery. The ostensible purpose may have been commercial prospecting – he noted that (like the Ethiopians) the Muscovites, Livonians and Lithuanians drank mead as their main liquor, which tasted like the wines of Malvasia and Candia (from the Canaries and Crete), and the northern regions had little knowledge of sugar, and so were a virgin market for Portuguese goods – but Russia held a much broader fascination for Europeans of this period. Since winning their independence from the collapsing Timurid Empire in the late fifteenth century, the Muscovites had offered yet another prospect for a miraculous Christian ally, and a number of European powers had cherished hopes that the Russians would open a second front against the Ottomans from the north. This had become especially urgent after the Battle of Mohács (1526) a few years earlier, when Suleiman the Magnificent had routed the Hungarians, bringing Ottoman forces right into the heart of Europe. While the death of the Hungarian king in this battle was widely lamented as a tragedy, perhaps the most worrying aspect of the defeat was the complete failure of the other European powers to rally around the Hungarians. Damião himself was involved in a Portuguese effort to fund German support for the Hungarians, which had been blocked by a papal legate because it meant dealing with the Protestant enemy. The Hungarians could not look for help from closer to home, as they were perennially engaged in territorial disputes with both the Poles and Muscovy, and the Tsars saw Hungary and Lithuania as natural Russian possessions. Far from launching an attack against the Ottomans, the Russians were far more interested in making headway into Polish territory using the support of a Muslim ally – namely, the remaining Mongol Tatar forces in the Crimea. Though many saw resolving the intractable antagonisms in this region as key to the safety of western Europe, even the smallest steps were difficult, and Paolo Centurione's first efforts to open a Russian route for spices had been blocked after vigorous Polish lobbying at the Vatican. The Russians, for their part, were happy to keep eager European powers on the hook while ceding to few of their demands. Tsar Vasiley III seems to have given mixed messages about whether he would welcome an alliance with Western Christendom and the Pope's recognition of his sovereignty, or whether he disdained the authority of the Vatican, whose pope he refused to refer to by any other title than 'doctor'. While a five-year truce had been brokered between Muscovy and Poland around the time of the Hungarian defeat, even this was due to expire during Damião's stay in the region.[3]

Whatever Damião's mission was, it did nothing to change this longstanding political quagmire, and his remit and itinerary were unclear, though contemporary sources suggest that he not only visited Moscow but may also have travelled through the southern valley of the Don, still under Tatar control, and visited on his return those regions of Norway and Sweden for which the Magnus brothers had created an appetite. What is clear is that his exploration of the region had a profound effect upon him, and he was later to draw upon this knowledge regularly when writing his histories of Portugal. He was not alone in his fascination with Russia, and he was connected through Olaus Magnus to the two other European authorities on the region, the Polish historian Jacob Ziegler and the German diplomat Sigismund von Herberstein, whose much more extensive writings allow us to fill out what Damião would have seen.

As one left the cosmopolitan familiarity of Gdansk, the country-side quickly turned from a land sea of wheatfields which fed the rest of Europe to glades of silver birch, like the bare ruined colonnades of abandoned marble churches. All of the European accounts of this period give a distinct impression of stepping beyond the looking glass, perhaps at the moment when, on the borders of Lithuania and Russia, the traveller passed Zlotababa, the little golden statue of a woman to which offerings were made by wayfarers. In the winter this strangeness was compounded by sled-travel and bodies waiting until the ground was soft enough to dig graves.

If Europeans were hoping to find in Russia an extension of their customs and beliefs, they would be severely disappointed: while Western Christendom argued over whether it was acceptable for priests to marry, they would find that in the Russian Church marriage was a requirement, and even more disconcertingly the priest's wife seemed to be the bearer of his consecration – the man was not allowed to give the sacraments if his wife died; what was more, if she remarried, her new husband would be obliged to become a priest as well. And neither side in the fierce Reformation debate could look for support from the Russians, who considered them all schismatics from the true – Eastern – Church, condemned their 'Judaising' use of unleavened bread in the sacrament, and followed a completely different regime of fasting, which included a diet of *ikhri* (fish entrails) during Lent, a ban on eating strangled animals at any time, and strict vegetarianism for religious leaders. The Russians even followed the Greek calendar, with years counted from the moment of creation at 5508 years before the birth of Christ, a full 308 years earlier than the Portuguese date.[4]

The hopes that Russia would be an ally in European attempts to build empires and resurrect the glories of Rome were also wildly misplaced, given that Vasiley considered himself rightful heir to the legacy of Rome – as suggested by the fact that he was the first Russian sovereign to use the title 'Tsar' (Caesar). His mother, after all, was Sofia Paleologa, the heir to the last emperor of Constantinople, and this allowed him to assert an unbroken link to Rome far superior to any claims descending from the long-since fallen Western Empire. This claim was heavily contested, both by the Ottomans who saw the legitimate power as vested in the city of Constantinople itself (so authorising their use of the title *Qayser-i-Rum*, Roman Caesar), and even by the Shah of Persia, who could claim descent from another branch of eastern emperors and who styled himself the new Alexander. Machiavelli provocatively wrote that the virile Ottoman culture was more truly the heir of *romanitas* than European Christian humility. The Muscovites had their own form of classicism to underpin their imperial ambitions, and had recruited scholars and artists from far afield to advertise them, just as European monarchs had. The architect Aristotele Fioravanti had been lured from Bologna during the height of the Italian Renaissance to build the Cathedral of the Dormition in Moscow, and a leading humanist named Michael Trivolis (known in Russia as 'Maxim Grek') had left his post in the greatest printing house of the age, where he had helped Aldus Manutius to bring ancient Greek writings to western Europe, and had gone to work in the Kremlin instead. There, it was said, Maxim was astonished to find a great library of Greek writings unknown to western Europe, the fabled 'Golden Library of the Tsars', which disappeared at some point in the eighteenth century (though it is thought by some still to be hidden beneath the Kremlin).[5]

The otherworldly aura of the Tsars was enhanced by reports from the few ambassadors granted audiences with Vasiley, who was customarily surrounded by an entourage of 'angels' – beardless youths dressed in gold and white robes – and flanked by his boyar aristocracy in tall fur hats. These reports said that Vasiley had chosen a wife by having 1,500 nobles' daughters paraded in front of him, only later to replace his wife when she failed to produce an heir – a scandal that, like that of his counterpart Henry VIII, brought him close to breaking up the Church, but which did bring with it the desired heir, Ivan (some day 'the Terrible'). European observers were astonished by the obsequiousness of those at court towards the Tsar, with courtiers being required to hit their heads against the floor in front of him and to refer to themselves as his slaves, even though these accounts of the Tsar as a godlike autocrat seem to have been misunderstandings of local formalities. They could, however, be forgiven for some confusion, given the extremely heavy drinking that accompanied banquets of roast swan and buttermilk, which involved pledging not to leave any more drink in one's cup than one hoped to find blood in the enemies of the Tsar. Damião was to recognise, in fact, that the

Persian banquet he had chronicled was far closer to the customs he had witnessed in Poland and Russia than to the customs of western and southern Europe. This strangeness seems to have been compounded, for Damião and other Europeans, by the presence of Mongol Tatars at the court, whose dress and manners were a reminder that Russian interests faced south and east as well as – or even instead of – towards Europe. Damião was later to record the similarity between the Tatars' silk robes and those being seen in China, though the dawning awareness of this dimension of global politics did little to help Europeans understand this nomadic people whose common curse, it was said, was to damn people *to reside in one place continually like a Christian, and inhale your own stink.*[6]

It was not only European notions of culture, religion and history that began to break down as one headed east: certain reports tugged at the very fabric of what Europeans understood reality to be. Perhaps most striking among these were claims of new sightings of the legendary 'vegetable lamb of Tartary', which became a topic of heated discussion in the subsequent decades. From the melon-like seed of this plant, which was understood to grow near Astrakhan or on the Caspian Sea, was said to sprout *something very like a lamb*, attached to the stem at the navel, and with a head, eyes, ears, horny hooves, and even wool which was used for making caps. This animal born from the soil had blood when cut into but no flesh, its body being like crabmeat, though it was still hunted by wolves and other predators. Antonio Pigafetta, chronicler of Magellan's fleet in its voyage around the world, had also reported a plant in Borneo, the leaves of which *are alive and walk*, having *on both sides two feet*. After keeping them in a cage for nine days, he noted that *they have no blood, and if anyone touches them they run away*. Astonishing though the prospect was of animals sprouting from the ground like soldiers from dragons' teeth, these

Opposite: Image of a Tatar couple from the *Boxer Codex* (c.1590).

reports were more deeply problematic given the war that was raging in Europe over diets and fasting. If the vegetable lamb sprouted from the ground, bled like a beast but had the flesh of a crab, it presented a problem for European systems of classification: as the eccentric French polymath Guillaume Postel asked: *Is it a plant, an animal or a fish?* This might seem like a mere matter for abstract speculation, until one considers whether eating it during Lent would or would not constitute an act of sacrilege. The precise distinction between fish and beast, between animal and plant, was already being troubled by encounters with manatees and sea slugs elsewhere, but reports of creatures like the vegetable lamb threatened to make a mockery of religious laws, suggesting that this new world had never been imagined by the authors of the scriptures. Europeans would, in time, turn these ambiguities to their own ends: the Jesuits in China, for instance, would use the bloodlessness of crabs to argue that the Buddhist vegetarian diet was based on a false distinction between animals and plants.[7]

The most unsettling revelations on the route from Gdansk to Moscow, however, may not have required the traveller to reach Russia at all, or even Lithuania, where observers recorded a species of sacred lizard and the habit of recognising as god the first thing encountered on any given day. At Frombork, on the road from Gdansk to Vilnius which Damião travelled more than once, there was a tower overlooking the immense and placid Vistula Lagoon, a tower in which a new universe was being kept secret. It was to this tower that the cartographer, economist, mathematician and astronomer Nikolaus Kopernik (Copernicus) had retired some twenty years previously, and shortly afterwards developed a new model for the movement of the heavens, though he had so far declined to publish it for fear of the reaction it might cause.

Copernicus was a sophisticated calculator and made contributions to many fields of knowledge, but his greatest breakthrough was in many ways achieved by playing dumb. The astronomy in which Copernicus had been trained, at Kraków and Padua, involved mind-bending complexities directed towards what was referred to as *saving appearances*, that is, producing mathematical rules that accorded with what was apparent to the viewer – namely, that the stars moved erratically through the sky above a stationary observer. Copernicus mocked the absurdity of one of these models by saying that it required the astronomer to believe that the road from Athens to Thebes was different from the road from Thebes to Athens. His daring counterproposal was that the motion of the stars could in fact be explained with a much neater and simpler set of rules, if only one were to drop the assumption that the earth sat still at the centre of the universe, and replaced this with a universe centred on the sun.[8]

Copernicus was, as it turned out, wrong to fear an immediate backlash against his ideas, and the response was largely favourable when he was finally coaxed into making them public. This was in part because the elegance and simplicity of his model made it extremely useful, but also because the profound logical consequences of his theory took almost a century to make themselves felt. It was not just that this model of the universe contradicted the Bible – which apparently made Luther uncomfortable – but also that it struck at the relationship between human experience and knowledge. In order to explain the counter-intuitive proposal that the ground beneath us, the very bedrock of our lives, was in fact in motion, Copernicus conceived of an exquisite *dance of the planets*, in which the earth whirled in just such a way as to make it seem as though she was standing still and everything else moved about her. But if this self-evident truth was merely an illusion, it begged the question of how many other systems had been elaborated merely to preserve our conviction that we are at the centre of things. Copernicus' calculations also suggested that the 'fixed stars' – those heavenly bodies that did not appear to move – were unthinkably far away, that the universe was almost infinitely large, and that the earth (by extrapolation) was almost infinitely small by comparison. There is no evidence to suggest that Damião met

Copernicus when passing through the region, though he was close friends with his cousin and his patron, who later sent Damião an early publication on the Copernican celestial model. But Damião shared with Copernicus something more profound than any incidental meeting could have conferred – an openness to, even a pleasure in, the lurching sensation of a universe shifting from its centre of balance.[9]

By Christmastime that year Damião was back in the Low Countries – in Brussels rather than Antwerp – and as perhaps his last official duty he was given the singular honour of waiting upon the Emperor, Charles V, at a banquet to celebrate the birth of a son and heir to the Portuguese king. As guest of honour, the Emperor had been escorted from his palace along torchlit streets, through triumphal arches bearing the arms of Portugal and past fires burning bundles of cinnamon, to the ambassador's residence, where a wall had been knocked through to allow as many dignitaries as possible see His Caesarean Majesty drink the health of the new Portuguese prince. The church tower of nearby Notre Dame du Sablon had also been torchlit for the occasion, and the windows of the residence had been blown out by the force of the artillery fired to commence the festivities. At the head of the table of honour was the Emperor's sister Mary, recently named regent of the Netherlands after having completed her period of mourning for her husband, the same king of Hungary who had been killed at Mohács by Suleiman. The Emperor himself sat in the middle of one side, under a golden canopy, the other side being left empty so as not to obscure the view. Behind him was a model of a castle set about with fireworks and other *fochi stranii* – strange, exotic pyrotechnics, still unfamiliar in Europe – and in front of him a window through which he could watch the *juego de cañas* (game of canes) in the street below, a form of mock battle that the Spanish had inherited from the Arabs. The two teams were distinguished by their costumes, with one side being dressed as Moors and the other as Turks. While Damião would certainly have been put through his paces managing the pastry cases set in front of the Emperor, filled with live parrots and other birds to perform a miracle of resurrected food when opened, there was nothing demeaning about being asked to wait on Charles. Indeed, it gave the opportunity to overhear what was being said between Charles and his neighbours at table – the Prince of Denmark and the Marquis of Villafranca – and perhaps to mention to the Emperor, as he served him with Malvasia wine, that they drank something very like it in Russia. The food, like the entertainment, was a taste map of Portuguese expansion, with wines from the Canaries and Madeira, thirty-two dishes of Portuguese cuisine (and a further three specially prepared for the Emperor) including gilded pigs' heads; confectionery made out of malagueta pepper from western Africa and black pepper from India and Malacca; and indeed *all the drugs* gathered by the Portuguese fleets.[10]

The drinking and feasting spread out over three days, and by the third day had become almost hallucinatory, with trick confections filled with garlic to surprise the lady diners and a masqued jousting contest undertaken at least partly in drag. Though the Emperor excused himself after the first night, the luxuriance of the feasting continued to build to a crescendo, with the ambassador making his way through 6,000 ducats in entertaining his guests. On the third night, in front of a gathered audience of diplomats from two dozen countries and the papal legate Cardinal Campeggio, the festivities climaxed in the performance of a scandalous play by the most famous Portuguese writer of the age, Gil Vicente. Only fragmentary reports of the production survive, but it caused such raucous hilarity (it was said) that no one could eat or drink any more for their bellyaches. Though the play, called *Guerta de Jubileu* (Jubilee Garden), was a love farce, the laughter was mostly prompted by Vicente's excoriating satire of the Church, led by a character in a hat that had been borrowed from the cardinal himself under a false pretext. The furious report of the evening to Rome – cursing the evil times in which they lived – spoke of how the laughter was so loud and open and universal, mocking the Pope as nothing better than an indulgence-monger who used damnation to drive up sales, that it seemed as though they were in the midst of Saxony, in Luther's country, rather than in the Emperor's own domain. The papal party complained, and demanded the head of whoever was responsible for staging the play, but the Portuguese refused to supply this information. Between the Ottoman threat, the contending versions of the faith that seemed to be sprouting everywhere, and the suggestion that the earth had shifted from its traditional place at the centre of the universe, it must have seemed like all the world was coming apart around them. That we have no further knowledge of the play-text is largely down to the fact that it was soon afterwards entered into a Library of the Damned, containing such books as were considered a threat to the Holy Faith, and no copy of it survives. This library was to prove a key element in Damião's downfall.[11]

X

Prince of Ghosts

I t was probably during Camões' absence on the Persian Gulf beat that a holy corpse almost caused a riot in Goa. Whether he was there or not, Camões never mentioned the crowds who pressed forward to see the body of Francis Xavier lying in state in the Jesuit College, who broke the grilles that were supposed to separate the anointed from the common man, straining forward perhaps to see if the body really was uncorrupted in the monsoon damp or if the smell was simply masked by all the incense. Xavier was not just any Jesuit but one of the six original companions, the founders of the order who had on an August day in 1534 met in Paris' Montmartre district and sworn amidst the turmoil of the Catholic Church to make a pilgrimage together to Jerusalem before offering themselves to the Pope as a new form of religious warrior. Among the largely Spanish companions led by the soldier-turned-mystic Ignatius Loyola there was also one Portuguese student, a man named Simão Rodrigues, who would go on to found their Portuguese chapter. Damião was to come to know this man very well indeed, if in fact he had not already met him shortly before the Montmartre oath.[1]

Xavier's body had been carried through Goa in triumph but his life was one that ended in frustration. Though he was the closest companion to Loyola and had been entrusted with one of the pillars of their mission, heading out as a new Apostle of the East

133

while Loyola remained in Rome to cement the institutional fabric of the Company of the Name of Jesus, the early fantasy of lost Christian kingdoms soon evaporated, and even hopes of new flocks which would ecstatically convert to Christianity proved illusory. Far from making new inroads for the faith in India, Xavier had in fact become anxious that those who had arrived in the east as Christians were falling away from the Church, and were only interested in fanatical preachers whose behaviour was almost as troubling as that of the heathens themselves. There was a further false dawn in Japan, where Xavier felt he had found a light-skinned, highly fastidious people who would surely welcome the Word, but the initial optimism slowly drained away as it became clear that the Jesuits' welcome owed more to political manoeuvring among the *daimyo* warlords than to any genuine interest in the faith. Xavier had, however, become convinced that he was merely starting in the wrong place, and that clearly he needed to follow the spiritual laws of Japan back to their place of origin in China, where Christianity could correct these religious errors at the source, and all would flow outwards from there. This theory was never to be tested, as Xavier's mission to China was halted when he died of a fever on an island a short way from the port of Guangzhou (Canton).[2]

Francis Xavier was not alone among Europeans in chasing phantoms of Christianity as they vanished across the world. The Portuguese factor at Safi in Morocco had sent reports of a race of Christians who lived in the 'Clear Mountains' and who had an ancient library of Latin texts, perhaps a garbled report of the great Islamic libraries of Timbuktu. During the early years in India the Portuguese, fresh from their disappointments regarding Prester John, had grasped eagerly at traces of St Thomas, the same doubting Thomas who was supposed to have stuck his fingers into the wounds of the risen Christ and then headed east to convert the Indies to the new faith. Signs of the Apostle were even encountered in Brazil, where the Jesuits recorded finding a petrified footprint which, according to tradition, had been left by a bearded white man known as 'Zomé', whom they quickly identified as their own São Thomé (St Thomas). The Portuguese hunger for an unbroken link with the early Church, which would suggest that they were merely completing the work of conversion begun by the companions of Christ, often had to contend with the fact that the Christianity to be found in India had its own practices and history, linked to the Armenian Church, which did not fit easily into this neat narrative.

A flicker of hope had however been kindled in the 1540s, when the dying Indian bishop of Cranganore had entrusted to a Portuguese official the knowledge that there existed certain copper tablets which recorded the doings of St Thomas in the region, but that in a moment of desperation the bishop had pawned them for twenty *cruzados* and had not been able to redeem them since. A hunt was immediately set in motion for the tablets, which were indeed recovered, but could not be read for the antiquity of the script. The tablets – whose story was recorded in loving detail by Damião – were about a palm and a half in length by four fingers wide, of fine metal and inscribed on both sides, locking the precious writing in a form that could resist flames, damp and the rapid decay of organic materials. After much searching, and having almost lost hope, they found an old Jew who lived in the Western Ghats and who spoke many languages and who pronounced, after much work, that the copper books were written in three languages – Chaldean, Malabar (Malayalam) and Arabic – and provided a transcription, a translation of which was sent to Damião for safe-keeping in the Torre do Tombo. The Portuguese convinced themselves that the 'Thomas' named in the copper books was none other than the Apostle, and secreted the precious artefact away for further study. The copper plates subsequently disappeared, much to the dismay of the Syrian Christian community, whose founder Thomas of Cana was actually the figure named in the document, a document that was also the oldest witness to the rights granted them by the local ruler.[3]

135

More troubling than the trails gone cold were those echoes of Christian history that had been transformed by long residence in India. When the Portuguese finally did reach Mylapore (Chennai), the resting place of St Thomas, they found that according to local tradition he had spent some time in the wilderness in the form of a peacock. In Ceylon, Christian and Islamic travellers reported a gigantic footprint that was said to have been left by Adam, the father and progenitor of mankind. After one ascended the mountain using the chains installed for climbers, there was a deep pool and nearby a foot-shaped hollow in the rock, which was held to be Adam's last contact with earth before he ascended into heaven. The Ceylonese footprint was a site of pilgrimage for members of all the Abrahamic faiths, Muslims particularly considering the lake to have special powers of purification and absolution. However, as the Moroccan traveller Ibn Battuta recorded when he visited the spot in the fourteenth century, this was not the only story associated with the print: the Buddhists venerated it as Sri Pada, the sacred mark left by the foot of the Buddha, and others with Shiva; yet another tradition held that this was the place spoken of in a climactic scene in the *Ramayana*, where the monkey warrior Hanuman landed after his great leap across the ocean in search of Rama's consort Sita, who was being held by the *rakšasa* (demon) king Ravana. The tendency of familiar things to begin to slip, to metamorphose into forms unthinkable to European Christians – saints and biblical figures transforming into animals, breaching the strict separation between man and beast in the Abrahamic faiths – was highly alarming to many observers, and there were increasingly widespread suggestions that the symmetries between eastern religions and Christianity were part of a diabolic temptation aimed at undermining the faithful.[4]

These joint feelings of wonder and dismay were nowhere more powerful than in European encounters with Indian temples, and pride of place among them was given to the island of Pori in Maharashtra, known to the Europeans as 'Elephanta'. The many accounts of Elephanta agreed at least that this was one of the wonders of the world – perhaps the greatest of them – and that what was seen there was beyond the realm of mere human capability. Camões' friend Garcia de Orta may have been the first European to visit the temple complex. At Elephanta, he writes, there is at the top of a hill a great underground monastery carved out of the living rock, surrounded by patios and cisterns, and all around the walls there are sculptures of elephants and lions, and women like Amazons, in which *it seemed that the devil used his best ingenuity to make people want to worship him*. Another account suggests that the stonework was so fine it could not have been better had it been carved in silver or wax, and records that the thin coating of blinding white lime contributed to the marvellous nature of the place, a contrast to the dark and heavily painted churches Europeans were used to. The most astounding of the figures was a vast trunk of stone with three heads and four arms, wearing a crown over hair plaited with jewels and carrying four symbols (a cobra, a rose, a globe, and something else that could no longer be made out) – the *Siva Mahesamurti*, considered by many to be the crowning artistic achievement of the Kalacuri period a thousand years before. The *Codex Casanatense*, a series of watercolours likely produced by Indian artists for a Portuguese patron around the time of Camoes' arrival in the east, portrayed not only the varied peoples of India but also the three gods of the Trimurti, though the European scribe struggled to label the figures of Vishnu, Shiva and Brahma correctly. Many European travellers also remarked on the statue of the elephant god after whom the island was called – though his name, Ganesha, was mangled to 'Ganesson' or 'Gaves' – as well as a statue of a great queen whom they took to be one of the Amazonian warrior women of classical antiquity.[5]

It was not necessary, however, for Portuguese travellers to go as far as Maharashtra to experience the wonders of Indian religious art. At Salcete near to Goa there was another immense subterranean temple, more impressive (writes Orta) than any religious

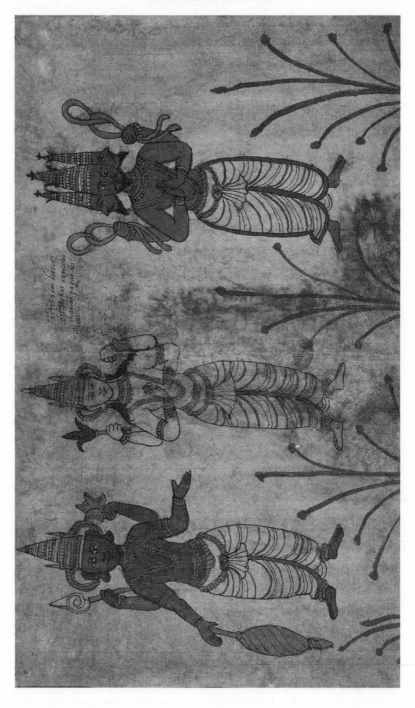

Opposite: Contemporary image of the *Trimurti* (Shiva, Vishnu, Brahma) made for a Portuguese patron in India during Camões' time in India, from the *Codex Casanatense*.

building in Portugal, where in more than 300 rooms there were a great many idols carved in stone, diabolic things in the shadows which made his flesh tremble. Goa itself was littered with toppled statues, including ones of the *gramdevata* (local deity) Vetal, the well-hung 'Prince of Ghosts' with 3,000 names and a necklace of skulls, whose statues were traditionally carved from wood of the Arjuna tree. There were also the hero stones that could be found everywhere in the Deccan, three-tiered friezes showing the fall of great warriors in battle and their ascent into the heavenly realm. Many artefacts made their way back to Europe, such as the golden idol described by Damião – covered in jewels including a ruby the size of a rosary cross embedded in his chest, with emeralds for eyes and a mantle of beaten gold – and the Sanskrit inscriptions that one retiring governor took back for his country seat near Sintra.

Just across the river from the palace of the Portuguese viceroy at Goa, on the island of Divar, there were the remains of the temple destroyed by the Portuguese in 1514 – the very one whose sculptures the Medici agent was eyeing for his patron – though the main statue of the elephant god Ganesha had been smuggled out to safety by the Brahmin. The destruction of these temples had clearly scarred the memory of the local community, as suggested by a striking tribute paid by another fascinating figure Camões knew in Goa – the mapmaker Fernão Vaz Dourado, who was quietly producing some of the most beautiful and accurate charts the world had ever seen, halfway across the world from where the European cartographic revolution was supposedly taking place. Renaissance maps strove to set themselves apart from what had gone before by presenting themselves as highly technical, plotting unprecedentedly exact measurements within imposing grid lines of latitude and longitude, and sweeping away all of the imaginative and historical information that had cluttered old maps, the fantasies of dog-headed men in distant places and the sites of great battles and vanished wonders of the world. Vaz Dourado was among the pioneers leading this purification, but he made a poignant exception on his maps just north of Goa where he lived, where among the names of major cities is found a label that says *O pagode queimado vam de Goa* – 'the burnt pagan temple of Goa'.[6]

Camões would have had ample opportunity to contemplate the island of Divar, as it was directly across from the Goan jailhouse where he was a regular resident and which with cruel irony was also named the Tronco, the same as the Lisbon lock-up where he had done time. This view across to Divar is thought to be captured in a short poem by Camões about a river island *whose plants feed the cattle and my eyes*, and the cell from which he contemplated it is captured in an extraordinary painting labelled *Prizam, 1556*, which may be the earliest surviving depiction of the poet.

In this unusual portrait, which feels very much drawn from life, Camões sits at a trestle table near a grated window, from which the masts of ships riding on the water outside can be seen. He is immediately identifiable by his missing eye, and his clothes are as we would expect: a study in ruined gentility, with rips and tears in the expensive black cloth of his jacket. On the table in front of him are dishes holding a few crumbs, a pot with quills, and sheets of paper on which he is composing; on the wall behind him a shelf has been affixed with room for four thick books. The titles of the books cannot be read, but we can see a map on which are shown two Portuguese ships, and a title is visible at the top of one of the pages in front of him, which reads 'Canto X'. We know this is the Goan prison – rather than one of the others with which Camões was familiar – because the artist has peeled away the wall behind his right shoulder, showing from a different perspective the outside of the jail, with a palm tree in front and a loincloth-clad porter

Opposite: Camões in Prison, in a portrait thought to be contemporary.

passing by. The books, the maps, the writing, and the leg iron visible in the corner of the portrait suggest that this was no overnight imprisonment, but rather a good solid stretch in which a poet down on his luck might begin something very ambitious.[7]

As ever, Camões' frequent incarceration makes it hard to put later stories of his troubles into any kind of order, and he was not important enough for his arrests to merit much of a record. There is good reason to believe, however, that it was his pen that got him into trouble this time, rather than the temper or money troubles that did for him on other occasions. Evidently hoping that his literary talents would win him a reprieve from the drudgery of shipboard life, Camões had written several pieces to celebrate the installation of a new Portuguese governor, including the *Auto de Filodemo*, an elegant and typically Renaissance play of shipwrecked twins who are subject to various confusions before they win love and discover their true identities. It seems to have been the first Portuguese play performed in India – though the settlers' theatrical culture took root soon afterwards – and very possibly the first European play performed in Asia, and all might have been well had Camões stopped there. But he seems also to have written a short sketch for the same celebration, a mockery of the leading citizens of Goa and their drunken debauchery. The skit took the form of a joust in which each of the participants was more intoxicated than the last, and each the subject of rather cutting jokes, like the one who claimed he was drunk only because he couldn't stomach the local water. The jousters were each given symbols – a bat, a palm frond, a salamander – which referred in various highly arcane ways to the sloppy lushness of these Goan personalities. The surviving account of the performance, which Camões wrote down after the fact, feigns surprise that anyone could have read slanderous things into these (very unsubtle) jokes, and at one point he even blames a local craftsman's poor command of Portuguese, which led to the salamander's motto, *I live in fire*, being written out as *I drink firewater*.[8]

142

That Camões may have been writing his epic poem about the Portuguese voyages while sitting in the Goan prison and looking out across to the ruined temple on Divar, as suggested by that first portrait, gives a particular sharpness to the act of erasure he was beginning to perform in his *Lusiads*. It was clear from the start that there would be some difficulty in making a heroic legend of Portugal's encounter with India, and his time in Goa could only have confirmed this impression, with its squabbling factions of *casados* and *soldados*, debauched and decadent officials, and weakening grasp on the ocean trade. It was also unclear how this strange Indian culture and its wondrous artistry fitted into the narrative. But Camões was a storyteller, not a historian, and as such had various moulds at his disposal into which the past could be fitted, patterns that would associate the figures and events of Portuguese history with heroism in the minds of his readers. One of these has already been mentioned – the story of Jason and the Argonauts, an eastward quest by semi-divine heroes in search of miraculous treasures – but there was another classical story that also helped European observers to place India within a framework they could understand: the legendary conquests of Alexander the Great. The historical facts of Alexander's military campaigns, which had indeed reached the Indus, had long been overshadowed by the myths that had grown up around them – which included half-memories of Indian yogis ('gymnosophists') and marvellous stories of a submarine voyage – and in the thousand years during which Europe had been all but cut off from India these stories had become central to European imaginings of the east. The stories did not, however, lose their power when the Portuguese arrived in India and had first-hand experience of the wonders they described; rather, the model that Alexander offered of a European conqueror of the east made the stories if anything more popular, and travellers were determined to find evidence of classical Greece wherever they went. Early witnesses attested that a mosque and burial ground in Gujarat, which was said to have 100,000 headstones, was the site of a great victory won by Hercules over the Amazons, despite the problems with reconciling the dates of the classical hero with Islam. Damião similarly confirmed that Gujarat accorded with Arrian's description of the place where Alexander halted, noting horses that were fed on fish, and beaches so gently sloping that a running man or even a horse could not escape the incoming tide with its *macareo* – a word for the sound of waters jostling. Many of the female figures of Indian sculpture were also associated with the Amazons, and soon it was even being suggested that Elephanta itself was not a product of Indian genius but rather a monument built by Alexander to mark the furthest point of his advance.[9]

It was in just this vein that Camões, fully aware as he was of the Indian monuments on Divar and Elephanta, wrote in his epic a description of Indian art that gave the lie to everything he had seen and heard during his time in the east. In a passage that closely echoes descriptions of Elephanta by Doctor Orta and other Portuguese contemporaries, Camões has da Gama encounter a relief bustling with *figures of gods carved in wood and stone, in various postures and colours, as if the devil had made them*, including ones with many faces and many arms. The gods depicted, however, are given not Indian names but classical Greek and Roman ones, and in the passage that follows all trace of India has vanished, replaced by a series of sculptures celebrating great invasions, *made with the skill of Daedalus* – the legendary Greek architect and creator of the Labyrinth – culminating in the victories of Alexander, whose flags flew beside the Indus. At the end of this frieze Camões refers to a series of blank panels on which the images of new conquerors will be carved, and we are left in no doubt that the Portuguese are to be seen here as Lords of India in the tradition of Alexander the Great. In Camões' rendering of the scene, then, the Indians have been almost wholly written out of their own history – the names of their gods are gone, their art is given over to the Greeks, and they are present only as the subjects of a long series of conquests, of which the Portuguese is the latest.

144

The disappearing trick that Camões performed upon the temple of Elephanta was in a sense simply a version of what was happening all around him in Goa. Several thick volumes in the Goan archive preserve the *Provisões a Favor da Cristandade*, the *Measures Taken to Promote Christianity*, which give a glimpse of the net that was tightening around those who held out against conversion. The edict against the Brahmins preaching their doctrines within the Portuguese-controlled territories had tightened, with new provisions that anyone reporting offenders would receive half of their possessions, and the offenders themselves would be committed to the galleys. A law sent out from Lisbon announced that *whereas much offence is caused by the gentiles of Goa and surrounding territories adoring and publicly celebrating their idols and temples and using their diabolic rites*, no idol was to be made in stone or wood, or of copper or any other metal, that no rite was to happen either inside a home or in public, that the Indians were not to perform their ritual washings or burnings or celebrate the festival of *aregueria* – possibly a reference to a famous ceremony where devotees allowed themselves to be crushed beneath the wheels of the enormous processional carts – and that any household suspected of infringements should be searched. The Portuguese religious authorities were clearly also concerned that gentile ideas would be smuggled into Christian worship on the sly, and banned any non-Christian artisans from making any sacred object, not paintings nor crucifixes nor candelabras nor other metalwork. While the official ordinance cited as the reason for this the lack of reverence the gentiles felt for these holy things, it was also the case that the local artisans included in their extraordinary works elements from their own traditions, such as the Kotte ivories, which blended Ceylonese motifs with Christian ones (some taken from engravings by Dürer), and the crucifix at Margão that incorporated an image of the goddess Lakshmi and her lotus-flower emblem.[10]

That early Portuguese hopes for religious harmony between west and east had been replaced with a terror of infection had much to do with increasing awareness of fundamental differences between Indian religion and Christianity. One of the most profound of these was the relationship between humans and other animals; the first thing noted about India in the *Lusiads* is that while *some worship idols, others adore the animals that live among them.* Early Portuguese accounts of India had fixated on the discovery that many parts of Indian society forbid slaughter and cannot even bear to see animals killed, holding it a terrible thing. In writing about India, Damião was to record the lovely detail that the Gujarati Banyans put lanterns around their candles so as not to harm the mosquitos that were drawn to them. The travel writer Duarte Barbosa noted that Muslim merchants were in the habit of torturing these Banyans by threatening to kill insects and small birds, which the horrified gentiles ransomed at great cost in order to set the animals free again. Christian missionaries were to take this cruel mockery even further, spreading cows' blood on religious sites in order to desecrate them and make them places of sorrow and pollution that could no longer serve as houses of worship.

The Indian relationship with animals, as seen in the animal gods, the tanks of sacred fish, the existence of protected species – was not only baffling to Europeans, but struck at the very centre of their system of beliefs. While affection for animals – especially domestic ones – was not unheard of in Europe, the treatment of animals as part of the spiritual economy was anathema to the Abrahamic faiths, for whom one of the most essential divisions was between man and beast, between the image of God and the animals above which he had been set. Much of European life revolved around rituals intended to maintain and reinforce this distinction, discouraging bestial appetites in order to purify the spiritual, uniquely human elements, with immortality as the promised reward. The idea that man's salvation might be tied up with his treatment of animals threatened to topple one of the ideas on which cultures were founded in (as the lovely Persian phrase for the west would put it) the *land behind the wind.*[11]

146

It was not only in matters of religion that the part played by animals seemed to change as one moved further east. The extensive essay written by Damião on the character of elephants, in which he recounted the battle he had witnessed in 1515 between an elephant and a rhinoceros, was mostly given over to reports arriving from India that justified his conclusion that, of all beasts, the elephant had the most natural wisdom. Among these were stories of a famous elephant in Cochin called Martinho, who acted as a porter, carrying things all over the city he knew so well and receiving cash-in-trunk payments that he then exchanged in the market for his meals. According to one of the many stories sent back to Portugal, Martinho had taken umbrage when a certain Portuguese merchant had refused to pay on delivery for a barrel for wine, claiming that it was for the king's fort and therefore exempt from fees. Martinho, it was said, knew he was lying, and in his anger smashed the wall of the merchant's house, retrieved the barrel of wine, and threw it so high in the air that it shattered into pieces upon landing.

Martinho may have been a famous personality, but he was not even the most impressive of these creatures. There were elephants who had learned to read and write – even in Greek, with which Damião himself struggled – such as those to be seen in Vijayanagara, where the horselords of the Deccan plateau kept elephants in the outsized stables of their wondrous city. Damião cites a highly trustworthy witness who himself saw an elephant brought into that king's presence who wrote his petitions in the dust using his trunk, asking for rice and betel. The economic and cultural behaviours that were supposed to set man apart from animals seemed to be in danger of slipping away, opening in their wake an abyss that threatened to devour a number of cherished beliefs. The Russian traveller Afanasy Nikitin wrote in his fifteenth-century account of India that the monkeys bore arms, staged punitive raids on villages that hurt them, were taught handicrafts and dancing by the peoples among whom they lived, and

147

spoke their own language. Indians were not alone in this recognition of personhood in monkeys: in Mozambique the Jesuits recorded that people there believed that the howler monkeys had once been men and women, and *called them in their language 'the first people'*. Even in their epic poems the Indians did not seem to recognise the dignity of man that was so central to the humanist ideas of the Renaissance, as Portuguese visitors could see in the great *Ramayana* murals being painted during the 1560s at the Mattancherry Palace in Cochin, which gave central and heroic roles to intelligent, articulate animals, including Garuda, the king of birds, and the monkey warrior Hanuman.[12]

In the story of Jason and the Argonauts, which provided a model for European visions of their travels east and which Camões always had in mind if not by his side, the heroes run the gauntlet of one of the most famous dangers of the classical world – the strange and enchanting song of the Sirens that threatens to pull the travellers to their destruction. While in the other famous encounter with the Sirens, Odysseus straps himself to the mast in order to feel the piercing song without being lured to his doom, the Argonauts are saved by another ploy. To guard them from these enticing foreign dangers the greatest poet of all, Orpheus, whose performances could make rocks move and rivers stand still, sang a song so powerful that it drowned out the voices of the Sirens. It was just such a song that was called for now, to save European ideas from their encounters with the east – a song that Camões had decided he was the man to sing.

XI

Dead Men's Shoes

And with the uncanny regularity that was to characterise the reversals of his life, Camões was free again, and once again headed east. It is unclear how he managed to convert his imprisonment into a highly desirable appointment, as the Warden of the Goods of the Deceased (*Provedor dos Bens de Defuntos*) for the Portuguese on the route to China and Japan. Despite the macabre title of the post, it was in fact one of the lynchpins of the Portuguese colonial enterprise, which guaranteed to sailors embarking on these often fatal voyages that even in the event of death their share of the profits would be safeguarded and given to their next of kin. It was crucial that this early form of life insurance be seen to work: if confidence in this mechanism failed, it would prove difficult to recruit the necessary manpower, given that the odds of shipwreck were in many cases about even. As well as being an important post, the appointment was also a highly profitable one: the Warden was entitled to a portion of each legacy and the entirety if the deceased was intestate, making the role one of the more lucrative offices in the gift of the Portuguese *Estado*. Camões evidently considered the post a great honour, one of the high points of his life – something we only know because, when he fell from grace this time, he recorded the scale of his loss, *from newfound expectations reduced to less than ever before*. For now, however, he was at least at liberty, free (in his words) to *turn the great sea over in his mind as they*

149

travelled, and headed to where the greatest private fortunes were to be made in the east.[1]

A decade after da Gama's arrival in India, the Portuguese had decided to push past the Malabar coast, closer to the heart of the spice trade, and Camões' route to China lay through the centre of Portugal's eastern operations in the port of Malacca. Following ten years of skirmishing for a foothold in India, the Portuguese once again gave in to fantasies that in Malacca they had found at last the endless and easy fortunes for which they had been searching. It was, according to early reports, the richest place in the world, and it was not unusual for the merchants there to have stockpiled a ton or two of gold in the course of doing business. The greater of these merchant princes had households with 6,000 slaves, and the harbour was awash with ships from Mozambique, Persia, Bengal and China. As had become customary, these first accounts mixed their delirious assessments of wealth with a litany of fantastical discoveries. An early voyage was foiled in its attempt to capture a junk when a *mineral fire* was launched at the Portuguese, a fire that *made a great flash but burned nothing*. There were also reports of magical bracelets that prevented the wearer from bleeding, Sumatran weapons which inflicted wounds that did not heal, and a fruit like an artichoke whose taste was so sweet and delicate that many travellers never left the region, staying there only to be present at its harvest. It is evident that in the flood of new things it was difficult to distinguish between what was real and what was not, between fireworks and the durian fruit on the one hand and mythical, magical objects on the other. What was beyond doubt, though, was that the extraordinary variety of plant life in the Malay peninsula and archipelago made them a treasure trove of spices, singularities of intense taste to bring the bland staple crops of Europe to life.

Once again, the Portuguese could not count on the element of surprise, as the Muslim traders of Gujarat and Java had already set the king of Malacca against the Portuguese before they even arrived. In the part of Damião's chronicle dealing with these voyages he records the accusations levelled against the Europeans: that they were *pirates and thieves, destroying even the towns who receive them as friends, making war everywhere and only sparing those who allowed them to build forts, and still upon those they used such tyrannies as have not been heard of from the most barbarous people*. Any attempt to deny these accusations was quickly undermined when they proceeded to do exactly as predicted. In a version of events that circulated in Malaysia, only to be written down later, the Portuguese tricked the king of Malacca by asking him to grant them one animal hide's worth of land, a seemingly modest request to which he unwittingly agreed. Armed with this promise, the Portuguese quickly proceeded to cut the hide into thin strips from which they made a rope, a rope which measured out enough space for a large fort, complete with cannon ports facing back towards their hosts. This legend of colonialism is striking not just because it neatly captures the Trojan Horse ruse seen so often in colonial ventures, but also because it is actually a retelling of a classical legend, in which Queen Dido gained the land for the city of Carthage in Tunisia by using the very same oxhide trick.[2]

Not everyone in Malacca was against the Portuguese. These voyages provided the first sustained contacts with Chinese merchants, who like the Persians appeared to be natural allies, seeming (Damião says) almost European – perhaps primarily in their love of drink, in which they indulged *just like Flemings or Germans*. There were, in fact, various European geographies of the period – jumbled understandings of the Mongol past – which suggested that China in its furthest western reaches bordered on Europe. The Chinese supported the Portuguese assault on Malacca, complaining that they had also been treated unfairly by the king, though they declined themselves to take part, begging off for fear of reprisals upon those of their nation. Once the Portuguese had gained control of the port, the Chinese also encouraged them to flood the city with settlers from Siam, tilting the population balance away from Muslim Malays and Javans and towards a more sympathetic people. But while the Chinese merchants were happy to use the Portuguese to further their interests in the region, this did not mean that the Chinese would welcome European traders to their own ports with open arms. China was both immense and geographically isolated, separated from others on the landward side by deserts and mountains, and the power of the imperial court came from the regulation of the vast internal trade, around which had grown an ancient culture of record-keeping and a bureaucracy of unparalleled sophistication. The period a century before, when the Chinese emperors had sent trade missions to Persia and eastern Africa and had welcomed *ten thousand countries* as guests, had given way to an intense aversion to foreign contact and interference, as the Portuguese had discovered when, in the years before 1520, they began to explore trading opportunities in the South China Sea.[3]

The first Portuguese expedition to mainland China had been a disaster. Tomé Pires, after writing the *Suma Oriental* in Malacca, had been dispatched on an embassy to the imperial court at Beijing, but during its fourteen-month absence the Portuguese crew awaiting its return near Guangzhou had descended into chaos. Reports of their attempt to build a fort and their continued trading during a period of Chinese national mourning reached the imperial court, where it was even being said that the Portuguese had purchased kidnapped children for the purposes of cannibalism. The embassy was turned away without ever being given an audience. When Pires and his companions finally arrived back in Guangzhou they were arrested, apparently forced to wear signs declaring that they were sea pirates receiving just punishment, and sentenced to imprisonment until such time as Malacca – a former Chinese vassal state – had been freed from Portuguese domination. Rather than opening relations with the Chinese Empire as the Portuguese had hoped, the Pires embassy resulted in a violent enmity towards European merchants that lasted almost three decades.[4]

The Portuguese had not, however, spent the whole of their time in Canton destroying relations between the two cultures, and the party that returned to Portugal in 1520 had brought back with them tantalising artefacts and intelligence. Damião had been present at the Portuguese court in Évora when they made their report, bringing with them books on Chinese rituals and paintings of the Chinese gods, including one of a prince who had left the palace for a religious life of such incredible goodness that he gained miraculous powers – a fragmentary description of Siddhartha, who would through his great virtue become the Gautama Buddha. A version of this story was actually already known to Europeans, through the popular medieval tale of *Josaphat* (a corruption of 'bodhisattva') which had made its way along the Silk Roads, though it had become so garbled in the retelling that its eastern origins were only later recognised. More prized than these paintings, however, were reports of the silk-rich trade fairs at Guangzhou, as well as of the strong demand for Japanese silver. This was to be the opening that the Portuguese were looking for: trade between Japan and China was forbidden on both sides, meaning that an opportunity awaited for a third party to act as a middleman. Francis Xavier and the Jesuits had begun to make inroads into Japan in the late 1540s, followed by trading expeditions, and Portuguese relations with China had healed enough by the 1550s that the idea of a trading station near Canton could once more be broached. The long-desired concession had finally been granted in 1554, with the Jesuits claiming it as a miraculous result of Francis Xavier's death just short of the threshold of China. The 1557 fleet – to with Camões' post seems to have been attached – would be the first contingent to establish a Portuguese factory at Macau, at the mouth of the Pearl River where it opens into the South China Sea after passing Guangzhou.[5]

Overleaf: Map showing Guangzhou, from an Atlas of the Ming Empire (c.1547–1559), similar to the one available to Damião in Lisbon.

The route to Macau is briefly sketched in the *Lusiads*, with Camões noting the meagre information with which Europeans tried to keep the region in order. Ships proceeded down the Strait of Malacca keeping the island of Sumatra on the right, which was believed by some to have once been part of the mainland, and to be the region named *Aurea Chersonesus* by ancient geographers, one of the sources of Solomon's legendary riches in the Bible. They turned around the point of the peninsula at Singapore, where the coast curves up towards the kingdom of Siam, whose main river was believed to flow from a marvellous lake called Chiang Mai which could be reached only by passing through a swamp region ruled by birds and then a mountain range entirely given over to wild beasts. Heading east, the ships passed south of where the Mekong delta separated Cambodia from Champa, land of fragrant woods, and Cochinchina, the Portuguese name for the Dai Viet (Great Viet) kingdom, after which began *that proud Empire, glorious in untold lands and riches, holding sway from the fierce Tropics to the Arctic Circle*: China.

From the very first, the European imagination was fixated by the way in which China was both boundless and completely enclosed. The Portuguese went to great lengths to obtain Chinese maps and books, and even a translator, who was brought to Lisbon to help them make sense of these documents; but given that they were starting from almost no knowledge, progress in understanding Chinese geography and culture was very slow indeed. There was no need for a translator, however, to see the Wall, which was marked out clearly on these maps, noted frequently in European accounts of China, and which Camões described in astonished terms in the *Lusiads*:

> Look at the Wall, an edifice built between
> one empire and another which strains belief:
> The ultimate assurance and certainty
> of sovereign power, pride and wealth.

It is unlikely that Camões ever saw the Wall, as most European activities were confined to those port cities open to foreigners, but the idea of a barrier that would cocoon an empire from the outside world was long to hold sway in the western imagination.[6]

Given the difficulty of penetrating beyond the coast of China, where the Portuguese were allowed no further than Guangzhou, their understanding of Japan developed far more quickly than that of its vast neighbour. Records of Camões' time in the Far East are almost non-existent, and like so many aspects of his life we can only puzzle out the details from the stories he later span. It seems likely, though, that on Camões' voyage they followed the protocol that was to become standard, and that he remained in Macau while the main trading vessel – the 'Great Ship' – went on to Hirado in Japan, where cargoes of silver were loaded ready for transport to Canton.

Whether or not Camões himself ever set foot in Japan, he could hardly have avoided the mesmerising Portuguese accounts of Japanese culture, such as the detailed comparison of Japanese and European manners compiled by the Jesuit Luis Frois, who arrived in the region soon after Camões, as part of the global spread of Jesuit informants who created a paper network of letters and reports. The Portuguese were for the most part favourably impressed by the mannered reserve of the Japanese, and bemused by certain startling differences – Japanese men cooked, for instance, and food was brought to the table already carved into bite-sized pieces, a procedure that was considered both an art and a task with which great honour was associated. While Japanese women covered up their necks, which were considered attractions reserved for moments of intimacy, they wore sleeves so wide that their breasts were often visible, and Japanese men openly warmed their buttocks by the fire in the wintertime. These women were free to leave the house without any reference to their husbands, and were free indeed to leave their husbands; they controlled the household finances, wore the same clothes as men, drank deeply and publicly, often terminated pregnancies and were, for the most part, literate – though for any Japanese person literacy was a life-long process of learning the infinite characters which could be added to the forty-eight syllabic symbols. The culture of documents particularly intrigued European observers. The Japanese did not sign their letters, as the calligraphy alone was enough to identify the sender – a tantalising prospect for Europeans, who were struggling with the problem of forgery – and they responded to letters simply by writing between the lines of the letter they had received. They were astonishingly concise in their expression when compared to European prolixity, and they had more than fifty different types of paper, whereas Europeans would recognise only four or five. They even made their handkerchiefs from it, throwing them away after only one use, and separated the rooms in their houses with paper, as if leaving the room was the same as turning a page.[7]

Most baffling of all, perhaps, was the way in which the Japanese engaged with the material world around them. While Frois was somewhat disingenuous in his surprise that the Japanese drank alcohol with the aim of getting drunk, his confusion at their treatment of food was undoubtedly genuine. As suggested by his descriptions of the *chanoyu* – 'the way of tea' or tea ceremony – and the intricate rules for serving food, the Japanese blending of philosophy and the culinary arts was a revelation. The link between food and thought should perhaps not have been so surprising, given the central parts played by eating and drinking in European religious and social practices, but it was at first not obvious to the Europeans how they themselves used rituals of consumption – from the Eucharist to hierarchical seating plans – as ways to make intangibles like 'God' and 'class' more solid. Even more striking was the way in which the rites of the Japanese tea ceremony flowed without interruption into the appreciation of art, with the very tea

Opposite: *Bird on Tree* (*Haha-chō*), attributed to Shūkō (active 1504–20).

sets being designed not to astonish by their costliness and complexity but rather to encapsulate certain simple essences of the world – 'chill', 'withered', 'lean', on the border between warm and cold, life and death, dearth and plenty – which could serve as a focus for contemplation. The fact that Europeans – who routinely gathered in front of religious art for the ritualised consumption of wine and bread – thought this remarkable had everything to do with an increasing insistence in European culture that the things of the body could have nothing to do with the intangible powers of mind and spirit. And while Japanese artists were soon reproducing copies of European art so exact that they could not be distinguished from the original, Europeans were nonplussed by the Japanese aesthetic, which favoured as few figures in a painting as possible, and placed a high value on pen-and-ink sketches, which in Europe were still largely treated as drafts for expensive, crowded and colourful paintings and tapestries.[8]

It may have been in response to this European desire for costly, hectic artworks that some of the most astonishing depictions of this cultural encounter were produced – the scores of giant folding screens that began to appear from the late sixteenth century depicting the *Namban* or 'southern barbarians', records of the yearly arrival of the Portuguese Great Ship on its trade visit to Japan. These paintings observe a set form, using their shape to draw out a narrative across the breadth of the screen, from the arrival of the *kurofune* (great black ship) to the people pouring out of its swart sides down the gangplanks and into the life of the Japanese port. The detailed observation of dozens of small exchanges on these screens are very like the highly popular village scenes of the same period by Pieter Breughel the Elder, though the effect is strikingly different: unlike the muted, earthy tones of Breughel, the stark contrast on these Japanese screens between the two main colours, black and gold, gives them the feel of religious icons, as if these quayside encounters were not just moments for trading but rather parables in the life of a culture. The arriving

Adoration of the Magi (1501–6) by
the Portuguese painter Grão Vasco,
featuring one of the first European
depictions of a New World inhabitant,
a Tupinambá man like those whom
Damião met in Lisbon soon afterwards.

A sixteenth-century painting of one of Lisbon's busiest streets, the Rua Nova dos Mercadores (Merchants' New Street), showing the diversity of the early modern city.

The Battle of Mohács (1526), between Hungary and the Ottomans,
as depicted in the Ottoman visual epic, the *Süleymanname*, from 1558.

A sixteenth-century ivory salt cellar produced in Benin for the Portuguese market, featuring West African portrayals of Europeans.

The 'Robinson Casket', produced in Kotte, Ceylon, c.1557, and featuring Ceylonese deities as well as figures copied from engravings by Dürer.

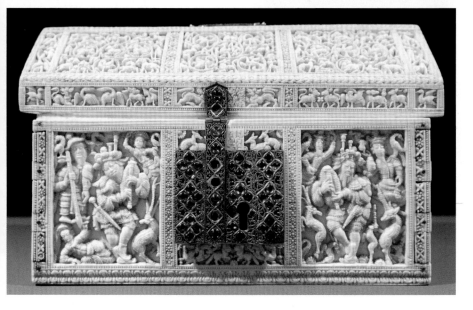

A detail of the screen, c.1600, by Kano Naizen showing the arrival of the Namban (Southern Barbarians, i.e. the Portuguese) into a Japanese port.

Triptych of the Temptation of Saint Anthony by Hieronymus Bosch, likely one of the two Bosch paintings owned by Damião.

crews are easily distinguishable from the Japanese, with the ballooning trousers and big noses of the Portuguese setting them apart; and the diverse life of this fleet is clear from the large number of African slaves up in the rigging or fanning the reclining officers or carrying the goods from the ships. The Japanese painters also have a keen eye for the part played by animals. In the screens by Kano Naizen, now at Kobe, it seems as if for every Portuguese there is an animal under his control – a horse being reined in, an elephant being steered, a dog on a leash, a tiger being carried behind him in a cage. These are not, however, expressionless beasts present only to show the master's authority, but rather (as in the sculptural tradition soon to blossom in the miniature *netsuke* form) their faces are studies in intense feeling, from the whinnying panic of a rearing horse to the bounding joy of a dog who has not had the run of dry land during a long ship's voyage.

The Portuguese had their own surprises to offer in return for the marvellous discoveries they were making in Japan. Here, as elsewhere, one notable introduction by the Europeans was time itself – or, rather, a particular means of measuring it, as when in 1551 Francis Xavier had presented to Yoshitaka Ohuchi, *daimyo* of Suo, Japan's first mechanical clock. Christian life in Europe was highly regulated by time, with particular observances being required at certain hours of the clock – where many faiths would go by the position of the sun or moon – and missionaries were eager to impose their own notions of time on non-Christian nations, to prepare them for thinking of the world in this way. To justify this imposition it was often necessary to claim that these heathen peoples had no sense of time of their own, or at least that their timing was very defective, as when Olaus Magnus had suggested that the Lapps until very recently had no way of dividing up the days and hours. It mattered little that this wasn't true – the Lapps had their own way of structuring the day and night into four hours, and the Japanese had a twelve-hour system measured by water clocks – or that the European division of day and night into twenty-four hours was itself highly arbitrary: as Olaus Magnus admitted, the the division of the equinoctal day into twelve hours was believed to be based on an ancient observation that a certain Egyptian animal urinated exactly twelve times during the daylight hours. The marvellous mechanical clocks that the Jesuits carried with them were enough to suggest, however, that this European time was in some sense more exact, more objective, more true than the flimsy and variable times of other cultures.[9]

It was not only in divisions of the day that Europeans found notions of time to be inconsistent as they moved out across the globe: more unsettling still was the wide variation in ideas about the age of the world and the timespan of history. Though there were squabbles among the Abrahamic faiths about exactly how far back to place creation, and whether to count years starting from that or the birth of Christ or the Hejira – Muhammad's move from Mecca to Medina – they were at least vaguely in agreement that the world was between 5,000 and 7,000 years old and that the end of historical time was near at hand. The Chinese, by contrast, were regularly heard by Europeans to wish each other 10,000 years of life, and there were reports that Tatar history covered events 74,000 years in the past. The Chinese themselves, it was discovered, believed that the physical world had existed eternally, and that mankind had been around for more than 100,000 years. Most worrying of all were the beliefs of the gentiles in India – published in Europe by incredulous Jesuits – that the current age would last almost 400,000 years longer, and moreover was only one of four ages, with the previous three having totalled 3,624,006 years. Muslims were also deeply troubled by these assertions, as suggested by the Persian historian Firishta's alarmed refutation of the Indian belief that 100,000 years had passed since the time of Adam, and by al-Biruni's mockery of the assertion that the world, in its present state alone, had existed for some 1,972,948,132 years. Though for the most part these beliefs were ridiculed and roundly dismissed by Europeans, it nevertheless meant that they were contending with people whose sense of their place in history was profoundly different. It was one thing to call upon people to repent when the end was nigh, and quite another when there were 400,000 years still to settle up accounts. Similarly, the providential narrative of history, moving from creation to salvation and judgement within a countable number of generations – few enough that most European monarchs had family trees drawn up starting with Adam and Eve – looked quite different when framed within a notion of time that stretched for millions of years. In one telling incident, the crew of a Japanese vessel were recognised as Christian converts by the Portuguese when they were heard to state that it was *past the middle of the middle of time*.[10]

While Camões may have had to rely on second-hand reports of Japanese culture, Macau itself offered a wealth of novel and unfamiliar things, and his new post involved a large amount of listless and unoccupied waiting. Though the year would be punctuated by periods of intense activity – the biannual trade fairs in Guangzhou, from which the Great Ship took silks to Japan in May and returned with silver in November – the intervening months would have left little to occupy the Warden of the Dead, especially since his job was simply to safeguard the portions owed to the casualties of trade and collect the requisite fees. If this was a time of swelling expectations for Camões, whose share of the annual take of 60,000–80,000 *pardaus* would be enough to make him a rich man, there was not much that could be done to increase this fortune or to make it arrive more quickly. His earnings, after all, accrued from tragic accidents and he would at least have had to put on a respectable show of wanting them not to happen. In the meantime, this limbo gave him ample time to explore nearby Guangzhou, which appeared to Portuguese eyes little short of an utopia. Two accounts written in the years immediately before Camões' arrival – one by a Dominican friar, the other by a Jesuit, and both published in Portugal shortly afterwards – provide a minutely observed description of how the city appeared to western eyes. Both emphasised that Guangzhou was a very minor city in the Chinese scheme of things – only about the size of Lisbon – but had a gridlike network of streets that stretched as far as the eye could see, each irrigated by freshwater channels and planted with trees as though it were a garden. If the tallest building in the city was a minaret, the Christians were relieved to learn that the Muslims hadn't had much success with conversion; the Dominican gleefully surmised that the local love of pork made the adoption of Islam unlikely. At the end of every street was a triumphal gate – the Jesuit estimated there were at least a thousand – each of which had been erected by a local governor at the end of his term. These governors served only three years and had to be from another province, and were further prevented from corruption by a network of royal surveillance. Everyone, the astonished correspondents wrote, is employed, even down to the blind who are given grain to mill to keep them from begging. The Jesuit and the Dominican were in agreement that the major weakness of these industrious and ingenious people was their lack of belief in reward and punishment hereafter. This was taken as evidence that they had no understanding of the world, as if they did they would surely have been led to deduce the true nature of God. It also explained the Chinese addiction to pleasures of the flesh, in service of which they held their feasts during the diabolic darkness of the night (as opposed to European feasts, which happened in the day).[11]

The language barrier was a major obstacle to learning about the local beliefs, and a Jesuit who was in Macau at the same time as Camões gave up trying to learn Chinese after its difficulties destroyed his health and mental stability. But the Portuguese were accruing piecemeal an understanding of many aspects of Chinese culture, including one which Camões had ample chance to experience at Macau, for all that the island was little more than a collection of grass huts and a thatched church built the year before his arrival. Facing the Portuguese factory across a narrow stretch of water was a great shrine to a sea goddess – the temple of A-Ma the *Celestial Spouse of Universal Salvation, Wondrous Numen, Brilliant Resonance and Magnanimous Benevolence, Protector of the Country and Defender of the People*. A picture of this goddess had been among the first Chinese paintings to reach Europe. Among those Damião saw presented to the king in 1520 was *the image of a woman, whom they take for a saint, whom they call Nāma, who is intercessor before God for everyone, both on land and sea*. Though the European understanding of this goddess was often distorted by the desire to associate her with the Virgin Mary, Damião's brief record suggests that Portuguese information on this legendary figure was actually quite accurate. Tian Fei or Mazu, known locally as A-Ma, or 'grandmother' – and after whom, indeed, Macau, the 'bay of the goddess A-Ma', was named – was the deified form of a real woman who had lived in the tenth century, a prodigy of extraordinary memory whose mental prowess grew so great as to allow her to project herself across vast distances and act upon the world with extraordinary force, something she first demonstrated by saving her father and brothers from a storm at sea without ever leaving the home in which she was sitting. Since then she had grown into the protector of those whose lives were threatened at sea, and indeed had gained her most recent and elaborate title – *Celestial Spouse, Protector of the Country and Defender of the People* – in 1409 after she had saved the great Chinese admiral Zheng He from a storm, appearing *swiftly as an echo* to hover at the mast in the form of a glowing lamp and bringing a sudden calm upon the waters.

This miracle – along with others duly recorded in the Bureau of Sacrificial Worship – allowed Zheng He to return home with the findings from his pathbreaking voyages across the Indian Ocean, some ninety years before da Gama's voyage in the other direction. The goddess was said, on these voyages, to have *purified and tranquilized the searoute*, and to have helped with the capture of those barbarians who were resisting the *transforming influence* of Chinese culture. A literature had grown up around Mazu, and the

Opposite: Mazu saving the Chinese fleet during a storm, from a
seventeenth-century compilation of the Miracles of Mazu.

doors of her temples were guarded by the sea monsters she had
subdued, Qianliyan (Thousand-Mile Eye) and Shufeng'er (Fair-
Wind Ear), giants with green or red skin and yellow fangs.[12]

With all the marvels offered to Europeans in this part of the
world, one of the greatest enigmas is that Camões makes almost no
explicit mention in his writings of his time in Macau – one of the
most extraordinary acts of suppression he was to visit upon the
world he had seen. In part his silence was, perhaps, because the
astonishing nature of Chinese culture sat uncomfortably within a
story of the Portuguese nation as elect and heroic, but it may also
be because of the shadow cast by the one event he does mention,
an accusation that cut short his stay and put paid to the hopes he
had allowed himself to build up. While in his writings he only
gestures darkly to an *injustice executed upon him*, it seems clear
from contemporary documents that he was deprived of his post
and ordered back to Goa to face charges that he had misused the
funds in his custody, which were meant to be set aside for the
families of the deceased. Camões as ever furiously protests his
innocence, and certainly in this case there was good reason for his
superior, the captain of the fleet and first governor of Macau, to
want him out of the way: the same governor had complained that
the profits of Camões' post rightly belonged to him, and after
Camões' dismissal the fees were permanently absorbed into the
governorship itself, providing much of the wealth that accrued to
this lucrative position. Not only was the hope of a fortune now
slipping away, prison once again beckoned to the inveterate jail-
bird. Camões was to insert into his epic a plea for a place where *a
poor man can live his short life in safety, a little piece of earth safe
from the falling sky*, and with bitter irony he was granted just such
a little piece of earth in the prison cells that were his most constant
address. Yet when he was brought in this time he would have good

reason to see the prison as a haven of safety; the journey back to Goa gave him both a lowest point from which to stage his return and the beginnings of a legend, a recipe for the fame that had long eluded him.[13]

XII

Our Dying Gods

After leaving the service of the Portuguese crown in Antwerp, Damião had installed himself at the University of Louvain, to join the Collegium Trilingue (College of the Three Languages) which had made this minor town an epicentre of the northern Renaissance. The collegiate university was an opulent monument to learning, though Damião's college was a rather more modest affair, albeit one with a wholly immodest ambition. The Collegium was dedicated to the revival of the classical tongues – Latin, Greek and Hebrew – and research into non-Christian knowledges, for so long held at arm's length in western Europe. Damião would never be more than a middling scholar of the classics, having begun too late, at thirty, to achieve the fluency displayed by the most celebrated humanists, but the growing interest in other tongues (including Arabic) at the Collegium might have given him reason to hope that his fascination with the Lapps and the Ethiopians would find a welcome there. Yet Damião arrived in a Louvain at a time of lengthening shadows. Erasmus himself had been driven from the town some time before, after a long campaign against him by the conservative theologians; in one incident he had been deep in conversation and had failed to remove his hat before the crucifix, prompting mutterings that this proved his allegiance to the Lutheran schismatics. Shortly before Damião arrived, Erasmus' books had been banned from Louvain. Damião's Latin tutor at the

Collegium had also fallen afoul of the growing intolerance, and had spent a year in prison before recanting and being released.[1]

Along the public highway a short walk from town were displayed the bodies of those who had not been so lucky, as a warning to the people who passed them. As we know from a detailed account left by one of Damião's fellow students, most of these people had died by hanging, and because of that their skin remained unbroken as they slowly rotted within; it was a common mistake, the observer wrote, to think that the bodies were eaten by birds, as the skin was too tough to allow this, and in general the birds only pecked out the eyes. He wrote this to explain his excitement when he found a body that had indeed been stripped clean by the birds, on account of it having been somewhat burned before being displayed. Now it hung, a failed scarecrow, from its pole, rather like the figure of the Crooked Christ in the town's cathedral, which dangled half-attached to the cross, miraculously suspended (the legend said) as he reached down to catch a thief in the act. Damião's classmate took it upon himself to steal the skeleton by the highway, pulling it down bit by bit and secreting it back at their lodgings, until all that was left was the thorax, which was tied with a chain and was too big to hide. To obtain this last piece the bodysnatcher allowed himself to be locked outside the city walls at night-time, before climbing up the stake and working the torso free.[2]

The walk home, in the dark and with a body over his shoulder, must have felt eternal; just such a walk as is imagined in the Indian vampire legends, in which a possessed corpse asks an endless series of riddles to the person carrying it. Having smuggled the torso home, he tells how he found the ligaments too hard to cut through, and he resorted to seething the bones *in a secret manner* to get them clean. The risks taken to retrieve this body and the occult procedures performed upon it were neither black magic nor reverence for a martyr, but rather the rituals of a new movement, founded upon the precise observation of isolated specimens from the physical world. The author of this grisly account was a man named Andries van Wesel (Andreas Vesalius), and later – when both he and Damião had moved to Padua – he was to use just such scandalous behaviours to change profoundly how humans and their bodies were understood.[3]

Damião's first residence in Louvain did not last long, and after a little more than a year he went to look for the presiding spirit who had left this vacated temple, managing to arrange an audience with Erasmus in the spring of 1533. Erasmus had by this time removed from Basel to nearby Freiburg; after the incident of the egg fight, when Erasmus had condemned both those who ignored the Church laws and those who enforced them, the Protestants had taken over in Basel and made the celebration of their rites obligatory. Erasmus had long since decided that *his was never the spirit to risk his life for truth. Not everyone has the strength needed for martyrdom*, he wrote in a letter to a friend: *when popes and emperors make the right decisions I follow them, which is godly; if they decide wrongly I tolerate them, which is safe.* This, he decided, was an acceptable position when there was no hope of better things.

The Erasmus that Damião met in the spring of 1533 was much in decline, suffering from gout and kidney stones, afflicted by continual fevers, and no longer at home in the world. His masterful *Colloquies*, which had been celebrated across Europe for the eloquent and playful ways in which they gave speaking parts to both sides of an argument, were now damned on both sides. He was accused by Catholics of having sowed *the worst seed in the field of the Lord*, making it acceptable to ridicule the Church establishment, and also condemned by Luther and his followers for not joining in the zealous destruction of the same. The urbane blend of scepticism and tolerance which Erasmus had offered was now itself a form of treason to Luther, who believed that *one should take delight in firm assertion or one is not a Christian.* Yet if Erasmus would not take up arms for either side, he also could not resist periodically making public his disdain – increasingly for both sides – as in his 1529 work *Epistola contra Pseudevangelicos* (On

False Prophets), a curse on both their houses, both the rotten Church and those who would *rather break the rope than slacken it and keep it whole*. Damião was delighted to find the frail and besieged master in dire need of secretarial help, and though the young acolyte failed to make any impression on Erasmus at their first meeting, he persisted, returning all the way from Lisbon where he had been summoned to fill a prestigious post, giving it up against the advice of Erasmus and resuming his stay in the older man's house as his guest, his companion and his apprentice.[4]

The relationship that grew up between them over the two remaining years of Erasmus' life is touching to witness and was to remain lodged in Damião's heart until his death. He was to keep the letters exchanged between them when apart in a special case containing his most treasured objects, which also included a portrait engraving of Erasmus by Dürer. The younger man was full of projects, proposing without much delay that he undertake to edit and publish the complete works of the master and urging Erasmus to draw up an authoritative catalogue of the same, so that his legacy could conform exactly to his wishes. As an antidote to Damião's puppyish enthusiasm, Erasmus created exercises for the younger man in Latin and Greek, guiding him through the different ways of constructing an argument, how to attack or defend a man by exaggerating or minimising his faults. There were also exercises in translation – slightly more ambitious given that Damião would be writing in his mother tongue – poignant marks of the curious affection between the two. Under Erasmus' guidance Damião rendered from Latin into Portuguese Cicero's tract on old age (*De Senectute*), a defence of the dignity of those in declining years, and an argument that those in the full flush of youth and captive to the senses have much to learn from those in whom the fire of appetite has been dulled. Doubtless Erasmus, who was still

Opposite: Portrait of Erasmus by Hans Holbein, produced as a print by Johannes Froben, 1538.

·ER·ROT·

TERMINVS

turning out an enormous amount of work, including more of the play-like *Colloquies* which had made and marred his name, saw himself in a number of Cicero's anecdotes – such as that of Sophocles who, taken to court by his heirs in his old age with a view to declaring him senile, simply read aloud his newly completed play *Oedipus at Colonus*, and asked the judge whether that seemed to him the work of an imbecile.[5]

For all that Erasmus had a sense of his own importance, he was not above needing the approval of the younger man. Though Erasmus was married to his work, he had at many times in his life developed passionate friendships with other men, and Damião seems to have filled this role in his last years; their flashes of worry over each other's health, and the ease with which Erasmus could be wounded by Damião's clumsy loyalty, suggest that their expressions of feeling for one another were more than simply the standard flourishes of humanist correspondence. In one lovely episode, Damião thought to flatter his mentor by urging him to *perfect his style and approach Cicero more closely*, little realising that Erasmus would take this idea of him as the new Cicero as an insult. The younger man, with his enthusiastic half-knowledge of Erasmus' enormous body of work, had evidently missed the fact that the maestro considered himself long since to have surpassed Cicero – had, in fact, been engaged in a long-running battle with the Ciceronians of the literary scene, whom he considered to be mere parrots incapable of speaking to the here and now. Erasmus responded to Damião's suggestion by having a go at another author for whom his protégé had expressed admiration, saying that the writer had *dulled the impression of his piety by his polish*, and that really *mysteries require their own style*.[6]

Damião immediately recovered from this scolding, announcing his ambition to write the official biography of his hero, and to do so in such a style *that future generations will not only praise your life but also the thread, warp and woof of my speech*. The idea was a preposterous one for many reasons, and not just because Damião was the newest, greenest and least qualified for such a task of Erasmus' many followers; to write the life of Erasmus would be nothing less than to address the divisions that were tearing apart the Christian west, and attempting this posed considerable risks even for a much cannier person that Damião. But Erasmus also seems, in his last years, to have turned away from the intimacy he once allowed his readers by having so many of his writings – even his letters – published. We get a sense of this when, to everyone's surprise and against Damião's protests, Erasmus wrote nothing in response to the execution of his dear friend Thomas More; perhaps this was a grief he did not feel the public deserved to share. Erasmus also reacted violently to Damião's suggestion that the younger man was going to publish the exercises in Latin and Greek his master had set him: *if you were my deadly enemy*, Erasmus wrote, *you could not do anything more inimical to me than to publish the notes I have marked only for you … take care you do not do it, to the great disgrace of my name!* It is unclear what these exercises contained that Erasmus considered such a threat – evidently something that could be read between the lines, which worried the older man, who was a jealous guardian of his public image.[7]

Erasmus did, however, respond to Damião's desire to improve his writing style, to approach the language for mysteries that Erasmus had made his own, setting him as another translation exercise the gorgeous biblical book of Ecclesiastes, which Damião would publish as the only rendering of the scriptures into Portuguese in this age of great Bible translations. Ecclesiastes, Damião wrote, with its warnings against the fickleness and vanity of this life, was the appropriate choice for a man in the middle of his life, who might be tempted to trust in his own strength and vigour to make his way in the world and to make the world in his own way. In the haunting words of the text, supposed to have been spoken by Solomon, wisest of kings:

I returned, and saw under the sun, that the race is not to the swift,
nor the battle to the strong, neither yet bread to the wise, nor yet
riches to men of understanding, nor yet favour to men of skill: but
time and chance happeneth to them all.

We can sense Erasmus hovering above Damião's shoulder while he
works, as when Damião notes that the word rendered as 'vanity'
– the vanity of worldly things, in which we should not place our
trust – is in the original Hebrew given as *hevel*, which means *a
most delicate vapour that soon disappears*. Vanity, vanity, all is
vanity – all is mist, vapour, breath.[8]

But for all his dutiful attention to Erasmus' warnings about the
unshakeable injustice of the world, Damião was still too full of
hope to be deterred, and he tried repeatedly to interest his master
in the causes close to his heart. He had presented Erasmus on their
first encounter with his pamphlet on the Ethiopians and the
Laplanders, and continued to ply him with works on Baltic history
in the hope that Erasmus would lend his considerable weight to
the demand for charitable treatment of these non-Christian neighbours. Damião was also at work on a new, longer treatise on the
faith and customs of the Ethiopians. During his brief visit to
Lisbon in 1533 he had met with an Ethiopian named Zagazabo
(Sägga Zä'ab), an 'archpriest' of the Abyssinian Church, and with
his usual interest in the outcast Damião had taken on his cause.
Zagazabo had tearfully reported to Damião that though he had
been in Europe for seven years, he had not received Communion
during that whole time, as he had found no one willing to share it
with him. He had waited seven long years to be granted an audience with the Pope, who in the end had shown little interest in
Zagazabo's pleas to unite the Ethiopian Church with the Church of
Rome, and the stranger had returned to a hopeless limbo in
Portugal. In meeting Damião, whom he addressed in his writings
as his *dearly loved son*, he met one of the few Europeans who
shared his belief that surely the many things that Ethiopians and

Europeans had in common were more important than the ways in which they differed. Damião was eager to clear up any misunderstandings he had created through his previous pamphlet, which Zagazabo said was mistaken in many respects, but forgivably so given that his informant Matthew was not a priest or even an Ethiopian, and both were convinced that a fuller account of Ethiopian culture would open the path to mutual understanding. Even though Zagazabo would have to work without access to his books, which had been lost in a shipwreck on the passage from Ethiopia, he set about writing a lengthy account of Ethiopian culture, which Damião would translate and publish, and so enter into the public record of Europe.[9]

There were many reasons for Damião to think that Erasmus might be recruited to the Ethiopian cause: Erasmus had, after all, often enjoyed the provocation of telling Europe that there were others whose behaviour was more Christian than its own – the Eastern Orthodox Armenians, for instance, or even the Turks themselves – and took the broadminded view that truth, wherever it was found, should be attributed to Christ. The Ethiopia described by Zagazabo, moreover, held out a mouthwatering prospect for biblical scholars like Erasmus: not only did the archpriest report that the Ethiopians had certain books written by the Apostles at their councils – books which might help to resolve the contentions over Church rituals that were setting Europe ablaze – but he also brought the first account of an even more miraculous survival. Reviving hopes that the Abyssinian ruler was the hoped-for priest-king after all, Zagazabo related the tradition that the royal house of Ethiopia was descended from Solomon himself, out of a union with their queen who went to pay him homage – known in the Bible as the Queen of Sheba but to them as Maqueda. It was furthermore held by Ethiopians that when Maqueda had departed from Solomon, the priest of the first Temple, Azarias, had received a premonition of its destruction by Nebuchadnezzar, and so had decided to steal from the Ark of the Covenant the Tables of the

Law themselves – inscribed by God and Moses together on Mount Sinai – and carry them into safekeeping in Ethiopia. Azarias the priest had secretly forged an identical set of tables and swapped them for the originals, which he took with him and only revealed to others when they had arrived back in Ethiopia. There they were shown to Maqueda and David, her son by Solomon, who danced along the road before them, *exactly as his grandfather David had done* in the Book of Samuel. The tablets had been kept by David's descendants, according to Zagazabo, in a convenient (but unnamed) place during the 2,600 intervening years. Erasmus and his contemporaries were possessed by the idea of recovering lost books, so much so that one of his close companions employed a medium to help him locate missing manuscripts, but this was a discovery of a different magnitude.[10]

Yet even the prospect of God's own archive could not tempt Erasmus to enter into the fray. Though he could not resist making promises to his friend, little came of it; and, to the end of his days, the most prominent thinker of the day remained largely silent about the world beyond Europe, even though his adult life coincided more or less exactly with the great voyages of the age. In part Erasmus' disinterest in the world beyond Europe was doubtless because his mind was elsewhere – on his health, on the many projects he was bringing to completion – and because of his constant fear that if the challenge to the status quo was too great there would be a backlash, and the freedom to study non-Christian works (even while protesting their worth for underpinning Christian values) would once again be withdrawn. But there was also a sense in which Humanism saw itself as part of a never-ending struggle between light and dark, civilisation and barbarism, its battlefield the former Roman Empire and Rome its citadel, part of the drama of history in which the rest of the world could be offered only supporting roles. Even curious minds like Damião's constantly fell back upon arguments that these distant people were, in fact, part of that drama, only in ways that had not yet been understood;

the idea that there might be other histories, centred around places and events completely outside Europe's bounds – which even threatened to make Europe's history seem of secondary importance – was for most simply unthinkable.

If Damião absorbed his mentor's belief that a historic battle was underway, he did not imitate Erasmus' caution or share his pessimism regarding the possibility of reconciliation. During the four months Damião stayed with Erasmus, his host became increasingly alarmed by the careless way in which the younger man inserted himself into the fiercest contentions raging across the continent. Whereas Erasmus had withdrawn from Basel to nearby Freiburg to avoid a confrontation over his attitude to Protestant church services, Damião regularly made the forty-mile trek between the two cities, carrying letters between Erasmus and his friends. Putting himself up at the Inn of the Stork, Damião immersed himself in a thrilling intellectual environment, though one which was also fiercely Protestant. Some of the schemes in which he involved himself seemed harmless enough, such as the collaboration with a friend of Erasmus who was determined to prove that polyphony was not some modern invention but rather had been known to the ancients, that the sinuous blending and harmonising of different parts had been a feature of the Greek world. Though Erasmus was one of those who looked askance at polyphony – doubting its claims to classical roots and worrying that it obscured the understanding of the words being sung – Damião was to contribute a composition to this project written in imitation of his hero Josquin. But being in Basel also put Damião in the way of more dangerous encounters. He was later to claim that he met the great Lutheran geographer Sebastian Münster in the doorway of a Basel bookshop, and also found the Protestant theologian Simon Grinaeus reading a book of philosophy at the entrance of his inn, and *did not go with him to his house.*

Many of Damião's encounters did not even have the convenient excuse of coincidence. During his travels back and forth from

Erasmus' house he had presumed upon his acquaintance with Luther and Melanchthon to write a letter of introduction for a Portuguese friend who wanted to see the famous heretics for himself. Damião had also visited Strasbourg where, by his account, he had acquiesced to the suggestion of his innkeeper that Martin Bucer and Caspar Hedio – two of the more aggressive Reformers – be invited to dine with him, a form of intellectual tourism that seems to have been common in the period. His meeting in Geneva with one of the most extreme Reformers came about (he said) because they were staying in the same lodging house; this man (Guillaume Farel) had told Damião that the Reformers understood the Gospel better than St Paul himself, and was probably behind the notorious 'Affaire des Placards' shortly afterwards, the anarchic attack in which the French royal household was infiltrated and Reformist propaganda pinned to the door of the king's bedchamber as he slept. It mattered little that Damião's friend who wanted to meet Melanchthon believed that he could convince the heretics of their errors, or that Damião claimed to have spent his meal with Bucer and Hedio telling them about the beliefs of the Ethiopian Christians, and how these suggested paths towards conciliation in Europe. The perception back in Portugal would nevertheless be that Damião was breaking bread with the enemy, and – worse – leaving a paper trail as well. Erasmus wrote in alarm to Damião warning him that, while innocence (feigned or otherwise) would provide a certain amount of cover for his recklessness, there would be no helping him if he continued to correspond with the likes of Melanchthon and Grinaeus. Erasmus' circle of friends were also worried that his young apprentice was putting the great man in danger, and that the careful distance Erasmus had maintained from the Reformers would be for nothing if Damião was thought to be visiting them on Erasmus' behalf. A plan was hatched to send Damião on to Padua, where he could continue his studies without drawing undue suspicion upon himself and others.[11]

Many years later, after he returned to Portugal, Damião would see a worrying memento of these heady days in the form of a notice nailed to the door of every church in Lisbon: a catalogue of forbidden books that read like a roll-call of Damião's encounters. All of Luther's and Melanchthon's writings were included, of course, and most of Bucer's, along with works by Münster and Hedio; also Gil Vicente's play the *Jubileu de Amores*, which had brought the house down in Brussels. Most of the letter 'D' was given over to works by Desiderius Erasmus of Rotterdam, and to make sure that there was no getting around the order to turn these books in for burning, there was also a general interdiction against all *books without titles, or without the name of the printer, or without a named author.*

Portugal was the first country to issue an index of forbidden books, a grim monument to the power of reading in the form of a Library of the Damned, which sought to seal off certain volumes from the world. The Portuguese example was to be followed by other countries, and finally by the Vatican itself, until much of Europe was subject to such restrictions. It was no longer a question of whether a person's actions or words conformed to what was deemed acceptable; the banning of books aimed at no less than the regulation of people's silent places, seeking to make certain ways of seeing the world invisible and certain thoughts unthinkable. These lists threatened to blunt the sharpness of the written word as a tool for thought: *if I am not allowed to debate modestly with educated people*, one contemporary wondered, *I do not know why I learned to read*. The making of these lists, however, also advertised the fragile nature of orthodoxy, whose collective delusions could be shattered by too many people asking the wrong questions. With a grand irony these indexes also created one of the most entrancing imaginary libraries ever conceived, a locked room or sealed ark filled with all the thoughts you were not meant to think, and before long inclusion in the list was no longer a mark of notoriety but rather a badge of pride. Among the test cases for the Portuguese index, and perhaps the first books to be subject to a ban on the printing or import, were Damião's translation of Ecclesiastes and his treatise on the customs of the Ethiopian people.[12]

XIII

Inside a Dog

D amião had already been living in Padua for a few years when a series of house guests descended upon him unexpectedly and with unfortunate timing. The first of these was Roque de Almeida, the man he had dispatched from Paris with an introduction to Philip Melanchthon and who apparently hoped that he would single-handedly argue the Reformation to a halt. Roque had turned up in Padua in a state of dire poverty, having also shed his monastic dress and changed his name to 'Jerome of Pavia', and Damião had agreed to put him up out of charity. The second was Simão Rodrigues, one of the six original companions of Ignatius Loyola who had sworn in Paris to reach the Holy Land and open a new chapter for the Church Militant. The fraternity had not managed to get any further than Venice, where in 1537 they spent a year stranded and waiting for a ship to take them to the Levant. Simão was later to claim that he and Damião and Roque were at one point all great friends together, though this was only to clarify that the accusations he made against them were not animated by any spirit of inveterate malice. Whatever the case, it is apparent that the situation in the household rapidly deteriorated. Although Roque was to boast that he had crossed swords with Luther himself and that the great man in despair had become angry and said that all Hispanics were merely sophists, it was clear that he had come away from his time in Wittenberg with more than a touch of the local scepticism. Simão, on the other hand, had been captivated by the example of Loyola, who developed spiritual exercises to drive away the sadness that hung about him like a cape and bring on pious ecstasy, exercises that won for him a fiercely loyal following. Roque took to mocking Simão for his constant praying, saying that he would be better off spending his time reading the scriptures he professed to adore so much, and to offering Simão bites of the cheeses and meats that he insisted on enjoying during days set aside for fasting – fresh cheeses, Simão was to remember, to distinguish perhaps the braided *mozzarelle* or sheep's curds, rather than the aged Padano cheeses that were local delicacies. Roque also goaded Simão about his monastic vows of chastity – presumably having dispensed with his own at the same time as his habit – and took to quoting the scripture about how it is better to marry than to burn. If Damião did not take the lead in all of this, he certainly does not seem to have reined in the provocateur, and he even lent Simão a volume of Luther's writing on Ecclesiastes to help him better understand the position of these northern schismatics.[1]

Erasmus had sent Damião to Padua precisely because it offered a safe haven for careless talkers – something increasingly rare in the continent – but this also meant that it was a place where antagonisms that elsewhere festered under the surface came out into the open. The university town of the Republic of Venice was a strange place, not least in the sense of being entirely under the sway of *stranieri* – foreigners – who had built for themselves an enclave there free of outside influences. Following the model of Europe's oldest university at Bologna, local Paduans were banned from holding professorships or even being admitted as students, and in fact all citizens of the Veneto were subject to exclusions designed to preserve the cosmopolitan character of the institution. The university was instead governed by two student bodies, the *ultramontani* from above the Alps and the *cismontani* from below them, with the *ultramontani* – dominated by German students but also counting large contingents of Poles, Hungarians, Frenchmen and

Englishmen – firmly in control. The students also had significant power in choosing those who would give the lectures, including the daily talks on philosophy and history at which Damião was a regular attendee. And now that Bologna was under direct papal rule, Venice and Padua were among the few places that were beyond the power of the Pope and the Holy Roman Emperor. The peculiar status of the university had made it a draw for students and scholars across Europe, from the likes of Copernicus and Vesalius to Francis Walsingham and Reginald Pole, as well as the second-most famous humanist of the age, Pietro Bembo, into whose care Erasmus had resigned his young charge with some jealous reluctance.[2]

Padua also had a claim to being the spiritual home of Humanism, where the movement to resurrect the learning of Rome had begun with the literal resurrection of the Roman historian Livy, a native Paduan whose supposed final resting place had been discovered by Lovato Lovati and later dug up with the support of Petrarch and Boccaccio. Lovati had also discovered a tomb that he claimed belonged to the legendary founder of the city, the hero Antenor, who had fled from a burning Troy to found a new settlement on the Adriatic coast, and both of these finds had been turned into monuments to the classical heritage of Padua, places of pilgrimage for those who wished to immerse themselves in *romanitas* and soak up the Greek and Roman essence of European culture that had long been buried. Included among these were all the great and good of Venice, who though they were barred from being registered as students, frequently made the twenty-mile trip to Padua to listen to lectures at the university. Damião was later to record his astonishment at the fact that *men of fifty, sixty, seventy years, key men of the Council and all the government of the Republic,* took time out of their days to listen to lectures on history and philosophy before returning to the business of state in Venice. Damião however was a dissenter from the belief that this was a specifically European practice inherited from Rome, suggesting instead that the model came from the Islamic world, citing examples at Ksar el-Kebir in Morocco, and at Hormuz where people crowded daily to hear lectures on Islamic philosophy and their own histories of Darius and Alexander.[3]

If Simão had come to Padua from Venice to console himself with the company of his fellow Portuguese, he would have found Damião's house anything but a home away from home. Instead, it was an extraordinarily cosmopolitan place even for Padua. Although he occasionally played host to countrymen like Roque, Damião seems to have formed part of the *ultramontani* group at Padua, sharing digs with a number of former students from Louvain, including at least one who was an open and professed Protestant. Among Damião's other associates at this time was the French poet Clément Marot, who was seeking refuge in the Veneto after having been implicated in the anarcho-propagandistic attack on the French king's bedchamber. These were men who shared none of Simão's passionate desire to sacrifice himself in the service of the Roman Church, and Simão clearly saw the tolerant and permissive atmosphere of Damião's house as a test of his faith and a mockery of his intense convictions. It is not clear whether it was the cheese or the talk of priestly sex or the loan of a heretical book that drove Simão over the edge, but it is clear that he snapped in such a dramatic and outrageous fashion that Ignatius Loyola himself came down from Venice with his followers to apologise to Damião in person for the behaviour of his hot-headed companion.[4]

The future saint and soon-to-be founder of the Jesuit order was at a crossroads in his life at the time when he and several of his followers came to stay with Damião. He had metamorphosed once before, when as a young man a battle injury had put paid to his dreams of military glory and he had in fevered convalescence reconceived these dreams in terms of spiritual glory, which would require the same ardour and physical suffering but directed against inner demons rather than enemies of flesh and blood. Over the course of the following fifteen years, Loyola had lurched across the continent as a student and holy ascetic, denying himself comfort and inviting pain, spending long periods praying in a cave, letting his hair and nails grow long and unkempt, being imprisoned on suspicion of heresy and attempting to settle in Jerusalem, all the while developing as he went on his spiritual exercises intended to attune the faithful to the voice of God within them. Along the way, he had acquired one set of disciples and then lost them, and then a second set, the group of ten who had set out from Paris on the way to the Holy Land. But the period the companions spent waylaid in Venice, prevented by war with the Ottomans from proceeding on their intended path, saw Loyola begin upon another transformation. While his unworldliness and the untempered acts to which it gave rise inspired passionate loyalty in those around him, it was a struggle to direct and give order to an energy which after all came from the abandonment of restraint. Loyola was coming to see the ship that did not sail for Jerusalem as another test and another exercise; and just as he had turned from literal war to spiritual war, so he began to pivot from advocating complete submission to God to demanding complete submission to the fellowship and – perhaps more importantly – to its leaders. Giving in to religious ecstasy was now to be seen as a temptation of its own, and a doctrine emerged that God spoke to some more than others, providing Loyola and his old roommate Francis Xavier, through certain *movements of the will*, with instructions to be communicated to the rest.[5]

Though the emphasis on discipline and obedience would become ever more central as the Jesuit mission took on global proportions, not all of the original companions subscribed uniformly to this new order. As suggested by the dramatic displays of religious fervour that would take place in Coimbra when Camões was a young man – during that brief period in the late 1540s and early 1550s when Damião and Camões and Simão were all in Portugal at the same time – the chapter that Simão went on to found there had not relinquished the extreme behaviours of the early days, and a collision course would be set between the leadership of the increasingly powerful and respected institution in Rome and the Portuguese chapter, which was at once renegade and held the keys to the world through its connection to the Portuguese global network. And while it was still many years before the differences between Loyola and Simão would break into open rupture, to have Loyola come to Padua from Venice to apologise for his behaviour, taking the side of those who had mocked and derided his piety, could not have been otherwise than humiliating for Simão, and not humiliation of the kind that could easily be turned to spiritual grace. This was likely no more than a matter of business to Loyola as he began to turn his vagrant band into an institution – Damião, whom Loyola may have known since his days begging alms in Antwerp, was, after all, much better connected than Loyola and in correspondence with many of the chief men of Europe, and Loyola was increasingly aware of the need for the support of the powerful as well as the devotion of his foot soldiers. But for Simão these were wounds that would remain open and festering for the next thirty-five years.

Loyola may have been less conciliatory had he known of the clandestine activities in which Damião was involved during this same period. While the battle lines between Reformers and those loyal to the Church of Rome were becoming ever more entrenched, there was a modest party of those who felt the rift was not beyond repair – among them Erasmus, who was optimistic that eventually the two sides would weary of it all and come to terms. Fresh hope was given to these *irenists* (peaceniks) by the news that the Pope had agreed to convoke a council at Mantua, an enormous step given the Vatican's reluctance to summon church councils (which were a threat to papal power), and especially given that Mantua was a fiefdom of the Holy Roman Empire and therefore part of German lands. The Reformers were being offered a meeting on their own turf, and there were even senior figures at the Vatican who were arguing for extraordinary concessions to end the schism, including allowing priests in Germany to marry and making the observance of fast days optional. And, at this tilting point of history, which might have stood a chance of averting the bloodshed that was to wash Europe for the next hundred years, Damião was identified as someone who was well connected among the Lutherans and liked by the chiefest among them. He had been approached through the association of German merchants at Venice – the Fondaco dei Tedeschi, near the Rialto Bridge – by Cardinal Sadoleto, one of the leaders of the irenic party in Rome, who used one of Damião's fellow students as a go-between, carrying a letter to him in Padua. The letter contained a simple request, but one of such moment that it can scarcely be exaggerated: that Damião open a back channel between the peace party in Rome and a person who was not named in the letter but whose identity was known to the messenger. This person was Philip Melanchthon, Luther's right-hand man, by whose humble poverty Damião had been so deeply affected during his visit to Wittenberg some years before. Sadoleto, his go-between, Damião and Melanchthon formed a skein-thin link that might just stitch back together a Europe that was swiftly falling apart.[6]

With his characteristic energy and optimism, Damião had accepted his part in the mission at once, writing to Melanchthon via an intermediary in Augsburg, conveying Sadoleto's proposal for the council at Mantua and enclosing a letter of his own to increase the chances of a favourable reception. Caught up in the excitement of it all, Damião went even further, using Zagazabo's tract on the Ethiopian Church that he was translating to argue that the moment should be seized not just to reconcile the Protestant and Catholic Churches, but all Christian Churches around the world, and that the council had the right to enforce the necessary concessions upon the Pope. Loyola was included among those to whom the tract was sent, in hopes that he might be recruited to the cause. If the council was going to find a way to repair the schism between these branches of Western Christendom, might not the opportunity be grasped to form a broader union with peoples across the globe, people who might have differences but who also shared certain core beliefs? Damião also travelled to Mantua himself to meet his friend Johannes Magnus, who would be attending the council as the leader-in-exile of the Swedish Church; perhaps the council could also be used to rein in the Swedish mistreatment of the Lapps, another cause close to the hearts of both men. All that Europe needed to set itself on a course towards a greater tolerance was for a few people who were willing to slacken the rope and keep it whole to outmanoeuvre those straining for it to break.[7]

It was perhaps never more than a fool's hope, and there was mercy in the fact that Erasmus did not live to see the caving-in of this last best chance for peace in Europe, a failure that was to have profound effects also for Western Christendom's attitude towards difference within its bounds and beyond. The great man had died in 1536, the year before the proposed council, and as Damião learned in letters from those who were close to him at the end, he had summarily refused to be fixed in his dying moments on one side of the divide or the other. Nothing more could be said for certain than that he died a good Christian, though perhaps in holding his tongue to the end he had in a sense attempted to carry some of the indignation out of the world with him, a martyr to even-handedness. Damião had been disconsolate, and was to keep the relics of their friendship close to him for the rest of his life; and though he dropped the plan to edit Erasmus' complete works when no record could be found of the author's wishes in this regard, the drive to convoke the council at Mantua was another way to honour the master's legacy. But the forces ranged against it were too great. Melanchthon never responded to Damião's letter; the French king

Opposite: The portrait of Erasmus by Dürer that Damião kept in a locked coffer until the end of his life.

sabotaged the council out of fear that the location would give the Emperor too much control; the non-Imperial German states also withdrew; and the whole house of cards fell in upon itself.

Damião's fantasy that the great variety of the world could be used to interrupt any easy narrative of 'us' and 'them', substituting instead a medley of echoes and contrasts, was quickly evaporating. Worse than that, the tide was turning the other way: these echoes could be used instead, by those so inclined, to argue not for an infinite variety that beggared attempts to divide it up, but rather to tar opponents with accusations that their ideas were dangerously foreign. If the Protestants could suggest that the statues and saints of Catholicism were like the idols of Indian polytheism, then orthodox Catholics could suggest that the Protestant hatred of these statues was suspiciously like Islamic iconophobia. Guillaume Postel, the esoteric Frenchman who was among those fiercely debating what the vegetable lamb of Tartary meant for Christendom, had newly returned from an embassy in Istanbul to join his friend Loyola in Venice, and would shortly write a detailed comparison between the ideas of the Reformers and those of the Muslims. Though there was, in the end, no place among the Jesuits for Postel and his increasingly outlandish religious theories, the language of crusade against the Reformers would come to be common, and it would gain further credibility when certain Reformers began to question the doctrine of the Trinity – following Erasmus' casting of doubt upon the authenticity of the one passage in the Bible that mentions the idea of a triune deity – in a manner which (for some) aligned them with the Islamic creed on the unity of God. Calvin, on the other side, came out against those who refused to take up arms for the Reformation, calling them 'Nicodemites', after the Pharisee who was willing to support Jesus only in secret. Both sides would soon turn not only against those who openly opposed them but also against those who kept quiet, and eventually even people whose behaviour was unexceptionable but whose heart did not seem to be in it. While Cardinal Sadoleto would continue the struggle until the point that he was identified as an enemy within and ostracised from the Church, Damião, at least, saw the writing on the wall at this point, and sought to dissuade Sadoleto from further efforts to contact Melanchthon, as well as asking the provocateur Roque to leave his house to avoid drawing any further attention. But there was no recalling the letters that had been sent, no hiding the hand that had been shown, no unrolling of the dice: the trap had been set, and Damião would live the rest of his life under stay of an increasingly certain execution.[8]

Not all of the dramatic events at Padua went on behind closed doors. One of the most spectacular performances of the age was being prepared at this time by Damião's old companion from Louvain, the body snatcher Vesalius, who would certainly have been part of the same group as Damião at Padua and may even have lived in the same household. As suggested by his macabre outings to acquire body parts in Louvain, Vesalius was part of an emerging generation of natural philosophers who saw close first-hand observation of the natural world as key to a greater understanding of their subject. Just as Doctor Orta in Goa was mocking pharmacologists who studied theory endlessly but had no knowledge of where their drugs actually came from, so Vesalius was convinced that great discoveries awaited close at hand for those with stomachs strong enough to make them. The central problem, as Vesalius saw it, was that the connection between practical anatomy – the dissection of human bodies – and medicine had been severed, with the dirty work being done (if at all) by lowly assistants, meaning that many so-called doctors had never set a hand inside the very human bodies on which they claimed to be expert. He was to call this *that evil fragmentation of the healing art ... importing into our Colleges that detestable ritual whereby one group performs the actual dissection of a human body and another gives an account of the parts; the latter aloft on their chairs croak away with consummate arrogance like jackdaws about things they have never done themselves but which they commit to memory.* This provided a tantalising opportunity for a man of ambition: it had been almost two millennia since Aristotle had proclaimed that *the internal parts of the body are for the most part unknown,* and while the late-classical author Galen had set the standard across much of Europe and Asia for the last thirteen hundred years, Vesalius thought he had spotted a chink in the master's armour. To celebrate the award of his doctorate from Padua late in 1537, Vesalius arranged a public demonstration of his prowess for all to see.[9]

The frontispiece of Vesalius' monumental work of anatomy published a few years later, *On the Fabric of the Human Body,* gives us some sense of his showmanship. The room is uncomfortably crowded, with people leaning forward from the balconies, hunched in expectation over the stalls, climbing the pillars to get a better look, surging forward and being held back at the very edge of the table itself, both straining to get a closer look and trying desperately not to be shoved forward into the gaping space of the open torso. At the head of the table is a grisly prop, a skeleton mounted to show the bone structure of the body, but posed in such a way as to be a ghastly reminder of the life it had lost, clutching a pilgrim's staff and looking upwards in a gesture of despair. Everyone is watching, and in the crowd we can see beardless students and men of gravity and position, wearing the caps of prominent Venetians and the cowls of the monastic orders. There is even a dog brought along by its master, and a monkey on a leash who seems on the point of leaping over shoulders and wreaking havoc. And, at the centre of it all, Vesalius himself, his hand resting casually on the place where the cadaver opens and the abyss of the bodily cavity begins, his glance directed right out of the page at the person holding the book. If the whole space looks like a theatre, that is not a

The Frontispiece to Vesalius' *De Humani Corporis Fabrica* (On the Fabric of the Human Body) by John of Calcar, showing Vesalius dissecting as Damião may have seen him do in Padua.

ANDREAE VESALII

BRVXELLENSIS, SCHOLAE
medicorum Patauinæ professoris, de
Humani corporis fabrica
Libri septem.

CVM CAESAREAE
Maiest.Galliarum Regis,ac Senatus Veneti gra
tia & priuilegio,ut in diplomatis eorundem continetur.

mistake: this kind of theatre was developed in the period as a space for anatomy and only later was adopted for stage plays, though there was perhaps a natural continuity in the way that both of them opened up the secret places of the human to the general view. And Vesalius was a master impresario, even having a series of posters printed for the occasion which captured in graphic fashion the things that most of the jostling crowd probably couldn't actually see. These underlined the nature of the great reveal, so that later people would know what to boast about having witnessed.

The scandalous and shocking announcement that was later to make Vesalius famous across Europe had all the elements of a great story, toppling a revered ancient authority and opening up to question all that people thought they knew, before swooping in to provide a bold and heroic new way forward. The foundations of our understanding of the human body, Vesalius would say, were rotten, and rotten because Galen himself had based his anatomy not on people – but on apes. *I am quite certain*, he proclaimed, *on the basis of the art of dissection now reborn, combined with careful reading of Galen's works and many textual restorations thereof, for which I make no apology, that he himself had never cut open a human body, and furthermore that, deceived by his apes … he frequently and quite wrongly finds fault with the ancient physicians who actually did their training by dissecting human material.* The idea that a great authority of classical medicine, and all the doctors in the centuries following him, were treating people like monkeys threatened to make both Galen himself and the whole medical community a laughing stock, and many across Europe reacted to Vesalius' suggestions with violent indignation. They were fighting a losing battle, however, as Vesalius would parade in front of the European public *the infinite multiplicity of differences between the organs of the human and the simian bodies* which Galen had not noticed, leaving any staunch Galenists in the uncomfortable position of endlessly admitting that they also did not know the body as they claimed.

196

Like many great claims to discovery, Vesalius' triumph was as much a matter of presentation as anything else. In truth, Galen had been quite open about the fact that he relied on simian anatomy, using the similarity between certain mammals (as advised by Aristotle) to get over the difficulty of finding human subjects for dissection. But the Renaissance was an age obsessed with the idea of the uniqueness of the human, driven by orations on the angel-like dignity of man and constantly debating what it was that made him quite so special – his place in God's plan, his power of speech, his political nature, his fondness for laughter or mathematics or even drunkenness, all possibilities being considered other than the unthinkable idea that there was nothing truly unique about humans after all. Vesalius was very much the man called forth by this age, capable of providing detailed demonstrations of how man was different from those apes who sat a little too close for comfort, and using it to announce the dawn of a new age in which the scales that had covered our eyes fell away to reveal new truths. It was convenient to ignore the fact that Vesalius' own work had weaknesses, particularly in cranial anatomy, his knowledge in that regard being largely based on the skulls of dogs. And his findings were not just perfectly suited to the age – they also set things up for a thrilling sequel, when three centuries later European science would congratulate itself on having discovered the exact opposite, namely that humans and apes were very closely related, a suggestion that equally shook deeply held convictions and was met with similar indignation and disbelief. As one philosopher has aptly put it, *it is not scientific discovery that changes our idea of nature, but changes to our idea of nature that permit discoveries.* Faced with an age of global encounters that cast doubt upon its own exceptional and unique status, European society was creating a new idea of history, nature and the world, a vision which would keep European man at the centre and whose truth was demonstrated by a cascade of just such theatrical discoveries.[10]

The abandoned church council at Mantua would eventually be replaced by the Council of Trent, in which the Lutherans would not be formally included, and which would take on a much less conciliatory approach to the matter of the Reformation. Roque sloped off to Venice, in hopes of learning the secrets of alchemy. And Simão Rodrigues would shortly be appointed the founding provincial of the Portuguese chapter of the Society of the Name of Jesus.

XIV

História Trágico-Marítima

The return passage from Macau found Camões at a very low ebb. The perennial obscurity in which he felt condemned to live had not only failed to lift but had in fact plunged from a false dawn into a deeper darkness yet. These vicissitudes of fortune, to which the caprices of power and patronage exposed young men like Camões, could only have been felt more keenly amidst the discoveries the Portuguese were making about the astonishingly meritocratic nature of the Chinese state. Unlike the European system, where ambitious young men had to navigate a corrupt and unaccountable system of patronage, China had long since allotted posts in its immense government through a series of rigorously fair examinations. The detailed reports on these procedures from the years of Camões' residence there record the standardised system of local, regional and national tests, with fierce penalties for cheating and ingenious methods of making the responses anonymous so that the examiners could not be bribed. The fact that the exams consisted of recalling and responding to the great classic works of Chinese literature and history must have been even more galling to the many European readers who had similarly been drilled in the classics but then left to work out for themselves how to make a livelihood from this training. The number of opportunities offered in the Chinese government was vast – one observer suggested that there were as many as 3,000 civil servants in each of the thirteen provinces, not including those employed in the central government – and created in their wake a literary culture far in advance of what existed in Europe. As the exams were highly competitive, there were for each government post many times that number studying the classic texts in preparation, creating demand for myriad copies of standard texts, a demand that had been met for six centuries by the use of print. The paper industry employed 36,000 people in one key production centre alone, and despite the wide variety of spoken dialects, all subjects of the Emperor read the same script, making it easy for written texts to spread across the whole territory. This had also prompted an immense system of state archives from which the histories of the realm were written. So powerful was this literate bureaucracy that Chinese culture represented the afterlife itself as a government department filled with legers and registers in which allotted lifespans were recorded, as we see in the classic novel of the period *Journey to the West*. Not that this bureaucracy was without its frustrations: the hero of the novel, the monkey king Sun Wukong, becomes immortal simply by crossing out his name in the right list.[1]

Consignments of Chinese books were beginning to make their way back to Europe: Damião's close friend, the historian João de Barros, had acquired a set of Chinese maps and books and a Chinese slave to translate them, and Damião himself had charge of the queen's library, which contained several Chinese chronicles. Soon afterwards, a library of Chinese books was on its way to the Philippines, there to be rendered into Spanish by 'Sangley' translators and sent on to Europe. Included in this library were titles on *The Antiquitie of the Kingdome of China, and of the Beginning of the World, and in what time and for whome it beganne; Of the number, and movings of the heavens; Of such kingdoms and nations as they have notice of, and of the particular things that are in them; Of how to play at tables, and at chess, and how to make sports of legerdemain and puppets; Of architecture, and all manner of buildings*; and so forth. The materials that these volumes contained offered new perspectives on virtually every aspect of life as it was lived in Europe, perspectives that would require an immense undertaking to translate and assess and digest. The sheer quantity and strangeness of the information can only have been daunting, and begged the question how European writers could respond to this epochal flood of new knowledge and ideas. For a vagabond poet like Camões to make himself heard in the noise and confusion of the age would require a story of quite some extraordinary power.[2]

It was precisely at this low point in his life that a series of entrancing legends begin to grow up around Camões. While some of the basic facts of these stories find echoes in the historical record, the obscurity in which he had languished now became one of his greatest assets: in the absence of other witnesses, the world had only his word for what had taken place. And, like so many romantic stories of the Renaissance, Camões' new life began with a shipwreck, in the South China Sea on his return from Macau. There are a few recorded wrecks that might be candidates for the one in which Camões was involved, though none can be said with certainty to be the right one. Yet though he was never to describe the event in great detail, it is clear that the experience underwrites the many sea disasters that appear in his epic poem, such as the storm he invents to heighten the triumph of Vasco da Gama's arrival off the Indian coast, where the sailors' puny attempts to reef the sails and bail the ocean from the ship are useless against the world-destroying power of the indignant winds.

> The ship is beyond man's force and art –
> the winds were such that
> they could not have shown more cruel
> impetuous force had they come
> to level the Tower of Babel.

The waves were breaking above the clouds, the secret innards of the deep were revealed, the four winds contrived to smash the machinery of the world, the black and ugly night was illumined by lightning with which the whole sky was afire. *How many mountains were levelled by those waves, how many ancient trees wrenched out of the earth by the wind, never thinking to have shown their mighty roots to the sky?*[3]

While the terror of the storm was enough to shatter a sailor's understanding of the world, it was at least preferable to the moment when the ship finally went down, leaving the survivor to float in the limitless expanse of the ocean, spreading in each direction for an eternity with no way of knowing how far away from struggling limbs were the seabed or the shore. If man has a familiarity with the infinite, it is here, a loss of scale that opens an abyss, but an abyss that is hard to shake off afterwards, and is always as near as simply closing your eyes. Camões described the experience of ocean swimming as a confusion of swallowing and being swallowed, like the passage through the intestines of a great beast – *fleeing in the curving waves, drinking the sea, and being thrown up on shore.* Perhaps it was a similar sensation that prompted the Japanese belief, which featured in contemporary reports, in a submarine kingdom of rational, vengeful lizards. The Jesuits scoffingly rejected this notion, proudly proclaiming that all such stories of water-dwellers were held to be just so much nonsense in Europe, though it is far from clear that this was true. The dark undersea zone beyond the looking glass of the water had long served as a parallel universe where the surface world could be thought through, as in the legend of Alexander the Great, where his pride in his conquests is humbled during a submarine adventure through the vast underwater kingdoms he could never possess. But this yawning abyss also offered great power to the person who could face it and come through, who lived on after to silence those who had not seen so much.

Camões evokes this sense of the vertiginous feel of shipwreck, and the blessed status of survivors, in the first of two mentions of his catastrophe, in which he describes *escaping to the shore with my life hanging by a thin thread, a life saved by miracle – no less than that Jewish king whose life was lengthened*. In comparing himself to the Old Testament king Hezekiah, Camões is claiming not less than to have gone as that king had *to the gates of the grave* and to have come back with a vision like that granted to his right-hand man Isaiah, *the voice of him that crieth in the wilderness*. For all the grandiosity of these claims, there is little doubt that being cast up on the shores of the Mekong delta, which we later learn was the place of the disaster, would have stripped any European to their spiritual core. The silted river bottom and the marshy coast-line presented a nightmare of indistinction, depriving the castaway of any real sense of whether they had actually reached the safety of the shore, or whether instead this was just another kind of abyss, waiting to suck the swimmer down into its heavy depths. The storms described in the great Cambodian epic *Reamker* – written at much the same time as Camões' epic poem – have the same nightmarish confounding of elements described in the *Lusiads: white horses broke out of the sea's surface, the water seemed to be the sky and the seabed to be the clouds, as the waves were inverted and turned to white foam*. Another contemporary Portuguese account of just such a swampland shipwreck describes how the survivors, shoulder deep in slime, *all began to wail and hit ourselves like men out of their minds and possessed at what had happened*.[4]

It is at this unlikely juncture that the manuscript of the *Lusiads* makes its entry. If there is anything to which the ocean is more inimical than man it is paper, to which the water's very touch is death – meaning that there was something almost miraculous in the claim that Camões was to make: that he also saved a draft of the poem from the wreckage, and carried it aloft as he swam ashore in a river estuary. At the very end of his epic, as part of a prophetic vision of the Portuguese expansion into the Far East after da Gama's time, Camões describes the Mekong, and so speaks directly about the shipwreck for the first and only time. The river, we are told,

> will receive calmly and pleasantly
> in its lap the verses that came
> soaking from a sad shipwreck, forlorn,
> escaped from a tempest, from
> hunger and dangers, when
> the unjust order was served
> to him, whose sonorous lyre
> will be more famous than rewarded.

The poem, even before its publication, joins an elect library of drowned books, and the even rarer company of those that have emerged from the waters, a survival that always suggests that they have been reserved for some higher purpose. Not thirty years before this shipwreck, the founder of the Mughal Empire stayed up all night drying papers by the fire when a monsoon hurricane almost destroyed his epic autobiography, the *Baburnama*. Babur describes how they gathered together the drenched volumes, *wrapped them in a woollen bedspread, and put them under the cot,* until they *got a fire going and then got busy drying out the papers and notebooks until dawn with no sleep.* Early editors noted the similarity between Camões' story and the one told of Julius Caesar, who was said to have swum ashore during a battle at Alexandria holding the manuscript of his *Commentaries on the Gallic Wars* above the waves. The suggestion that this makes Camões' story less likely to be authentic, however, misses the point – these stories are always, in a sense, an act of mythmaking, a ritual that weaves a new strand into the legendary fabric.[5]

The ritual by no means stopped there. It was later to be claimed that the portion of the poem that Camões had saved from shipwreck had been written in a certain cave on the island of Macau to which he was fond of retiring. This also placed the *Lusiads* in the genealogy of other such cave writings, which emerge from the dark places of the earth like Pythic prophecies, breathing out hidden truths: the Revelation of St John was supposed to have been written in a cave on Patmos, the Vulgate translation to have been undertaken by Jerome in a grotto near Bethlehem, and the Mallorcan polymath Ramon Llull was said to have unlocked the secrets of Arabic wisdom by isolating himself in a cavern with a Muslim slave for nine years. And another story, one likely told by Camões himself, added a tragic dimension to this part of the legend; it suggests that, while the poem had been saved from the wreckage, a woman whom he loved had been lost. The story, in fact, bears a striking resemblance to legends of drowned lovers from Viet literature taken away by the jealous water, like the wife in the sixteenth-century classic *Truyên Ky Man Luc* (Compendium of Marvellous Legends), who is stalked by an enamoured sea monster and long avoids water until, with one slip, she drains away into his liquid kingdom. Camões' drowned beloved is only referred to using the name of an ancient Greek water spirit ('Dinamene'), but was said by his contemporaries to be a Chinese mistress whom he was bringing with him from Macau.

> Oh, my Dinamene, have you left
> the one who never left off loving you?
> My nymph – I cannot see you now,
> as you did not care for this life.
> How could you depart forever
> from one who cannot do without you?
> The waves, that did not know your pain,
> could have better spared you …
> O the sea, the sky, my black fate! –
> Will I feel pain or care for anything
> when nothing more than sadness endures?

Whatever the truth of the story, there is no denying one heartrending fact – that there is no chance whatsoever that a search of the archives will produce details of the death of one poor Chinese woman, much less the circumstances under which she would choose to leave everything that she knew to travel across the world with a man down on his luck and headed for jail. But whether or not the account is in all its aspects true, Camões was to make central to his writing stories of nymphs who save sailors at sea, storm-quelling ocean goddesses who are given Greek and Latin names but who also bear uncanny resemblance to A-Ma, the protectress of Chinese sailors whose temple stood across the bay from the Portuguese station at Macau. Was the story of Dinamene fabricated by early readers who themselves fantasised about love affairs with exotic women, or was the loss of a real Chinese lover central to Camões' vision of a sea filled with women who could save men from the abyss? The idea that we can fix these things on one side or the other is in itself a fantasy; in reality, the dance of the imagination often suspends in both writer and reader any simple relationship between fact and fiction. Poetry is a way of lying to get closer to the truth, to what one really wants to say.[6]

The alchemical process of turning incident into myth, however, lay a long way in the future, and for now Camões was no more than a castaway on a unknown shore with a few fragments of a story and no way to make them pay. The Mekong delta in this period formed the boundary between the kingdoms of Cambodia and Champa, though Champa was slowly being swallowed by the advance of the Dai Viet kingdom to its north. The area was an unknown quantity to most European travellers – or rather it would be truer to say that it was forgotten rather than unknown, given that the Oc Eo civilisation of the Mekong had been in contact with ancient Greece and Rome, with modern excavations producing coins and medallions of Marcus Aurelius. The memory of this region in classical geography had in the intervening period become hopelessly muddled, and was of little use now. An ethnography of southeast Asian peoples compiled at the end of the sixteenth century noted only that *Kampuchea* (Cambodia) *is a sovereign kingdom and it borders on the kingdom of Siam*, adding that *Nothing is known at present about its rituals or customs*. There was, in fact, one garbled account of Cambodian culture, compiled by the same Dominican friar who went on to write one of the detailed early descriptions of Guangzhou. He had been drawn there by rumours that Cambodia was a kingdom ripe for conversion, but had been sorely disappointed by the resistance he encountered from the Brahmin elite. There seemed no use in offering them the Christian heaven when they already had twenty-six of their own, a labyrinth of afterlives utterly baffling to the poor Dominican. In one of these heavens the holy men who had lived in the wilderness were given the chance to spend eternity sitting in a refreshing wind, while in another lived spherical gods who granted to the virtuous the honour of also taking on the form of a ball.[7]

The Dominican made little headway with the Buddhist and Brahmin ideas that he encountered, but he does seem to have understood one key aspect of local belief, an article of faith that was also to capture the attention of Camões. Though the Mekong delta was to form a central part of Camões' mythic story, he dedicated only a few lines to it in his writings:

> See where Mekong cuts through Cambodia,
> called the Chief of Waters because
> one river has many tributaries.
> It floods the plain, restless
> like the cold and surging Nile,
> and its people believe that
> the glory and the torment after death
> comes alike to every sort of beast.

207

While the relationship between man and animal in south Asia had been a matter of astonishment to European observers for some time, the realisation that many considered animals not only to be involved in man's destiny but to share it equally took more digesting. Camões also alludes in the *Lusiads* to this animism – this belief that animals had souls and, moreover, souls of the very same kind as humans – when discussing the Brahmin priests in India, who he says *follow the famous teachings of One, who first gave science its name*. This cryptic allusion to the ancient philosopher Pythagoras – the main proponent of metempsychosis or reincarnation in the European tradition – indicates the danger of a doctrine that cannot even speak its name; for if the same soul could be incarnated in animals of different species – as they were constantly in the shapeshifting literature of the Viet – this suggested that there was no essential difference between man and beast. The record of Cambodian beliefs left by the Dominican gives some sense of the difficulty Europeans faced in understanding these unthinkable things. *They make seven and twenty heavens*, he writes, *to which they say all living things go, even the flea and the louse, as they say that, as they have souls, they must live in the other world*. The choice of the flea and the louse as examples shows the Dominican straining at the edges of belief, testing whether his interlocutors could really believe (as they seemed to) that God's image, man, shared the same spiritual essence as these most inconvenient of pests.[8]

The struggle even to conceive of such a belief as possible is testimony to the profound challenge that this presented to European ideas, not only in knotty matters of theology but in every ethical and philosophical idea that was extrapolated from them. If man was not unique in the possession of a soul that lived on, then there was little reason to believe that the course of history was tied to the drama of his salvation; there was also little reason to believe that he could become immortal simply by making himself less like other animals, eschewing those 'bestial' appetites that were to the

Abrahamic faiths the antithesis of godliness. The animistic belief that all animals had similar souls threatened to erase all boundaries between man and animal, as amusingly suggested in the episode of *Journey to the West* where the monkey king Sun Wukong peruses the ledgers of the afterlife:

> The legal official scuttled off and soon returned with a pile of volumes, including the registers of the ten species of living creatures. He went through them one by one: the register of the hairless and the short-haired; the hairy; the feathered; the crawling; and the scaly – no mention of our Monkey. Monkey, you see, was hard to classify. He shared some points of resemblance with humans, but not enough to be categorised alongside them; though his hair was on the short side, he did not belong to the kingdom of the hairless and the short-haired; although he was animal-like in appearance, he did not answer to the unicorn …
> He was eventually located in his own separate ledger, which Monkey personally examined, finding his name under the entry for soul number 1350.

The ideas that were being encountered in the east threatened to make a mockery of everything that Europeans held most sacred. The stakes involved in silencing these doubts could scarcely have been greater.[9]

It was not, in fact, strictly true that the same fate awaited all creatures, as the Portuguese writers suggested – the Portuguese themselves were increasingly seen by those in the region to be beyond the pale in spiritual terms, meaning that Camões was marooned in deeply hostile territory. A report from Cambodia contemporary with his shipwreck records how the locals saw the Portuguese as *that notorious race of bearded men who enrich themselves by spying out the land, acting like merchants, but returning later to attack and plunder like thieves*, who *set fire to our houses and fields with the sparks from those firebrands dangling from their mouths, turning into white ash as they puff on them*. This sense that Europeans were somehow unnatural was not an isolated thing. Muslim readers of the *Ramayana* had long thought that the capital of the demon empire Lanka was none other than the city of Rome. And stories were growing up on the edges of the South China Sea of certain mysterious creatures, called *yawas* or *Biri-biri* by the inhabitants of the Moluccas, who lived in the jungle and who were excluded from the economy of souls. These blue-eyed, long-haired monsters had once been kings, but had degraded to become less than any animal, whose laws they no longer observed. The *yawas* were said to be none other than the Portuguese colonisers and castaways, whose depredations of the places they landed were becoming the stuff of legend. So debased were these creatures believed to be that they were excluded even from the comfort of death: the stories of the *yawas* written down many centuries later did not claim that these were the descendants of the sixteenth-century Portuguese, but rather that they were the very same men who had arrived in these waters hundreds of years before and had lived ever since in the wilderness, a rogue undead beneath the level of other living things.[10]

The manner in which Camões escaped this fate, condemned to perpetual existence in the jungle, is not part of the historical record. This is probably because it was not very interesting, and so never found its way into the myths surrounding the poet: while the culture of the Mekong delta was to remain for some time a mystery to Europeans, there was regular sea traffic between the region's other major ports, and the Dominican easily found onward passage once he decided that Cambodia was a lost cause. And though his miraculous survival did not spare Camões the spell in prison which had been awaiting him, he at least now possessed the makings of a legend, which would tie his own fate to the future of Europe, together to sink or swim.

XV

The Land Behind the Wind

D amião returned to Portugal in 1545, at the age of forty-three,
and shortly afterwards accepted the post of *Guarda-mor* of
the Torre do Tombo, keeper of the royal archive. He had not
arrived directly in Portugal from Padua, instead spending a few
further years in Louvain, but the return to his native land was
increasingly inevitable. For all that he sought to put some distance
between himself and controversy, marrying a Dutch woman from
a prominent Catholic family and publishing works demonstrating
his loyalty to the Emperor, it was clear that the walls were closing
in on the cosmopolitan world in which he had previously thrived.
Things came to a head when a French army besieged Louvain and
Damião had risked his own life to save his adopted home, using his
role as a negotiator to bluff the French into believing that Imperial
reinforcements were coming to relieve the town. The French had
retreated and the town was saved, but Damião remained their
hostage and the ruse was soon apparent. His fate was to be the
same as the *poor, wise man* from Ecclesiastes, whose wisdom deliv-
ered the city, but who went unremembered. *Wisdom is better than
strength*, says the Preacher; *nevertheless the poor man's wisdom is
despised, and his words are not heard*. Damião's isolation was made
clear when no one came to his rescue, not his connections in Italy
or the Imperial court, not even the ungrateful city of Louvain, and
he was forced to beg the Portuguese crown to pay his ransom. He

211

returned a prodigal son to the country of his birth, was considered but passed over for an important role at court, and took on instead the thankless role of writing the chronicles of the realm, a position with little influence which had ruined many men before him. But while the protection of obscurity would delay his fate, it would not be enough to save him from an age itching to open old wounds – especially as he was now himself too old to leave well enough alone.[1]

The task of writing chronicles was an arduous and time-consuming one, but one in which the expectations were clear. In this case Damião was to write the history of the reign of Dom Manuel, whom he had served from the age of nine until that king's death in 1521. The chronicler was to gather together the notable events of the reign, and in these it had not been lacking, covering as it did the period of Vasco da Gama's voyage to India and Pedro Álvares Cabral's landing in Brazil, the conquest of Mozambique and Goa, the establishment of a trading factory in Malacca and the first contacts with China, the triumph of Christianity in Portugal, and an immense growth in the wealth and status of the *Reino*. The chronicle was, moreover, commissioned by Manuel's own son, the Cardinal-Infante Henrique, who was among the most powerful men in the realm, the head of the Portuguese Inquisition, and (during the latter period of Damião's writing in the mid-1560s) regent of the kingdom while his great-nephew Sebastian was still a minor. The remit, then, was plain: to bolster national pride and to flatter the ruling family by finding in the archive evidence of heroism, virtue and charity. And this Damião was willing to do – up to a point.

The archive was, however, not quite the inert and powerless place that it appeared. The recourse to written records, which allowed information to be transmitted across space and preserved through time with much less loss of detail than oral culture, was nevertheless a vicious cycle. Once the archive became the official record of happenings in the realm, anything not in the archive for

212

all intents and purposes simply hadn't happened, blotted from the Book of History as God was believed to blot sinners from the Book of Life. All the infinite transactions of the world meant nothing until they were given in writing. Other cultures had reached this stage of dependence on the written record long before Europe. The Islamic belief in a perfect archive – *al-lawh al-mahfoudh*, the 'preserved tablet' on which destiny is ineradicably written – is also testament to the anxiety that human records were constantly threatened by erasure and loss. Vasco da Gama noted that the zamorin of Calicut was followed everywhere by a team of scribes who wrote down in palm-leaf books everything that happened in his presence. When the Portuguese arrived in China, the newly built imperial archive housed a ten-year tax register in 60,000 volumes in thirty temperature-controlled storage rooms behind two-tonne doors and walls ten feet thick, with duplicate copies in a series of islands off Nanjing where 1,400 people worked. China was in a sense nothing more than a shared record system: the Jesuits who visited noted in astonishment that though many Chinese people could not understand each other's speech given the bewildering variety of dialects, the country was united by its writing, which could be read in all parts and was the only mode of communication between the government and its provinces. It was all very well to speak of 'Portugal', or 'China', or 'the Catholic Church', but to understand what that actually meant you would have to visit the archive. Although very few had access to these documents, their presence nevertheless underwrote all the claims of the state with the assurance that those claims could, if needed, be checked against the archive, like a gold deposit that gives value to a currency.

Yet this also gave the microcosm of the archive a kind of sympathetic magic, a power to manipulate the world beyond by meddling with the documents within, like a voodoo doll whose stick pins are felt elsewhere. Recognising this power, the emperors of China had formed a habit of destroying the records of the

213

previous dynasty once the official chronicles had been written, making sure that no one could revisit the past and change its meaning. The English crown exercised strict controls over who could access the state archive in the Tower of London and elsewhere, denying access to those whose histories might subvert the official versions. And the Portuguese had developed their own version of this in what has come to be known as the 'conspiracy of silence', the royal edicts that forbade information about the lands that they were encountering across the globe from being disclosed to foreigners. Damião was at the heart of this labyrinth, managing the release of documents that had been licensed for circulation by the king, and guarding the mysteries to which even the scribes of the archive – who were already sworn to secrecy – were not allowed access. The classified material consisted of royal correspondence and the maps and reports that ensured Portugal kept its advantage over other nations in the matter of global trade, leaving its rivals to wander around in the darkness of an uncharted world; but it also meant that, after half a century of annual Portuguese fleets to India, there was still remarkably little available to the wider public about exactly what they had found there. There were, then, two ways in which the magic of the archive worked upon the world – both by controlling what was allowed in and became part of the official record, and also what was allowed out to form the knowledge of the world. The history that Damião was expected to write was supposed to be a distillation of the archive, and that in turn reduced the bewildering variety of the world to the perspective of one man, by placing the correspondence of the Portuguese king at the heart of it. The world, as seen from this archive, might be nothing more that the sum of the contracts, reports, and accounts sent back and forth between the crown and its agents.[2]

Yet controlling the world in this way was easier said than done, and was getting harder every day. Though Damião's tower was meagre compared to the imperial archive in China, being only

214

nine metres high and thirteen around and staffed by a mere hand-
ful of people, the size of Portugal's overseas operations had resulted
in an explosion of paperwork. While the core collection was relatively modest, numbering only 1,860 items in 1532, arranged in
certain drawers (*gavetas*) and further reduced into thirty-seven
volumes of key documents, there was a second, less orderly part of
the archive, in which tens of thousands of letters and memoranda
were arranged only as best as possible into a rough chronological
sequence, documents with which the Torre do Tombo was reaching saturation. Damião had over months and years begun to sort
the chaos of it all, dividing the piles up into the more secret and the
less, and then into packets and making a note of their contents,
before distributing them into chests and coffers and desks, and
again labelling each of these. And among this extraordinary profusion there were documents that didn't quite fit in the official order
of things – often quite literally, given that other cultures tended to
use different sizes of paper or parchment, or even different materials entirely. Whereas rules had been developed in the Chinese
archive regarding the precise shape of each kind of document,
certain things stuck out in the Torre do Tombo, such as the
four-metre long letter from Oman or the ornately folded square
missives from Malindi. This did not mean the Portuguese archive
was open to everything: there were innumerable ways of recording
the world, from tattooing to facial scarring and the Andean *quipu*
books of knotted string, which were simply too strange to
European eyes to merit inclusion in a repository of knowledge.
Many documents, translated early into Portuguese and on the
more familiar surface of paper, nevertheless introduced unofficial
histories into the archive, testimonies from those outside the
government bureaucracy whose way of seeing the world was not
shaped by the standard protocols.[3]

It was these other voices in the archive that distracted Damião
from the task he had been assigned, just as his attention had been
drawn aside from his guide to Lisbon to record the stories of

mermen. As he gathered documents on the Portuguese conquests in northern Africa, he became fixated on the story of Yahya ben Tafuf, the Maghrebi hero from Safi who had revolted from his own people for love and served the Portuguese loyally, only to be betrayed in the end by those who could never fully trust him. Damião's desire to tell this story led him not only to search the archive for ben Tafuf's letters and to copy out their complaints against the ungrateful Portuguese, giving the dates according to the Muslim Hejira calendar, but also to seek out an account of how this story looked from the other side, which he found in the writings of ben Tafuf's countryman Leo Africanus. He also had at his disposal a manuscript history of the Moluccas, left as a legacy by a friend who felt that the civilisations of the east outstripped those of the west, and who evidently saw Damião as sympathetic to his cause. When Damião came to write of the conversion of Kongo, a victory for the Christian faith and evidence that Portugal's expansion was a divine mission, he found the letters of its king, who went by his Christian name Afonso, and transcribed them into the chronicle, word for word and at great length. In the face of the documents Damião included, it is hard to see exactly where the triumph of the Portuguese was: instead we have the letters of a man who still felt bitterly the fact that he had been spurned by his own people for his conversion to Christianity, and by his father who with *great contempt and much misery exiled us in lands far away, where out of his sight and his grace we lived a long time.* While Afonso returned from his exile with an extraordinary religious conviction – knowing the Prophets, Gospels and Saints' Lives better than any European, sleeping with his books and forgetting to eat and drink – he was now held in contempt by a people who rebelled against him and attempted to depose him in favour of his brother. The anguish of this stranded figure, who even considered his own people to have been *discovered by the Portuguese* and who all alone a world away was imposing a foreign faith on an unwilling people, is hard to avoid. The same can be said of the king of

Cochin, one of those allies to whom Portugal was a fair-weather friend, but who remained loyal till his death to a people who cared little for his sacrifice. *The Greeks and Romans* [Damião comments] *can write whatever they like about Emperors, Kings, Princes, Republics, cities and private citizens to whom great praise is due, for keeping their word, as the public faith required: but I do not think that the truth, and faith with which the king of Cochim protected and defended our people is inferior to any of those of whom they write in their books with great admiration.*[4]

In Damião's hands, the history of Portugal, and even of Europe, began to come loose at the seams. So full are his chronicles with accounts of the kingdom of the Monomotapa, the customs of the Gujaratis, speculations on the giant stone horseman found in the Azores, the genealogy of Shah Ismail of Persia and the beginnings of the Shia faith, and descriptions of the eating habits in Hormuz and Malacca, that it is difficult to say precisely whose history this is. Fewer lines are given to the character and virtues of King Manuel than to the character and virtues of elephants, who are the subject of a 2,000-word section detailing their wisdom and extraordinary talents. And Damião contrived an elegant remedy for the fact that his account of Ethiopian religion and culture had been banned for sale in Portugal by simply including much of the same information in the official chronicle of the realm: over twenty densely set pages in two columns, placing the testimony of an Armenian and a black man – who had been scorned during their visits and refused even the courtesy of shared Communion, starved of the chance of salvation which was elsewhere preached so fervently – at the centre of Portuguese history. In these pages we also find testimony to the learning of black women, in the accounts of the books written by the Queen Mother Eleni of Abyssinia, and the sister of the king of Kongo who taught at the school erected for a thousand nobles of the realm.[5]

The inclusion of other voices is accompanied by a corresponding desire to temper the triumphalism of Portuguese and European narratives of history. Damião opens his account of the voyages of Vasco da Gama by saying that *though many Portuguese make the mistake of saying that they were the first* to sail this route, it was merely *a route forgotten to mankind for a long time*. Most provocatively, particular moments of national disgrace are placed as crescendos at the end of the first three parts of the four-part chronicle. Perhaps most affecting of these is the long and detailed account, at the end of the first part of the history, of how on Easter Sunday 1506 a mob had turned against the New Christians – those Jews who had accepted conversion rather than exile – and had over the course of two days killed more than 1,900 people. The chronicle unflinchingly describes how citizens of Lisbon and German sailors, led by two friars, had dragged the New Christians with their wives and children into the streets and thrown them alive or dead on to fires stoked by youths and slaves, *evidence of the cruelty of which even our children, even young people in the crib, are capable, taking them by the legs and ripping them to bits, and drunkenly throwing them at the walls*. The mob stuck not to drag people from churches and pillage their homes, and to settle scores as well with others who were not even converts. Nor does Damião allow this atrocity to be an isolated and extraordinary event, elsewhere giving several pages to the cruelty with which Jewish children were separated from their parents for reinstruction, a work (in Damião's words) *of great terror, which not only provoked much sorrow and sadness and many tears among the Jews, but also much astonishment from the Christians themselves, as no creature will suffer to have its children parted from it, and strangers who see this done feel almost as if it is done to them, especially rational creatures, to whom nature's laws are apparent*. These laws forced many of the Old Christians to be deeply affected by the roaring and the sobbing and the laments of the Jews.[6]

If Damião's notion of history was provocatively unconstrained by the borders of his nation, his household was no different, and in the periods of rest from composing the chronicles his rooms at the tower were *bursting with foreigners and those from outside the city*, something of which he boasted. All were welcome, especially musicians – there was a Fleming called Erasmo, and *Jacques que faz os oculos* ('Jack the lensgrinder', a Frenchman), Hans Pelque a Pole, and a German called Tibaldo Luis – and after meals they made a habit of performing Masses and motets in the *canto de organo*, the polyphonic music in which Damião had become expert but which was still foreign to most Portuguese ears. Damião's own compositions included a soaring setting of the *Song of Songs*, where the bursting spirit of the lover is called forth by the swooping notes and singing birds and fruiting trees and tendrils reaching out from vines: *the winter is past, the rain is changed – the time of the singing birds has come; the fig tree has brought forth her young figs, and the vines with their small grapes have cast a savour.* But there were also pieces of a darker note, such as the foreboding words of the Prophet Micah, set as a lament emerging from the shadows of imprisonment:

> Rejoice not against me, O my enemy:
> when I fall, I shall arise;
> when I sit in darkness, the Lord
> shall be a light unto me.

Perhaps Damião explained to those unfamiliar with polyphony how the music could be understood like the flowing of water, a comparison he had used in his praise poems for his idol Josquin des Prez, and which he had once expounded at greater length to two friends while on a walk in the woods outside Louvain. *He called them to a stop by the river that flows through Hever*, one of them recalled, *and said that out of the glorious surging of the rustling stream, bouncing off the pebbles and rocks, it was possible to hear marvellous harmonies, as if the spirits were singing beneath the waters, their voices all gushing out at once.* What seemed merely babble to the hurried and unheeding ear was actually a miracle of counterpoint, with an emerging current giving rise elsewhere to a corresponding depth, each sounding its own path and incomplete the one without the other.[7]

Damião was not alone in finding in fluid movement a voice that spoke against a notion of harmony as complete agreement reducible to precise and static laws. Over in France, Michael Servetus, who like Vesalius challenged the authority of classical medicine and was among the first to describe the circulation of the blood in the body, had been burned at the stake and put on the Index of Forbidden Books for his ideas, including the suggestion that the vital principle of man lay not in his brain, heart or liver, but rather in the flow of blood through his veins, an 'animal spirit' that brought him troublingly close to other creatures, restoring the full sense of *anima* (spirit) to the animal. Leonardo da Vinci's fame rests upon the extraordinary precision of his draughtsmanship, captured for many in the *Vitruvian Man*, which promises to unlock the simple but elegant geometry of the human body; but Leonardo spent his final years obsessively sketching the shapes of cascading water and describing the structure of lunular waves, mesmerised by the infinitely complex and fleeting nature of their symmetries. The idea that the material world was in flux, unstable and unchartable, had been a dangerous and revolutionary idea in ancient philosophy, and it was against this that Plato had posited his idea of a fixed, unchanging metaphysical world – the only world that was worth knowing, or in fact even could be known – an idea subsequently adopted by Christianity. The idea that flux had a significance of its own, and was not just a foil to set off the perfections of that which was eternally fixed, threatened to erode the foundations of how the world was understood, putting in its place a history which could not be divided into regions and periods, a history like water, before which all existing structures might be swept away with their attendant beliefs.[8]

As he put the finishing touches to his chronicle, Damião wrote a preface in which he laid out his task as he saw it as well as a consideration of the nature of history. He had decided to take up the writing of the chronicle, despite his weak judgement, because he did not think that in commissioning him the Cardinal-Infante Henrique was requiring him to recount *all* the deeds of King Manuel, but instead only those that were substantial and fitting to a chronicle; and, moreover, that it was his duty to give truthfully to each its praise or reprehension as it was deserved. *Many historians, he says, begin their chronicles by praising history, but these praises always sell the matter short: because history is infinite, and so its virtues are also interminable, and cannot be confined within any limits.* The infinitude of history made a mockery of attempts to reduce it to laws, rules and precedents, delusions of order achieved only by ignoring most of the world. Like attending to a confluence of rivers, history was for Damião a matter of becoming immersed in the babble, attuning one's ear to the counterpoint of similarity and difference, each sounding its own path and incomplete without the other.[9]

XVI

The Tale of the Tribe

There was, however, a different way to tell the story. The bewildering multiplicity of the archive, with its myriad voices and lack of obvious governing logic, creates an opening for those who offer reassurance, a way of looking at things in which the world makes sense. This singular perspective, at which the chaos of the world aligns, provides a totem uniting all those who share the same vision. But the construction of this communal destiny requires a rearrangement of the past, an ordering of the long and doubtful voyage such that it seems clear that it could only ever have had one destination.

We next see Camões in 1569, when Diogo do Couto – future chronicler, and founding *Guarda-mor* of the Portuguese archive in Goa – came across the poet on his way back to Portugal, in the river estuary fortress newly built in eastern Africa by one of the future architects of the Escorial Palace in Madrid. *In Mozambique* (Couto wrote many years later) *we found that Prince of Poets of the age, my fellow traveller and friend Luís de Camões, so poor that he was reliant on friends for food, and we got him outfitted so that he could make it back to the Reino. That winter in Mozambique,* Couto records, *he was putting the final touches on the* Lusiads *so that it could be printed.* How (or even when) Camões had made it back to India from the Mekong, what charges he had faced for malfeasance in Macau, how he had fallen back into poverty and yet managed to secure a passage at least as far as Mozambique – he drew a veil over all these things, leaving only those fragments of his life that fit the story, though rumours persisted that his money troubles followed him across the globe, and that he was stranded in Mozambique pending payment of 200 *cruzados* of debt he had run up in Goa. Whatever these missing years had held for him, they had left him exhausted, and the final book of his poem begins with a prayer for help *in this last work,* asking that he be given back *a taste for writing, which I have lost,* and for the strength to finish before age and sorrow *carry me off to the black river of forgetting, and eternal sleep.*[1]

The poem that Camões was finishing off at Mozambique also began there, opening, as the epic style required, *in the middle of things*, with Vasco da Gama halfway to India on his voyage of 1497–8. *Having committed to the doubtful sea in brittle wood, through unused ways*, the opening scenes find da Gama arriving in the Indian Ocean and being approached by a flotilla of small vessels carrying an innocent people who are delighted by being served wine in glasses, and who declare themselves to follow the law *that is taught by the great descendant of Abraham, who now rules the world, son of a Jewish mother and a heathen father*. The cosmopolitan and heavily Arabised culture that da Gama had actually found in Mozambique is nowhere to be seen; in its stead is a wide-eyed and simple people – strangely reminiscent of Columbus' descriptions of the Taíno he had met in the Caribbean – who reveal only coyly and cryptically to the unsuspecting Portuguese that they are Muslim. This encounter sets the tone for what will in fact be an epic of forgetting, a masterful erasure of the world.[2]

In fairness, Camões tells us as much himself. Repeatedly in the poem it is announced that the deeds of the Portuguese will overshadow those of the ancient world, causing us to forget the heroic feats of Greeks, Romans, Assyrians and Persians; in fact, it is necessary that we do so in order for the poem to work. Gone is the evidence that these routes had been sailed before in the ancient world, and the many contending claims to the legacies of Greece and Rome: the voyage as Camões tells it is one of *seas never before navigated*, in which the Portuguese *open seas no race has opened before*, undertaken by Europeans who are surrounded by the *uncultured* regions of Scandinavia, Muscovy and Livonia. At the heart of this Europe is Portugal, at which forces from across Europe converge to expel the Muslims and so set in motion the destiny of the nation, which is to leave this enemy nowhere in the world to hide. So it is from the white sands of the Rio Tejo that Vasco da Gama and his Argonauts – as they are repeatedly called – set off across the world.[3]

The trick of the epic is to remove all the things that led up to da Gama's arrival in India – the competition over spices, the dream of a distant Christian ally – and replace them instead with a narrative of European and Portuguese history, taking up almost half of the poem, which culminates in this moment. In this version of the story, the coming into being of the nation is proof that it was destined to fulfil some role, and this, in turn, is justification enough for fulfilling that role, whatever the cost. The lives of individual people simply become collateral in the great drama of the nation, which plays itself out over the course of centuries. Gone are the episodes that blurred the boundaries between the Europeans and the cultures that they met, where the idols of Calicut and Macau were taken for the Virgin Mary and a glimpse was had of shared beliefs in the Trinity; in their place, Camões has substituted tricks played by duplicitous Muslims, who try to lure the Portuguese into idolatry by pretending to be Christians. Starting in Mozambique, where the Sheikh upon learning that they are Christian conceives *a certain hatred in his soul, a malice of thought* against them, the plot neatly divides the messiness of history into the black-and-white of religious war, a Manichean struggle between Islam and Christianity.

The criticism, widespread and thoroughly documented in accounts of the Portuguese encounter with the east by Damião and others, of faithless treatment of local allies, becomes in Camões' telling just another Muslim plot, an attempt to undermine the Portuguese by sowing malicious and unwarranted rumours that they robbed the people whom they pretended to approach in peace. Vasco da Gama, who laments *the tricks that have been played upon our good faith*, launches into a diatribe against this Muslim duplicity, cursing the suspicion that Muslims continue to foster against noble Christian acts: if his own motives were so base, *why would he commit himself to the angry sea, the frozen Antarctic, and the harsh suffering* of these places? Here the very scale of European ambition, which prompts the most outlandish expeditions, becomes proof that they are prompted by noble motives, without self-interest exploring the furthest reaches of the globe. This account of events would be rather hard to stomach for many of the peoples who had been the subject of European 'discoveries', but no matter – their very incredulity that the voyages were undertaken for these reasons, their inability to conceive of noble motives, is evidence enough of their inferiority.[4]

For da Gama and his crew to triumph over duplicity and ignorance, however, would hardly be enough to transform their story into epic. Instead, Camões takes the extraordinary step of introducing pagan classical deities into his poem, setting the historical events of the voyage to India within a mythical narrative centred on warring Olympian gods. In the words of the opening stanzas:

> As when the south wind or the north
> blows through the thick forest,
> breaking the branches in the deep black
> with uncontrolled and careless force,
> making the mountain roar with the susurration
> of breaking leaves boiling on the mountain,
> such was the contention of the Gods
> that erupted on Olympus.

The triumph of the Portuguese is opposed by Bacchus, whose own famous conquest of India they threaten to overshadow; but Venus, admiring their strength and their language, *which is but a little changed from Latin*, takes their side. Camões would later in the poem explain these gods away as a mere metaphor, a way of dramatising what was at stake in this voyage – an explanation that would satisfy the censor and save his poem from the Index of Forbidden Books – and we might be tempted to shrug off this oddity as mere poetic licence, if it were not for the fact that this fashion for play-acting paganism went on to become central to European culture for the hundreds of years that followed, precisely the period in which European nations grew into colonial empires. Whereas the interest of the early humanists in pagan religion and culture had been viewed with alarm, leading to accusations of atheism and even some excommunications, neoclassicism was to become from the late sixteenth century onwards the undisputed aesthetic movement not only across Europe but also across the world that European states began to colonise, filling the globe from Peru to Goa with white marble columns, Italianate grotesques and triumphal arches in the Roman style. It was the beginning of a realignment of the ancient world, in which the broad global reach of the Roman Empire and its wholesale relocation to the east were all but forgotten, leaving only the Augustan empire at Rome and its natural heirs in the empires of Europe.[5]

In this telling of the story, then, the Portuguese voyages to the east become a triumph over the forces of nature and of barbarism, here given the form of ocean gods. The sea-men who had so captured Damião's imagination are transformed into monsters, jealous of the threat to their global empire posed by Portuguese ships, and dredge up waves to throw da Gama off his path, goaded on by Bacchus, who fears that his wild rule over the pagan East might come to an end if the Portuguese are successful. The storm-struck Cape of Good Hope is here transformed into a monstrous giant called Adamastor (Untamed Man), *with a*

dark face and a squalid beard, sunken eyes, terrifying and mali-
cious in his aspect, skin the colour of earth, hair dirty and matted,
black-mouthed and yellow-toothed, a gargantuan incarnation of
fear that many have surmised was part of the inspiration for
Melville's *Moby-Dick.* Ranged against these demons, on the side
of the Portuguese, are the women of the water: Nereids and
mermaids who watch over the sailors, saving them from a
Muslim plot by drawing the ships back from the harbour of
Mombasa, and calming the winds that threaten to sink the fleet
just as it reaches India. At the head of these women is Venus, who
descends to hover over the ships and calm the ocean when the
Portuguese expedition is threatened, *flying from sky to sea like an*
arrow, in a short space descending to the open sea. And, in the
final part of the poem, as da Gama departs from India, Venus
arranges for the emergence from the sea of a magical *Ilha*
Namorada, an Island of Love where the sea-nymphs assemble to
give the sailors their long-overdue reward in an episode of orgi-
astic sexual consummation.[6]

The fact that this strange and disturbing fantasy was to become
in time an orientalist cliché, a vision of a world teeming with alluring exotic women patiently awaiting the conquest of European
men, might almost distract us from the fact that the story is a
highly personal one for Camões, for all that it is told through the
medium of gods and sea monsters and mermaids. All the pieces of
his humiliation are there, scattered beneath the surface of the
poem. The giant Adamastor's metamorphosis into the man-killing
Cape of Good Hope comes after he is tricked by a nymph with
whom he is in love, who (as Antonia Bras had with Camões all
those years before) arranges a tryst with him only to humiliate him
for daring to think his hideousness worth her beauty, transforming
him into a monster of shame and anger. The Nereids who swarm
about the ship at Venus' command seem a little less like make-be-
lieve when one remembers the drowned Dinamene, Camões' own
lover-beneath-the-waves. And, in the closing stretches of the

poem, Camões appears himself on the Island of Love, thinly disguised as a sailor named Lionardo,

> a well-made soldier,
> manly, chivalrous and amorously inclined,
> but to whom love had reacted with disgust,
> always treating him badly,
> and who at last was convinced
> that he had no luck in matters of love.

Even the nymph set aside for Lionardo in this fantasy shows little interest in him until, worn down by the mournful beauty of his Petrarchan lament, she finally agrees to exchange vows with him, the last sailor to find a girl.[7]

In the closing sequence of the poem, da Gama is given a vision of the glorious future awaiting the Portuguese Empire, and Camões announces that this ornate erotic fantasy has merely been an allegory for the reward of fame that awaits those who dare to set off across the world. The truth was perhaps a little more complicated than that. While Camões did clearly long for fame and the financial security that it would bring, his writing is also fixated in a way beyond the conventional on finding someone who will love him in return. The fantasy that he would find in the east the reciprocal love that had eluded him in his native Portugal had proved hollow, as perhaps was inevitable when relationships were formed on such unequal terms: the very power and privilege that allowed him to take lovers was also a constant reminder that it was the power and privilege that had sealed the deal, not any quality of his own, something that seems to have developed into an obsessive shame. *The great sin of this age*, he was to write, is *loving things that were made for use, and not using the things that were made for love*. Though Camões might have proved useful to a few people, he had never been anything more. The very personal fixations to which his life had given rise, however, were to provide in his epic poem an archetype for the colonial fantasy, which braided together the fame of noble deeds, the rewards of conquest and the satisfaction of emotional and erotic desires.[8]

The fact that Camões felt the need to write his obsessions off as merely an allegory for something nobler and more abstract – the pursuit of fame – was part of a wider cultural reckoning faced by Europe in its encounter with the east. If the first thing that Camões notes about India in his epic is the unthinkable centrality of animals to its culture, the second is the people's attitude towards sexuality, which was all but incomprehensible to Europeans. While the vegetarianism of the Brahmins was baffling to the Portuguese, even more so was the fact that their strictness in matters of diet was reversed when it came to sex:

> But in matters of lust
> they have more licence and fewer rules:
> the women are general, if only
> among the husband's family …
> they feel no jealousy.

This muddled and vague account of Indian sexuality was of a piece with the astounded reports sent by Europeans from the east of very different ideas regarding the relationship between sex and religion, the effects of which were powerful, even if they were riddled with errors and misunderstandings. Whereas the regulation and restriction of sexual appetite was at the very core of the Abrahamic faiths, with the denial of this most bestial of appetites being key to rewards in the hereafter, Europeans were astonished to note that there were temples set aside in Vijayanagara for sacred prostitutes, a practice that they also found among the nun-prostitutes of Japan. Jesuit letters reported the perplexing fact that in India holy processions were accompanied by *almost-naked dancers, men and women covered in oil*, and there were edicts issued at Goa against troupes who visited from the mainland to perform *obscene dances, and sing dirty songs, and other things that only the devil could have taught them, in service of their temples and their idols.* Even more astonishingly, same-sex relations were widely and openly practised in many places that the Europeans visited, as among the Persian merchants of Hormuz and the literati of the Chinese court. While the Portuguese tried to stamp these things out where they found them, driving the 'sodomites' from Hormuz with arrows stuck through their nostrils and fulminating against homosexuality to the Chinese, none of this could undo the subversion these things threatened to their own beliefs. As with the treatment of animals, this attitude towards sexuality represented more than just a disagreement over a matter of detail: the idea that our salvation is not strictly tied to the suppression of our deepest desires struck at the very foundations of western metaphysics, which constantly affirms its belief in a better world elsewhere by acts of self-denial, turning its back on the fallen and inferior things of this world. While it seemed that the suffering of abstinence was worth the price, given what was promised in the hereafter, the reverse was at least just as true: the things of God seemed so powerful because they were tied up with torturous feelings of shame and self-denial. As the Island of Love at the end of Camões' *Lusiads* suggests, these appetites never really went away: instead, they were merely transferred on to other things, producing a toxic confusion between lust and greed and hope.[9]

Camões arrived back in Lisbon in April 1570 aboard the ship *Santa Clara,* and was granted a licence to publish his poem on 24 September 1571. Six months earlier, on the last day of March, the Inquisitor General of Portugal had found that the rejection of the religious merits of chastity by Damião de Góis was sufficient cause for his imprisonment and an investigation into his beliefs, and had issued a warrant for his arrest and the confiscation of his books.[10]

XVII

When I Sit in Darkness

On the morning after his arrest, Damião requested an audience with the Inquisitors and asked to be told what the accusations were against him, so that he could know whether he was imprisoned with cause or not. He was informed that it was not the habit of the Holy Inquisition to accuse anyone. Rather, they examined the crimes with care, and only after they were well looked into and guilt determined would they send for the party to be apprehended, as had been done in his case. He was invited, for the love of the Holy Church, to tell them everything he had done and said and spoken against the Holy Faith, as he had hopes of their mercy.[1]

Damião proceeded to give an account of his life, dredging his memory for where he may have been at fault: how when in the service of King João III and on a mission to Denmark he had stopped at Lübeck and at Wittenberg on the way to Poland, and had met there various Reformers including Luther and his lieutenant Melanchthon, and how over lunch, Luther had said he did all he could to bring people to truth, and Melanchthon followed Luther because it seemed to him that he taught the truth, and Damião said that he did not respond to this but was brusque and showed himself unhappy with them. And how he had gone to Freiburg on the advice of doctors – he had been suffering headaches in Louvain – and had taken with him a letter of introduction

233

to Erasmus, and had met the Protestant geographer Sebastian Münster in the doorway of a bookshop and another man, Grinaeus, who was reading philosophy by the door of the inn where he was staying and he did not go to his house. And he had met other Protestants in Strasbourg and had told them about how the Abyssinians believed that the Pope was the head of the Church. And when asked whether he ever wrote to the Lutherans again he said that when he was living in Padua he had been approached by Cardinal Sadoleto, begging him to send a letter on to Melanchthon, and had done so, with one of his own.[2]

At the end of the examination, Damião was urged to confess all that he had seen and heard in the land of the Lutherans, and he agreed that he would do so willingly.

During the course of six further examinations over the following month, Damião was asked time and again to revisit the story of his life, and each point of his faith was probed in detail. At the end of every examination he was urged to confess, told to be mindful of his crimes, being warned that if he did not confess everything it would be necessary for the Procurator Fiscal to publish an indictment of him. Did he believe in the power of indulgences, in the intercessory power of saints, in the Real Presence of Christ in the Communion wafer, in priestly celibacy – did he think it was acceptable to eat meat on any day, even major fast days? Did he possess any of the volumes in the Index of Prohibited Books, and had he rooted them out from his library and turned them into the Inquisition, as was required? Repeatedly, Damião protested that he had told them everything, though their silence drew from him more and more memories, desperate attempts to find out of what he stood accused. He had purchased in Flanders a papal bull *da cruzada* which allowed him to eat meat and dairy on fish days to preserve his health (*To keep bodily health, even when not unwell?*), yes to preserve health as well as cure infirmity, and no he did not believe it was necessary to seek specific permission to use the licence. But certainly on the days that he ate meat he did not also eat fish; it was because the fish made him unwell that he had eaten the meat. He remembered that among his books there was one on geomancy, and a few books by Erasmus. Perhaps he had heard a sermon by Luther in Wittenberg, but he had not understood a thing as he did not speak the language. The Apostolic Notary intervened to enter into the record that in order to go to Wittenberg on the way from Schleswig to Poznań it would be necessary to go some three or four leagues – fifteen or twenty kilometres – out of the way. Damião did remember one time when talking with learned men in Italy saying that the Pope should call a council and dispense with the rule *De dilectu ciborum* so that everyone could just eat what they wanted and this was because he thought many heretics would return to the fold if the Pope did this. And he remembered an incident with a Danish councillor in which the man had mocked his piety and urged him to drink a toast from a consecrated cup but he did not *and if this is not as he says may fire come from the sky and burn him*. He may also have had a few books by one Stephen Dolet and he had not thought of these because they were dictionaries of the Latin language but their author was suspected. He did not have a licence to own these books.[3]

Damião urged the Inquisitors to search his chambers and they would find inside a coffer his will, signed and sealed, and they should break it open and see whether he was a Catholic or a heretic, and they would also find there a description or story of his life and of the people with whom he had dealt. Also they would find there five or six letters from Erasmus, and his own collected works in Latin which he had published in Louvain. The Inquisitors instead entered into the record several letters from the Cardinal-Infante Henrique, written in 1541 and explaining to Damião that, although his account of the Ethiopian faith was praiseworthy, it would not be licensed for printing or distribution in Portugal, for all that the cardinal believed Damião was a good Christian. But there were also certain superstitions in the book which were justified by Damião using *twisted reasons*, and it was dangerous to publish such errors in Portugal, where there were many New Christians and heretics who might be drawn to these ideas. For *it is one thing simply to relate the customs of another nation and another to try to corroborate them with false reasons without afterwards refuting them.* This would later be formulated into an official charge – *laudando hereticum, non vituperando* (praising heretics, not condemning them). Curiously, Damião's chronicles, which are filled with just such unrefuted praise for those of other faiths and cultures, were not brought in as evidence. Perhaps, as they were published by the official printer of the Cardinal-Infante Henrique, they were considered above reproach; perhaps, given that these things were scattered within a thousand pages of dense historical record, they were yet to be discovered.[4]

Damião was asked whether it was possible to believe heretical things in one's heart and yet in a Catholic country to do as Catholics do and as the Church said to do. Damião answered he did not remember saying to anyone that he thought these errors were good. The implication, though unspoken, was plain. It was not enough merely to establish Damião's outward conformity, for the fear was spreading of 'Nicodemites', those whose words were no reflection of their true thoughts. To fight this terror, of a yawning inward abyss beyond the control of official instruments, new tools were needed to draw out the innards of the soul. Damião was urged to confess his sins.[5]

In the meantime, the treasurer of the Cardinal-Infante, one Luis de Crasto, had been urged by his confessor to come to the Inquisition and break the secrecy of the confessional booth, recounting how Damião de Góis had said that there were many popes who were tyrants, and that many priests were hypocrites and more tyrannical even than secular powers, and he said this when talking about the *Company* – the Jesuits – many of whom he said did not live in a humble way as the founder of that order had done.[6]

After a month of questioning, the charges against Damião were published. The indictment pronounced that he was obliged particularly as an Old Christian to believe in the teachings of Holy Mother Church, and that instead he had spoken at various times of the Lutheran heresies, twisting authorities to support them, taking delight in doing so and attempting to draw others to his side. He was a great friend of the heads of the sects, whom he had gone out of his way to see and to share food and drink with, and had later received their letters and responded to them, and was held in high esteem by them, as suggested by the fact that a prominent person had asked Damião to act as an intermediary with the Lutherans. Damião had shown himself to have little affection for the Church and its laws, making clear by his acts that he thought meat should be eaten on all days without licence or urgent necessity. And his attachment to his errors was such that, not being able to speak with heretics because they were absent or dead, *he had communed with them through the medium of the prohibited books that he kept in his library*. And he had said in the hearing of one that *he would go to church and hear mass like a Catholic but that in his heart he would keep what was there.*[7]

With the publication of the charges it was finally possible for Damião to know the identity of his accuser. He had no shortage of enemies, as his unvarnished history of the country had led to a torrent of complaints from those who felt that the memory of their noble ancestors had been traduced. But the infection lay in a far older wound than that: Simão Rodrigues had lodged an accusation with the Inquisition against Damião almost as soon as he had arrived back in Portugal some twenty-five years previously. Simão had seen him coming out of a church in Évora in the summer of 1545 and had been struck because he had met Damião before in Padua and that with Roque de Almeida they had discussed matters of faith over the course of two months, and that Damião had agreed with Luther's disdain for the Pope and for the sacrament of confession, and had delighted in doing so, and had even lent him a book by Luther on Ecclesiastes. When he had confronted him about attending church like a Catholic in Évora,

237

Damião had said that *he would do as others did, but in his heart he would keep and hold what was there*. And Simão protested that he was not saying these things out of any malice towards Damião and that on the contrary they had at one time been great friends, but he feared that Damião might be of great danger to the faith, given his knowledge of Latin and French and Italian and perhaps Dutch and German. And Simão returned two days later because he had remembered more: that Roque had spoken with Damião present against monastic vows of chastity and that *yes*, it seemed to him when they were saying these things that they were trying to convert him.[8]

At that time nothing had happened. It has been speculated that one of the Inquisitors, being a relative of Damião, was able to shield him from the charges; or perhaps that these things did not merit a trial in the prevailing atmosphere in those days. Simão returned again to the Inquisition five years later, in 1550, to reaffirm what he had said, and to add a few more details, about how he had been offered meat and fresh cheese on a fast day in Damião's house in Padua (though perhaps Damião was not there), and also he remembered Damião citing certain verses from Corinthians in support of a Lutheran position on salvation. An unpublished letter in the Jesuit archive shows that Simão had written to Loyola in the interim, accusing Damião and his family of being at the centre of a ring of heresy in Portugal, announcing his intention to call the inquisition down upon them, and saying *'and I think that in truth I can do more'*.[9]

Again nothing happened, for more than twenty years, though when the Inquisitors finally decided in the spring of 1571 that the charges against Damião merited an investigation, Simão was ready to testify again, now from the Jesuit seminary in Toledo, where he had been living in exile since his expulsion from Portugal following the erratic and unstable practices he had been cultivating among the Jesuit novices. He affirmed everything that he had said in his previous depositions, correcting only that he had never meant that Damião had lent him a book by Luther, but only that Damião had tried to lend him one.[10]

With the charges public, the floodgates were opened, and a stream of witnesses filed through the Inquisitorial offices to report things that they had heard Damião say or had heard said about him. Each of them was asked at the beginning of their testimony to testify to whether they had seen or heard anything done or said that had scandalised them. Damião had been heard to say that he wished to go and die in Flanders, and that he wished for his sons to be educated there. A certain nobleman said that, when he had been considering paying for a chapel to be built in the monastery of Santo Domingo in Coimbra, Damião had suggested he would be better off doing so in his parish church, and it seemed to the witness that this was because Damião expected the monasteries to be suppressed in Portugal as they had been in Germany.[11]

One woman of good repute had heard from a gentleman of the king's household that one of his colleague's sisters had been at Damião's house on a fast day and that Damião had eaten a piece of pork with some orange juice, and once this sister had been tracked down she said that she had indeed been at Damião's house six years previously and that she had been pregnant and he had offered her pork, saying that surely she shouldn't eat alone. And after they had polished off the pork they had eaten the fish that had been prepared as well, though she now remembers that it was thirteen or fourteen years before, and not six. And she certainly had been scandalised and had said as much to her brother and her brother's wife, and had told them that Damião claimed that *what goes into your mouth cannot condemn you, but rather what comes out*. And her own father had said to her that Damião did not believe in God any more than this wall. The Inquisitors noted that they believed that *she spoke according to the truth*.[12]

Others who had been present at this meal were called, but they were less sure, could not remember much about it. Damião's daughter Catarina protested that she had only been nine years old at the time, and that she did remember that her father had said that *what entered at the mouth did not dirty the soul*, but that *he meant this with regard to eating much or little*, and that it was advice to his sons not to gossip. It was noted of these witnesses only that *they spoke according to their testimony*.[13]

Over the course of six further months, and while the drip of accusations continued, Damião was subjected to relentless examinations, during which he remembered that more than thirty years before he had had doubts about whether the Pope's indulgences were of any avail, though he never stopped attending church and taking the sacrament, and that yes he had praised foreigners, but not to say their errors were good. He had perhaps for four or five years had doubts about confessions and indulgences, but that was before he had begun to learn Latin, and when he had been in Padua he had discussed these things with learned men and had repented and confessed these doubts in church. Interspersed with these new memories, Damião begged the Inquisitors to reach a speedy conclusion to their investigation, as he was old and frail and dying in prison, and so asked that he be given the penance that would serve God and earn him forgiveness. He also begged to be given a book – any book – in Latin, as he was going mad with solitude. There is no evidence that the request for a book was granted. A second set of charges was published, the harvest of these latest accusations, and Damião now wrote to the Inquisitors in agony that the reports of Simão that had started all this should not be believed, as Simão had shown his inveterate hatred in accusing Damião of crimes to Ignatius Loyola – who had visited him expressly to apologise for this – and also had not reported him right away upon his return to Portugal twenty-five years previously, but only some months later and even then only to prevent Damião from being appointed as Master of the Wardrobe to the Infante, whom Simão served as tutor. He bewailed the destruction of his honour that nine months in prison had wreaked, as well as upon his body, being seventy years of age and hardly able to stand and so covered with scabies that he might be taken to be a leper.[14]

The second set of charges produced another wave of new memories from his accusers. Damião had boasted of seeing Melanchthon walking in front of Luther, singing verses and with an uncovered head, as if this were something impressive, and he had often had Flemings and Germans at his house. Others who lived in the castle precinct had never seen Damião attend Mass there, and, when asked, members of his household said that he went to another church for that purpose but also said that he was not a great *misseiro* – not a great attender of the Mass – and laughed at this. Some had heard him say that Erasmus had lived a sober and temperate life and Damião gave an account of him as a virtuous man. Foreigners were often at his house and a witness heard them sing things that he did not understand; only he heard the voices and the singing lasted a long time and that they were not the kind of songs that he was used to. And that Damião had from his apartments a gallery giving on to the chapel and he was never seen to use it to hear Mass but instead he kept there bacon and salted meats, and below this there was a cross with a figure of Christ to the right of the transept, and fat and brine dripped from the storeroom on to this cross, and one of them even thought that what had fallen upon the cross might have been urine. This lasted a long time and the servants of another woman upon seeing the crucifix in this state had said *Jesus do you see that?* and they had all been astonished and scandalised by this.[15]

In response to this suggestion, that he shared with the Lutherans and the Muslims their hatred of religious images, Damião asked for access to a certain document which listed all the paintings and statues and church fittings that he had owned and those he had given over the decades to the king and the queen and the Church, and even to a certain papal envoy, who had begged him to sell the paintings that he owned by Hieronymus Bosch, having never seen such things in all his days. And he called many witnesses to the fact that he had a room full of great pictures, for which he had paid immense sums, each listed in great detail, and people had come to his rooms specifically to see them. Also that the drippings in the chapel were not brine or oil but rather rainwater, caused by a certain drain that ran along the wall and which flooded every year, and his own barrels were not on the balcony but in the middle of the room, which was tiled, and so for all these reasons it was plain that he would not have let the brine and drippings fall upon the crucifix in the castle chapel, and begged them to consider his service to the state and his good character and to let him go.[16]

In response to his pleas, Damião was informed that he was not sufficiently penitent regarding many things that had been declared heresy five years before at the end of the Council of Trent. His excuses – that he had merely gone to see the Reformers out of curiosity, not out of any intention of adopting their opinions, that this was common among Catholics at the time, and that he should not be condemned for his friendship with Erasmus since Erasmus himself had not been condemned – were of little avail. He complained that the one who had set this all in motion – Simão Rodrigues – was *his deadly enemy*, and had poisoned people against him in order to prolong his time in prison. He asked to be allowed to face in person his accuser, for whom he hoped that God would give the punishments reserved for the iniquitous, quoting the words of the psalm:

> The proud have had me greatly in derision: yet
>   have I not declined from thy law.
> I remembered thy judgements of old, O Lord; and
>   have comforted myself.
> Horror hath taken hold upon me because of the
>   wicked that forsake thy law.
> Thy statutes have been my songs in the house of
>   my pilgrimage.

I have remembered thy name, O Lord, in the
night, and have kept thy law.

His request was not granted. In a mournful letter, submitted to the
Inquisitors after sixteen months in prison and suffering alternating
interrogations and periods in darkness and ignorance, he said to
them that he was very ill, and suffering from not one illness but
three: the scabies that covered him like leprosy, kidney problems
and vertigo. *Anyone who sees him,* he attested, *is driven to pity, and
there is no thing in his body that is whole.* In the letter he reminds
them that he had freely confessed the sins of his youth and
repented of them thirty and forty years since, and points out to
them that even Saints Augustine, Celestine and Jerome were all
heretics at one point before mending their ways. A month passed
before the response of the Inquisitors, which was to read to him
the charges against him and to urge him to confess to his sins.[17]

And then, in the nineteenth month of his trial, and with no
further events of any note, it was over. The Inquisition determined
that they would get no more from him, and in consideration of his
age and state spared him a public execution and instead committed him to perpetual confinement in the monastery of Batalha, in
order to prevent him from spreading further pollution in the
realm, and moreover confiscating his worldly goods for the royal
treasury. Damião formally abjured his heresy, and invited the full
fury of the law upon himself should he ever lapse or even stumble
in his penance, which was to live out his life praying and reflecting
upon his sins.[18]

The next we hear of Damião is on the morning of his death
fifteen months later, when he was found apparently having been
released from Batalha. He was evidently well prepared for the end,
as his tombstone had been engraved during the previous decade
with the Roman numerals MDLX (1560), which needed only to
have added on to them the remaining digits summing up the days
of his life. The final X and I and V for the year 1574 were never

carved into the stone, and he was buried on the same day as he died beneath a tombstone some fourteen years out of date. The surviving accounts agree on signs of violence, but disagree whether he was burned or strangled, whether he was at home or at an inn, and on other key details.

XVIII

All Our Scattered Leaves

In May of 1903, the Director of the Bibliotheca Nacional in Lisbon was interrupted at his work by a bibliophile of some distinction, one Sr Carlos Ferreira Borges, a man well known to those at the library. He had come to the esteemed director Xavier da Cunha with a proposal for the sale of some manuscripts, driven not (he made clear) by any financial difficulties, but rather by a desire to clear his shelves for other things, and to ensure that the valuable pieces in his possession were lodged securely in the national collection, and were not dispersed into a range of private hands. The intrigued director arranged a few weeks later a visit to the house of Sr Borges, accompanied by the Inspector of National Libraries and Archives, to undertake a detailed examination of the objects on offer. They were delighted to discover that the manuscripts possessed by Sr Borges contained many volumes from the library of the House of Vimeiro, most of which had been thought lost during the great Lisbon earthquake of 1755. The result of their visit was the acquisition from Sr Borges' collection of a group of sixty-six manuscripts and an enormous quantity of loose documents, and the prize among these was a letter by the young Camões, one of only four known to have been written by the poet. The contents of the letter were, to say the least, unexpected.

In the intervening three centuries, the fame of Camões had grown to unparalleled heights in Portugal and had spread throughout the world. During his own lifetime the poet had won little fame and only meagre rewards, and died in obscurity on 10 June 1580, probably of the plague that was sweeping Lisbon. He was widely reputed to have died in a paupers' hospital, a figure of the neglected artist: *Fate's knife*, Herman Melville was later to write of him, *hath ripped thy chorded lyre*. Yet to add insult to injury, Camões was to see an extraordinary rise to near legendary fame very shortly after his death. The *Lusiads*, first printed in a relatively modest form, was soon being published in grandiose editions crammed with notes that explained the poet's meaning and placed his works among the great authors of the European tradition, and it was before long translated into Latin, Spanish, English and French. Though Camões had published only three lyric poems in his lifetime, collected editions of his verse began to appear shortly after his death and enormous numbers of sonnets were soon being discovered and attributed to him on the slightest of pretexts, to the point where more than 400 poems were associated with his name. He was seen during the period following his death as the pattern of a warrior-poet, and became in the aftermath of Spain's annexation of Portugal (1580–1640) the centrepiece of Portuguese national pride, an emblem of their difference from and superiority to the Spanish. The Romantics adopted Camões as a model for their own ideas of the poet, as a wanderer and a figure of exile, and his story and writings served as inspiration to Wordsworth, Melville, and Edgar Allan Poe, with commentaries written by Friedrich Schlegel and Alexander von Humboldt and a translation by Sir Richard Francis Burton. Meanwhile, in Portugal, his ascendancy reached such heights that his native tongue was proverbially referred to as *the language of Camões* and Portuguese intellectuals argued fiercely about the idea of a *super Camões*, a writer who might some day perform the unthinkable feat of coming to rival or even surpass the status of the national poet.[1]

Camões' extraordinary rise to fame owed much to the vision that he offered to Portugal and to Europe in a period when their sense of their place in the world had been profoundly shaken. As well as stumbling upon a western continent unknown to the most revered authorities of the classical and Christian tradition, and facing theories that the earth was neither stationary nor at the centre of the universe, there were encounters with civilisations in the east whose cultural and technical sophistication disrupted any simple notion that world history centred around Jerusalem and Rome. Even the idea that Europe was the heir to the legacy of the Roman Empire was subject to challenges from any number of rivals, and these challenges were also reminders of how globally connected the ancient world had been; this in turn undermined any claims that new paths were being broken and muddied any simple narrative of Europeans holding out against barbarous foreigners. Encounters with myriad different religions in the east similarly challenged simple narratives of a Manichean struggle between the light of Christianity and the darkness of Judaism and Islam, and suggested instead that there were a bewildering variety of different approaches to the main things of life – food, sexuality, gender relations, spirituality – which were hard to categorise, let alone understand. Many adherents of these faiths put Christians to shame in the very acts of self-denial, abstinence and fasting which Christians saw as setting them apart from the rest of the world.

In response to this troubling loss of balance, Camões offered a vision of a world discovered and conquered by European heroism, easily sortable into treacherous Islamic foes and virtuous Christian allies, and presented in a neoclassical style that suggested an uninterrupted continuity between the Roman Empire and the new colonial empires of Europe. His vision of heroic nationalism made his *Lusiads*, according to Schlegel, *the most perfect of epics*. Camões, however, was only one part of a much larger drive to shore up a certain idea of history. If we still think of Europe as having been forged by various kinds of internal struggle – emerging triumphant over religion and despotism into ages of enlightenment, democracy and liberty – in which the rest of the world played only a supporting role, this is largely because of the immense efforts that went into crafting national and cultural myths that insisted upon the coherent, continuous and self-contained nature of the history of Europe and its individual nations (efforts later expanded to include North America). For more than two centuries during the growth of colonial imperialism, much of the energy of European culture was given over to the form of play-acted classicism deployed by Camões, marshalling architecture, education, literature and fashion to affirm the rightful inheritance of the mantle of Rome. The apparent Renaissance, in which long-dormant classical culture was reborn in western Europe, was achieved in large part by making the east disappear – even going so far as to revive the name 'Byzantium' for the city once called New Rome or Constantinople – replacing a continuity that depended on the east with a miraculous reawakening which owed little to others. Those early parallels noticed between the religions of east and west were replaced by Reformation and Counter-Reformation doctrines that distanced themselves from any perceived affinities, and which moreover justified imperial ventures to bring universal Christian truths to the rest of the world. The culture and thought of non-European peoples, when noticed at all, were the province of eclectic specialists, safely isolated from the canonical culture of Europe by the development of institutions to study them separately under the guise of 'orientalism' and (later) 'anthropology', though recent accounts have begun to uncover the global roots of an 'Enlightenment' once thought wholly European. In obscuring these encounters with the wider world, Europe also turned away from models of an existence which they would not come to conceptualise for many centuries: worlds conceived within a much vaster timescale, where humans were not the only species that mattered, and with very different ideas on sexuality and gender relations.[2]

The absorption of Camões into this realm of myth was greatly eased by how little was known about his life. For details of his biography, readers were largely reliant on the introduction and notes to the 1613 edition of the *Lusiads*, compiled by two scholars who seem to have known the poet in his final years, and to whom he apparently related the few fragments around which the legend of his life grew up: his appointment as Warden of the Property of the Dead and Absent, his unjust dismissal from his post in Macau, the shipwreck off the Mekong delta, the loss in the wreckage of a Chinese lover and the rescued draft of the epic with which he swam ashore. In the centuries that followed, a few trustworthy details and many tall stories were added, but the details of his early life remained largely shrouded in obscurity.

Among the papers acquired by the Bibliotheca Nacional in 1903 was a thick volume of miscellaneous letters from the sixteenth and seventeenth centuries, bound in dark leather by Sr Borges and given the label 'Various Papers' in gold lettering. In the first gathering of these was the letter by Camões that Director da Cunha published the following year in the *Bulletin of the National Library*, though with profuse apologies for its *not merely numerous but even scandalous moments of indecorum*. This rediscovery of this letter, written during the poet's early years in Lisbon, made clear his youthful involvement in the dark underworld of the city, and soon a number of other letters were found that confirmed both the authenticity of the first letter and the troubling character of its author. The second manuscript, acquired in England in the 1920s, added further copies of these juvenile letters, including a continuation of the letter discovered in 1903, in which Camões not only adds further gossip regarding the prostitutes of the city and the gangs of ruffians with whom he was involved, but even puts a name to the mastermind of this Lisbon underworld:

> The best assassins around are under the pay of Simão Rodrigues, men who at one time would have cooked his gizzard for him, but who now take payment from him at the treasury, in marmalade pastilles and jugs of cold water, accompanied by glimpses of his

lady sister. And though that kind of merchandise is forbidden by the captain of that fort, in these voyages to China more is made by stealing than in wages.

References to *assassins* being paid at the *treasury* in *marmalade pastilles and jugs of cold water* suggested the use of a thieves' cant most likely lost to us four centuries later. The possibility that the 'Simão Rodrigues' named here was the same man as the founder of the Portuguese Jesuits was so unthinkable that it was immediately rejected as impossible by experts on the period, and has never been the subject of serious consideration.[3]

The riddling language of the letter, however, might be less obscure than it at first appears for those willing to entertain the possibility that Simão Rodrigues, ringleader of fanatical novices and relentless persecutor of Damião de Góis over the course of a quarter-century, was capable of paying for violence against those whom official instruments had failed to reach. The Jesuits were, after all, working out of the household of the Cardinal-Infante Henrique – whose treasury was to produce more than one witness against Damião during his trial – in the early 1550s, until the foundation of the Jesuit College of Santo Antão o Novo in 1553, and they were famous for the severe restrictions on their diet, which were not relaxed even when the king of Portugal came to call upon them. The one exception that they made to this was certain sweets that they prepared for their major feast days, most famously *certain marmalade pastilles*. In this light, the banter in Camões' letter seems less like the slang of the underworld and more like a joke about the joylessness of the Jesuits, and about the irony that the pious outcast who would once have been an object of derision to the young bloods was now calling the shots. Similarly, the reference to *voyages to China* reads like an ironic gesture to the Chinese missions that had been the focus of Jesuit ambitions since the mid-1540s. Certain elements, such as the identity of the *lady sister* mentioned in the letter, remain elusive

– though Camões also suggests in his first Lisbon letter that the Jesuits acted as *Cupids*, arranging adulterous trysts for a commission. Yet perhaps sometimes the only code that needs breaking is our own stubborn insistence on thinking in a particular way about the past.[4]

By the time of Damião's imprisonment in 1571, Simão had been living in exile in Spain and Italy for almost twenty years, meaning that he renewed his accusations against Damião from a distance, being deposed to give testimony in Toledo. The events leading up to his exile are only partially known: they began during a 1551 reunion of the founders of the Jesuits in Rome to draw up the *Constitutions* governing the order, in which the simmering tensions between Rodrigues and the rest came into the open. Simão was accused by many of trying to usurp the authority of Loyola, or even of breaking away to form his own order; he, in turn, complained that his chapter, with its links to the Portuguese crown and the growing Portuguese trade empire, was subsidising the whole operation, and that perhaps he should break away. Loyola moved to outflank him, installing a new rector in the Jesuit College in Coimbra, and then replacing Simão as head of the Portuguese province, without informing him directly. His most loyal allies were expelled from the order or sent overseas; and Simão himself was denounced at the Portuguese court and ordered to Rome for a trial. Simão wrote to Loyola begging that he give no credence to the many slanderous things that were being said about him, though the exact nature of these accusations is unclear, as many of the letters from Simão to Loyola, as well as other documents related to his trial, have disappeared, despite being kept in the most secret, well-maintained and treasured part of the Jesuit archive. In the end, Simão was condemned to live from then on in obscurity at a number of Jesuit foundations in Italy and Spain. Until, that is – as revealed in an unpublished life of Simão in the Torre do Tombo – he returned to Portugal, late in 1573, a few months before Damião's death.[5]

There remains the matter of the contradictory reports of Damião's death, one of which suggests that he was strangled or suffocated, but mentions nothing further, and the other which relates how his body was found burned, but makes no mention of strangling. Despite the gap of more than twenty-five years between Damião's death and the publication of the report that he had been strangled, the details of his biography are otherwise wholly accurate, and may well come from the networks of the Antwerp printer Christophe Plantin, who received regular reports from Lisbon and also worked with Arnold Mylius, the printer of the life. In the matter of Damião's death, some aspects of the report were slightly off – it was unlikely that the culprits were servants, given that he had been deprived of all his property at the end of his trial – while others are cast into question by the differences in the other testimony.

What, however, if the reports were not contradictory, but merely two fragments of a picture that seemed not to make any sense? There was, in fact, a particular circumstance in which it was common practice to strangle someone *and then* to set the body on fire – this was the standard punishment for those convicted by the Inquisition of heresy, who had nevertheless confessed their sins and repented. The accused was strangled as an act of mercy in recognition of their confession and penitent state; the body was burned as a public warning to others. The mixed mode of Damião's death, then, would have been the perfect murder for someone who felt that he had not received the heretic's ending that had been his due, someone whose hatred of him was unquenched and who was willing to act outside the institutions of the law to see that justice as he saw it was done.

An anecdote written down in the mid-seventeenth century, which records Damião's death and suggests that his immolation significantly coincided with an *auto-da-fé* in Lisbon, is untrustworthy on the details, but may preserve contemporary rumours that his death was seen as a heretic's execution. Damião's death did indeed nearly coincide with the execution of fifty-seven people – thirty-nine men and eighteen women – by burning in Lisbon (on the following day, 31 January 1574), the first such execution in seven years. The half-burnt piece of paper in Damião's hand, mentioned in the other report, may also be an important clue. It is unlikely that we will ever know what was written on the paper, but perhaps we do not need to; the report made no attempt to determine what the contents of the document were. The fact that it was found half-burned is the important detail, and presumably what caused the observer to make note of it: the fact that it stopped burning halfway suggests that someone was there to put it out, someone perhaps who did not want the flames to wake the other people asleep in the house, once the flames had served their purpose in burning the body.[6]

What satisfaction can we have, though, in a case more than 400 years old, centring on two old men, and the dead man anyway near the end of life? No more, perhaps, than can be had on the question of whether Camões was inspired to create his ocean goddesses by the example of the Chinese deity A-Ma or whether the Greek monuments in his epic were really descriptions of temples that he had seen in India and beyond. Where so much interest lies in maintaining an appearance of piety, or of suggesting a pure and exceptional culture that owes nothing to others, final proof is likely to remain forever elusive. We must also beware the trick that murders play, by offering us a finite injustice to set right as a substitute for the infinite injustices against which we feel helpless. Yet murders can also show as in a lightning flash the hidden contours of an age: how the victim represented such a threat to a way of living in the world that things could not go on with them breathing freely within it. Solving the murder itself may matter less than what has been witnessed along the way, which amounts to little less than a conspiracy to hide the world.

To echo the great Portuguese writer Fernando Pessoa, we have reached Lisbon, but not an ending. Although the mainstream of European culture for hundreds of years chose the monolithic, Eurocentric vision of Camões over Damião's infinite, polyphonic vision of history, the open and inquisitive responses of some in the early sixteenth century to new cultural encounters was not entirely lost. At around the same time that Damião was being arrested by the Inquisition, another eccentric intellectual was confining himself to a tower full of papers and books after turning his back on the war-torn world outside, determined to think his way free of any self-deceptions that lurked within him. This man, Michel de Montaigne, was to say much more explicitly in his *Essays* what was only ever implicit in Damião's work: that the encounter with cultures across the globe which felt differently about so many aspects of life, from eating and fasting to clothing, time, astronomy, sex and gender, suggested that there was nothing inevitable, necessary or inherently better about many European ideas and beliefs. Rather, it was only the perspective from which one looked that made it seem like this was the only natural way to do things, a view constantly reinforced by other aspects of the culture, from table manners and dress codes to building styles and beyond. In fact, Montaigne was to go further than this, expanding his demolition of the Eurocentric into an assault on the assumptions of anthropocentrism. His analysis led him to conclude that the same practices that fooled us into believing in our cultural superiority had also constructed a false notion of our difference from other animals. *We are neither above nor below the rest*, he wrote: *there are differences, there are orders and degrees; but it is all under the guise of the same nature.* Though Montaigne read many books during the ten years that he secluded himself in his tower library, one of his most profound influences, and major sources for information about other cultures, was a volume by a Portuguese man named Jerónimo Osório da Fonseca, whom Montaigne praised as the greatest historian of the age. Though Montaigne seems not to have known it, Osório's *De rebus Emanuelis regis* was simply an almost word-for-word Latin translation of the chronicle of King Manuel written by Damião de Góis.[7]

Damião had, in fact, for some time been leaking information about the cultures encountered by the Portuguese across the globe. He had been contacted in the early 1540s by the secretary of the Council of Venice, Giovanni Battista Ramusio, who was attempting to put together the first comprehensive collection of travel reports from the recent European voyages across the world. At Ramusio's request, Damião had provided him with a copy of a detailed description of Ethiopia by the Portuguese writer Francisco Álvares, which went on to be published in Ramusio's ground-breaking work of global history, the 1550 *Navigationi et Viaggi*. Ramusio had struggled, however, to lay his hands on many of the detailed geographical descriptions gathered on Portuguese expeditions, given the so-called 'conspiracy of silence' that forbade any of this information being shared with other nations or made public. After Damião's return to Portugal, Ramusio finally managed to acquire a copy of the long-sought *Book of Duarte Barbosa*, though at the same time he also found one in Seville, probably in the great library of Hernando Colón, which may itself have been acquired from Portugal in an act of espionage. After Damião's installation as archivist at the Torre do Tombo, Ramusio also acquired the copy of Tomé Pires' *Suma Oriental* that he had been seeking, albeit with the most precious information about the Moluccas and the spice trade removed as a concession – *so much*, Ramusio lamented, *can the interests of princes effect*. Ramusio's travel compendium, heavily supplied with illicit documents by Damião, was later reprinted and expanded by (among others) Richard Hakluyt and Samuel Purchas, and would go on to become the cornerstone of knowledge about the outside world for Europeans inquisitive enough to seek it out. Through the likes of Montaigne and Ramusio, Damião's efforts were to bear some fruit in the decades to come: his poignant evocation of the persecution of Jews in Lisbon was to be used in arguments against anti-Semitism in Venice, the information he transmitted on Ethiopia would make its way into Polish world histories, and the sceptical relativism fostered by Montaigne was to survive and eventually provide a tradition for self-examination in European thought in the aftermath of colonialism and the world wars.[8]

There is no doubt, however, that the dominant impulse was to guard jealously a belief in one's own cultural superiority, and this impulse was not uniquely European. The Chinese destroyed records of Zheng He's contacts during his early fifteenth-century voyages of exploration, as it was felt they came from a period of dangerous foreign influence. In the century that followed Damião's death, the Ottomans were engaged in their own attempt to position themselves as sole heirs to Rome's legacy and rulers of a universal empire, and both Japan and China closed their doors to Europeans in an effort to hold off troubling ideas from outside. While the physical isolation of Japan and China appears bizarre and extreme to western eyes, their isolation was in some ways no more complete than the permeable barriers set up between Europe and the rest of the globe, which allowed goods and wealth to flow in but filtered out the ideas, testimony and protests of the world, often by the simple mechanism of recognising only those things that fit in European archives – paper documents, written in Roman scripts, submitted through official channels. Despite the recognition by some that oral histories (like those Magnus recorded among the Laplanders) could be just as ancient and valid as written records, oral histories – including the historical traditions maintained by singers of the Moluccas and by the *griots* of the Songhai kingdom in western Africa – were routinely despised and dismissed. Those foreign knowledges that did make it into the archive were filtered through European eyes, and often locked away as closely guarded secrets; the protocols of the Torre do Tombo were copied by the Spanish archive at Simancas after the union of Portugal and Spain in 1580, subjecting the records of the

Spanish Empire to a similar treatment. In some instances, documents of non-European life were miraculously preserved in an unsorted state – as in the Cairo *geniza* where the local Jewish community threw all writings in Hebrew to save the sacred script from destruction – but in many cases they were lost, their value being recognised only too late.[9]

There can be few demonstrations of this impulse more effective than the world in which we now live, which is freely and globally connected as never before, and yet relentlessly constructs for itself ways of limiting its vision beyond the intensely local and similar. Haven't we always been here, sitting in next-door rooms, pretending that we are in a world of our own? We live already in John Donne's dream archive, which *shall bind up all our scattered leaves again for that library where every book shall lie open to one another*; the challenge, it seems, is to tear ourselves away from what we are reading and allow ourselves to wander through the world that awaits us on the shelves.

ACKNOWLEDGEMENTS

The task of writing about lives as global, and occupations as varied, as those of Damião and Camões could only be undertaken with a vast amount of support and advice from a wide range of individuals, and it is a great pleasure here to thank the many people who helped me to write this book.

First and foremost, my thanks go to the Leverhulme Trust, whose award of a Fellowship allowed me to undertake much of the research and early writing, and to the Master and Fellows of Sidney, who allowed me to take leave from my teaching duties during the Fellowship year.

As ever, this project would have been impossible without the unfailing support of my wonderful editor, Arabella Pike, whose willingness to trust an author heading off in an unusual direction is rare and immensely important. The team at William Collins have, as usual, been unfailing in their good humour and support, and have produced a beautiful book, and my thanks for this go to Jo Thompson, Katy Archer, and the design team, as well as to Kit Shepherd, who patiently copy-edited my wilfully idiosyncratic prose. I benefitted as well from the early support and trust of several wonderful international editors, including Michele Luzzato, Francisco Martínez Soría, and Jorge Garcia. I continue to be immensely thankful to Isobel Dixon and her team at Blake

Friedmann, and I am lucky to benefit from their quiet work to conquer the world on behalf of their authors.

During the course of researching and writing this book I was fortunate to be able to draw on the advice and encouragement of a wide range of scholars in various disciplines: starting with an invitation by John-Paul Ghobrial to present some initial thoughts at a conference in Oxford, and there and afterwards I benefitted from important input by Giuseppe Marcocci, Jorge Flores, and the late and much-lamented Sir John Elliott. Among those who provided immensely helpful suggestions and pointers in the period that followed were Henrique Leitão, Anna Weerasinghe, John Marshall and Manjunath Hiremath; Julia Lovell, Charles Aylmer, Noga Ganany and Joe McDermott; James Womack and Jan Hennings; Bill Sherman and Claire Preston; Marcos Martinón-Torres, Rupert Staasch and Philippe Descola. I am sure that I will have forgotten people who deserve to be thanked here, and I ask their forgiveness for my poor memory and manners. Drafts of the book were read by Joe Moshenska, Giuseppe Marcocci, José María Pérez Fernández, Tom Earle and (as ever) Kelcey Wilson-Lee, and each of them provided crucial advice and saved me from many errors, though I am sure I have retained a great number, for which they cannot be blamed. Ambrogio Caiani remained an unfailing source of encouragement and friendship during the course of the project.

I owe immense amounts to the patience and excellence of librarians and archivists across the world, without whose effort this project would not have been possible, especially given the fact that at least some of the research had to be done remotely owing to the global pandemic and the resulting travel restrictions. My thanks, then, go to the staff at the Arquivo Nacional da Torre do Tombo, the Biblioteca de Ajuda, the Arquivo Historico do Estado da Índia, the Archivium Romanum Societatis Jesu, the Vatican Archive and Library, the Plantin Museum and Archive, the Pierpont Morgan Library, and the Newberry Library, and of course as ever the Cambridge University Library and the British Library.

ACKNOWLEDGEMENTS

The writing of much of this book during the COVID pandemic and associated lockdowns, which involved extensive periods of home-schooling as well as increased demands at work, would have been unthinkable without the support of my family, centrally the willingness of my wife Kelcey to indulge my writing by allotting it at least equal time as her much more important work. This book is dedicated with all my love to our sons Gabriel and Ambrose, from whom the world was kept for too long, but whose inquisitiveness and spirit of adventure will doubtless help them to find their way out of the maze.

SUGGESTIONS FOR

FURTHER READING

While readers can follow the references in the endnotes to learn more about specific topics, this note is intended to provide suggestions for those looking for further reading on the general subjects of this book.

There is a stark difference in the existing scholarship on Damião de Góis and Luís de Camões, owing to the variation in both their fame and the amount of documentation available about them: the amount scholarship on Damião is relatively modest, and for the most part of excellent quality, whereas writing on Camões is vast, and extremely variable. Modern scholarship on Damião begins with Marcel Bataillon's essays in his Études sur *Portugal au temps de l'humanisme* (Coimbra: Por ordem da Universidade, 1952), though for English readers the major work is Elizabeth Feist Hirsch's *Damião de Gois: The Life and Thought of a Portuguese Humanist, 1502–1574* (The Hague: Martinus Nijhoff, 1967). Though Hirsch's study is somewhat dated now, particularly in its intense interest in whether Damião's allegiances lay with the Protestants or the Catholics, the quality of research by this fascinating woman (a German Jewish émigré who studied under Heidegger and lectured on philosophy at Bard College) is outstanding, and readers will find excellent treatments there of some of the more recondite areas of Damião's writings which are not discussed here. Hirsch's findings were given further detail, largely in terms of political and intellectual connections and contexts, in a series of essays in Jean Aubin's *Le Latin et l'Astrolabe: Recherches sur le Portugal de la Renaissance, son expansion en Asie et les relations internationales, vol. I* (Lisbon: Centro Cultural Calouste Gulbenkian, 1996).

Though many translations have been made into English of Camões *Lusiadas*, the best is probably Landeg White's *The Lusíads* (Oxford: Oxford Worlds Classics, 2008). White is also the translator of the *Collected Lyric Poems of Luís de Camões* (Princeton, NJ: Princeton University Press, 2008); there is another excellent selection in the bilingual collection *Luís de Camões: A Global Poet for Today*, ed. and trans. Thomas Earle and Hélder Macedo (Lisbon: Lisbon Poets & Co, 2019). The most comprehensive study of Camões available in English is Clive Willis' *Camões: Prince of Poets* (Bristol: HiPLAM, 2010), where readers will find not only translations of the canonical letters, but also astute discussions of the many biographical and textual issues facing Camões scholarship.

Though much of the best scholarship on the Portuguese encounter with Asia is understandably in Portuguese (such as Luís Filipe F. R. Thomaz's *De Ceuta a Timor* (Linda-a-Velha: DIFEL, 1994)), English-language readers are richly served in the works of Sanjay Subrahmanyam, beginning with *The Portuguese Empire in Asia, 1500-1700: A Political and Economic History* (New York: Longman, 1993). Subrahmanyam has followed this with a large number of exceptionally good studies of the period, from *Explorations in Connected History: From Tagus to the Ganges* (Delhi: Oxford University Press, 2004), to the most recent, *Empires Between Islam and Christianity, 1500-1800* (New York: State University of New York Press, 2019). An excellent study of how the same encounter looked from the Ottoman side can be found in Giancarlo Casale's *The Ottoman Age of Exploration* (Oxford: Oxford University Press, 2010). More specifically on questions of Indian art, readers should consult Partha Mitter's superb *Much Maligned Monsters: A History of European Reactions to Indian Art* (Chicago: University of Chicago Press, 1992).

On writing history in the sixteenth century, and the broader context of globalizing history in which Damião belongs, readers should consult Giuseppe Marcocci's *The Globe on Paper: writing histories of the world in Renaissance Europe and the Americas* (Oxford: OUP, 2020), and a substantial introduction to current attempts to study history at a global scale can be found in Jerry H. Bentley, Sanjay Subrahmanyam and Merry E Weisner-Hanks, eds., *The Cambridge World History, Volume VI: The Construction of a Global World, 1500-1800 C.E.*, Parts 1 and 2 (Cambridge: Cambridge University Press, 2015).

NOTES

List of Abbreviations
AHEI – Arquivo Historico do Estado da Índia, Goa, India
ANTT – Arquivo Nacional da Torre do Tombo, Lisbon, Portugal
ARSI – Archivum Romanum Societatis Iesu
BNP – Biblioteca Nacional de Portugal
CJ – *Chronica do Principe Dom Ioam, Rei que foi destes Regnos segundo do nome … composta de novo per Damiam de Goes* (Lisbon: Francisco Correa, 1567)
CM – *Chronica do Felicissimo Rei Dom Emanuel composta por Damiam de Goes, Dividida em quatro partes* (Lisbon: Francisco Correa, 1566–7)
Dicionário – *Dicionário de Luís de Camões*, ed. Vítor Aguiar e Silva (Alfragide: Caminho, 2011)
Er. Epist. – *Opus Epistolarum Des. Erasmi Rotterdami*, ed. P. S. Allen et al., 12 vols. (Oxford: Oxford University Press, 1906–1958)
Inéditos – *Inéditos Goesianos*, ed. Guilherme João Carlos Henriques, 2 vols. (Lisbon: Vicente da Silva, 1896)
Opúsculos – Damião de Góis, *Opúsculos Históricos*, trans. Dias de Carvalho (Porto: A Portuense, 1945)
Lusiadas 1613 – Luís de Camões, *Os Lusiadas do Grande Luis de Camões … commentados pelo licenciado Manoel Correa* (Lisbon: Pedro Craesbeeck, 1613)

All translations in the book are my own unless otherwise noted.

I. A Death in the Archive

1. The earlier report appears in a prefatory life written in *De Rebus Hispanicis, Lusitanicis, Aragonicis, Indicis & Aethiopicis* (Cologne: Birckmann for Arnold Mylius, 1602), sig. [*7]ᵛ; see ch. XVIII below for further discussion of the source of information used by Birckmann and Mylius. The second report was discovered by Bernardo Carneiro Vieira da Sousa, the antiquarian and *Desembargador do Paço* (High Court Justice) in the late eighteenth century, in 'a book of notes from Alenquer', and was printed in *Inéditos* II, 140–1, drawing on ANTT PT/TT/GMS/F25, 342–3, which in turn cites Bernardo Carneiro Vieira da Sousa as its source. The second report is undated, but was accepted by Vieira da Sousa as contemporary, and bears the hallmarks of the late-sixteenth/ early-seventeenth *Livro de Linhagens* style. The third report comes from a book of anecdotes in the Biblioteca de Ajuda (51-IX-22, fol. 130ʳ⁻ᵛ) dating from around the mid-seventeenth century; see further discussion of this in ch. XVIII below.

2. *Inéditos* II, 83. Sun Wukong's visit to the archive in *Journey to the West* (late sixteenth century) is discussed in ch. XIV below; a similar episode occurs in Nguyên Du's *Vaste Recueil de Légendes Merveilleuses* (sixteenth century), story X. The power of deleted records also, of course, forms the premise for José Saramago's novel, *The History of the Siege of Lisbon* (1989).

3. *Inéditos* II, 63–4 and 85–90, for the charges against Damião. His Inquisition trial is discussed in full in ch. XVII below.

4. António Joaquim Dias Dinis, 'Relatório do Século XVI sobre o Arquivo Nacional da Torre do Tombo', *Anais*, 2nd series 17 (Lisbon: Academia Portuguesa da História, 1968), 133, 152–3. Although the Torre do Tombo archive was surpassed by the Venetian state archive and the Vatican Archive in scale, it was unrivalled in terms of geographic scope and (especially) in its interchange with cultures with their own traditions of textual record keeping. The wider history of the development of archives and archival practices in Europe has been given in an immense number of excellent recent studies, which have provided a basis for much of this work, though references are made only to specific ideas and information taken from these publications; the most important include Markus Friedrich, *The Birth of the Archive: A History of Knowledge*, trans. John Nöel Dillon (Ann Arbor:

University of Michigan Press, 2018); Randolph C. Head, *Making Archives in Early Modern Europe: Proof, Information, and Political Record-Keeping, 1400–1700* (Cambridge: Cambridge University Press, 2019); and Liesbeth Corens, Kate Peters and Alexandra Walsham (eds.), *The Social History of the Archive: Record-Keeping in Early Modern Europe* (*Past and Present* supplementary issue 2016) and *Archives and Information in the Early Modern World* (Oxford: Oxford University Press, 2018); on archives and memory, see specifically Walsham's introduction to *The Social History of the Archive*, § VI.

5. The classic formulation of this question is in J. H. Elliott's *The Old World and the New, 1492–1650* (Cambridge: Cambridge University Press, 1970; rpr. Canto, 1992, 2011), ch. 1, and this study remains influenced throughout by Elliott's work.

6. The Casa da Índia in Lisbon was entirely destroyed in the 1755 earthquake, along with many of the records dealing with the Portuguese encounter with India, though most of the sources Damião used were in the royal archive at the Torre do Tombo. On the afterlife of the Torre do Tombo, see Pedro A. D'Azevedo and Antonio Baião, *O Archivo Da Torre do Tombo: Sua Historia, Corpos que o compõem, e organisação* (Lisbon: Imprensa Commercial, 1905), 7, 15, 28. On Napoleon's project to create a universal archive in Paris, see Maria Pia Donato, *L'archivio del Mondo: Quando Napoleone confiscò la storia* (Bari: Laterza, 2019).

II. Neither Fish nor Flesh

1. *Urbis Olisiponis Descriptio* (Évora: Andream Burge[n]sem, 1554), sig. aii^{r-v}; Damião de Góis, *Lisbon in the Renaissance: A New Translation of the Urbis Olisiponis Descriptio*, trans. Jeffrey S. Ruth (New York: Italica Press, 1996), 1–2. See Damião's account of the work on the chronicle of the reign of Manuel (*CM*; r.1495–1521) before it came to him, at *CM* IV, sig. F6^v; his complaint about Rui de Pina having taken the gift of some rings from Albuquerque to write about events in India is echoed by João de Barros in *Décadas da Ásia* II.vii.1. Damião was at work on the chronicle of the reign of João II (*CJ*; r.1481–1495) by 1556, as he mentions writing *CJ* sig. A3^v at this time. The prologue to the *Urbis Olisiponis Descriptio* suggests, however, that before he was assigned the task of writing the chronicle of the reign of João (and that of Manuel by the

Cardinal-Infante Henrique in 1558), he was working on the chronicles of the voyages of discovery, most likely assisting Barros on the composition of the *Décadas*; Damião later referred to Barros as 'hum de mores amigos que eu tive nestes Reynos', 'one of the best friends I had in this kingdom' (*Inéditos* II, 121).

2. *Urbis Olisiponis Descriptio*, sig. [aviii^r]–bi^r; Ruth (trans.), *Lisbon in the Renaissance*, 10–12. A copy of this contract is found in the *Livro de Mestrados* of the *Leitura Nova*, ANTT PT/TT/LN/0053, fol. 198^v: 'E se perventura algua balea ou baleato: ou serea: ou coca: ou Roas: ou musurana ou outro pescado grande que semele algun destes morrer en-se Simbra ...' ('And if by chance any whale or whale-calf, or siren [mermaid], or *coccinus*, or walrus, or serpent, or other large fish like these should die in Sesimbra ...'). A useful guide to early modern imaginings of sea life is provided in Chet van Duzer, *Sea Monsters on Medieval and Renaissance Maps* (London: British Library, 2013), on which see 26–47, 83, 88, etc. Note that Damião also seems to have discussed tritons with the Swiss natural historian Leonhard Thurneysser zum Thurn during the latter's stay with him in 1555–6; see *A História Natural de Portugal de Leonhard Thurneysser zum Thurn, ca. 1555–1556*, ed. Bernardo Jerosch Herold, Thomas Horst and Henrique Leitão (Lisbon: Academia das Ciências de Lisboa, 2019), 89. On the wider question of integrating oral accounts into written histories during the early modern period, and the specific importance of this to writing histories of non-European peoples, see Walter D. Mignolo, *The Darker Side of the Renaissance: Literacy, Territoriality, and Colonization*, 2nd edn (Ann Arbor: University of Michigan Press, 2003), ch. 3; Kathryn Burns, *Into the Archive: Writing and Power in Colonial Peru* (Durham, NC: Duke University Press, 2010).

3. On the difficulty of walking in Lisbon rain, see Eddy Stols, Jorge Fonseca and Stijn Manhaeghe, *Lisboa em 1514: O relato de Jan Taccoen van Zillebeke* (Lisbon: Cadernos de Cultura, 2014), 116.

4. The copy of *De Expugnatione Lyxbonensi* by Osbert of Bawdsey is Cambridge, Corpus Christi College MS 470, fols. 125^r–146^r, and can be viewed using Stanford University's excellent 'Parker Library on the Web' resource; the pressmark on fol. 24^r was deduced by M. R. James to have belonged to Norwich Cathedral Priory; on the provenance, see C. W. David (ed.), *De Expugnatione Lyxbonensi*

(New York: Columbia University Press, 1936), 27–8. Sanjay Subrahmanyam, *The Portuguese Empire in Asia, 1500–1700: A Political and Economic History* (London: Longman, 1993), 39. Jan Taccoen van Zillebecke visited Lisbon in 1514 on a pilgrim vessel; see *Lisboa em 1514*. Dinis, 'Relatório', 153.

5. *Opúsculos*, 118–19. On the reasons for malagueta pepper being less popular, see Garcia de Orta, *Coloquios dos simples, e drogas he cousas mediçinais da India* (Goa: Ioannes de endem, 1563), sig. Giii^v.

6. *Opúsculos*, 118–20; *CM* III, sig. K1^v (on the bark cloth) and sig. Q1^{r-v} (on the turban sent back from Persia). The global material culture of Lisbon has recently received a magisterial treatment in Annemarie Jordan Gschwend and K. J. P. Lowe (eds.), *The Global City: On the Streets of Renaissance Lisbon* (London: Paul Holberton Publishing, 2015), which contains a number of inventories of goods arriving in Lisbon in its appendices; see ch. 8 on the commonness of Chinese porcelain by the mid-sixteenth century, and ch. 10 on oliphants. As Lowe points out there, some of the figures on Sapi- and Bini-Portuguese ivories were likely derived from European printed images. On the burying of porcelain, see *The Book of Duarte Barbosa*, ed. and trans. Mansel Longworth Dames (London: Hakluyt Society, Second Series XLIV and XLIX, 1918–21), I.214; this misapprehension on the method of manufacturing porcelain was later corrected in Gaspar da Cruz, *Tractado em que se cõtam muito por esteso as cousas da China* (Évora: Andre de Burgos, 1569), sig. ciii^r, and C. R. Boxer (ed.), *South China in the Sixteenth Century (1550–1575): Being the Narratives of Galeote Pereira, Fr. Gaspar Da Cruz, O.P., Fr. Martin de Rada, O.E.S.A. (1550–1575)* (London: Hakluyt Society, Second Series CVI, 1953), 126–7; see Mary Laven, *Mission to China: Matteo Ricci and the Jesuit Encounter with the East* (London: Faber and Faber, 2011), 87, and Anne Gerritsen, *The City of Blue and White: Chinese Porcelain and the Early Modern World* (Cambridge: Cambridge University Press, 2020), ch. 10. Damião is listed as one of the 'Moços da Camara' in the 1519 'Pagamento de Moradias e Soldos', ANTT PT/TT/CRC/N/2/139, fol. 37^r, where the scribe has clearly begun his brother's name, 'Fr[uctoes]', before crossing it out.

7. *CM* IV, sig. C7^v–D1^v; Damião places this event in 1516, but it in fact took place in 1515. The event was also reported in Giovanni Jacopo

de Penni, *Forma, natura e costumi dello rinoceronte* (Rome: Stephano Guiliretti, 1515), which survives in a single copy in the collection of Hernando Colón (Biblioteca Colombina 6-3-29(29)). *Lisboa em 1514*, 118. For a near-contemporary analogue, see Christóvão da Costa's 'Tractado del Elephante y de sus calidades', in his *Tractado de las drogas, y medicinas de las Indias Orientales* (Burgos: Martin de Victoria, 1578), 411–48, and Ines G. Županov, 'Drugs, health, bodies and souls in the tropics: Medical experiments in sixteenth-century Portuguese India', *Indian Economic and Social History Review*, 39/1 (2002), 1–45.

8. *Opúsculos*, 119; Gschwend and Lowe (eds.), *Global City*, 61–73; see also *CM* III, sig. K2^v, where Damião describes the house of the governor of the Casa do Cível as full of 'escravas brancas', likely meaning Chinese, Japanese and Indian slaves. *Lisboa em 1514*, 116. On nature, personhood and ontology, see Philippe Descola, *Par-delà nature et culture* (Paris: Éditions Gallimard, 2005), 126–32.

9. Joseph Klucas, 'Nicolaus Clenardus: A Pioneer of the New Learning in Renaissance Portugal', *Luso-Brazilian Review* 29/2 (1992), 87–98; *CM* I, sig. Giiii^v (on the Brazilian bowmen) and sig. Hi^r (on Cojebequi, the Hormuz merchant whom Damião met at court as a youth); *CM* III, sig. N8 (on the Ethiopian embassy from Queen Eleni), as well as Damião's *Legatio Magni Indorum imperatoris presbyteri Ioannis* (Antwerp: Johannes Graphaeus, 1532), discussed more fully in ch. V below. On the myths arising across the Americas seeking to explain the European possession of firearms, see Alfred Métraux, *La Religion des Tupinamba, et ses rapports avec celle des autres tribus tupi-guarani*, ed. Jean-Pierre Goulard and Patrick Menget (Paris: Presses Universitaires de France, 2014), 49–50. A useful summary of the turn towards recovering subaltern voices in the archive is given in Head, *Making Archives*, 31–2. Damião provides a substantial ethnography of the Tupinambá at *CM* I, sig. Giiii^r–Gvii^r. The story of the 'halves' is from Montaigne's essay 'On the Cannibals'; see *The Complete Essays*, trans. M A. Screech (London: Penguin, 1991), 240–1.

10. *Urbis Olisiponis Descriptio*, sig.ciii^{r-v}; Ruth (trans.), *Lisbon in the Renaissance*, 27. On the growth of public notaries across Europe, see Alexandra Walsham's helpful summary in her introduction to Corens et al. (eds.), *The Social History of the Archive*, § III.

III. House of Smoke

1. *Lusiadas* VIII.lxxxvii. The lines seem to be partly inspired by the description of Medea in the *Argonautica* of Apollonius of Rhodes, III.754–7, though also by Virgil's *Aeneid*, 8.22–5.

2. Most of the reliable information on this incident is gleaned from the letter of pardon issued to Camões on 7 March 1553, which is ANTT PT/TT/CHR/L/2/20, fols. 296^v–297^r, though the pardon misnames the subject of the attack as 'Gonçalo' Borges, rather than Gaspar Borges; see Clive Willis, *Camões, Prince of Poets* (Bristol: HiPLAM, 2010), 187. The 'second Lisbon letter' mentions several attacks, including the one on Gaspar Borges Corte-Real, one on 'Dinis Boto' that took place a few days before, and one that took place on St John's night (24 June 1552) for which a 'mandado' has been issued 'pera prenderem a uns dezoito de nós'. This second letter is in BNP COD. 9492, fols. 155^r–156^r; references to all Camões' letters, however, are given to the transcriptions in Willis, *Camões*, where the relevant passage here is on p. 266.

3. The 'first Lisbon letter' from Camões is found both in BNP COD. 8571, fol. 27^v, and (with some variations) in COD. 9492, fols. 154^r–155^r, as well. See Willis, *Camões*, 253–9 and 262–6. For further discussion of the letters, see ch. XVIII.

4. It is unlikely that there were people who were openly Muslim or Jewish people about, so Camões may have been referring to *conversos*.

5. For Damião's account of the expulsion of the Jews, see *CM* I, sig. aviii^r–B[1]^r and sig. B5^{r-v}; 'Old Christians' were (at least in principle) those with a long-established lineage of Christian ancestry, a category which separated them from converts. François Soyer, in *The Persecution of the Jews and Muslims of Portugal: King Manuel and the end of religious tolerance (1496–7)* (Leiden: Brill, 2007), argues rather that Manuel was not driven by pressure from Spain; see also Giuseppe Marcocci, 'Remembering the Forced Baptism of the Jews: Law, Theology, and History in Sixteenth Century Portugal', in Mercedes García-Arenal and Yonatan Glazer-Eytan (eds.), *Forced Conversion in Christianity, Judaism and Islam: Coercion and Faith in Premodern Iberia and Beyond* (Leiden: Brill, 2020), 328–53, which mentions 'os d'area' on p. 342.

6. The records of the 1554–6 Inquisition trial of João de Melo are ANTT PT/TT/TSO-IL/028/01606; the information here is taken

from his 'Comfesão de Jo[am] de Melo turco de nacão', fols. 4ʳ–8ᵛ.
The town where he handed himself over to the Portuguese in India
is given as 'Chaleat', which I take to be a corruption of 'Chalia', the
Portuguese name for Chaliyam. His trajectory was not uncommon;
see, for instance, Damião's recollections of Miguel Nunez, a Muslim
born in Granada who was captured in the Maldives by Albuquerque
(*CM* II, sig. H[5]ʳ), and Nicolao Ferreira, born in Sicily, captured by
the Turks and encountered by Albuquerque in Hormuz serving as
an ambassador before being brought back to Portugal, where he
reconverted (*CM* III, sig. P7ʳ). On Sinan the Jew, see Giancarlo
Casale, *The Ottoman Age of Exploration* (Oxford: Oxford University
Press, 2010), 113.

7. Isabel Drumond Braga and Paulo Drumond Braga, 'A vida
quotidiana em Ceuta durante o período português', in A. Texeira, F.
Villada Paredes and R. Banha da Silva (eds.), *Lisboa 1415 Ceuta:
Historia de dos ciudades/História de duas cidades* (Lisbon: Ciudad
Autonoma de Ceuta – Consejería de Educación y Cultura/Câmara
Municipal de Lisboa – Direção Municipal de Cultura, 2015), 120–2.
Subrahmanyam, *The Portuguese Empire in Asia*, 86–7. Andrew C.
Hess, *The Forgotten Frontier: A History of the Sixteenth-Century
Ibero-African Frontier* (Chicago: University of Chicago Press, 2010),
45–54. Natalie Zemon Davis, *Trickster Travels: The Search for Leo
Africanus* (London: Faber and Faber, 2006), 21.

8. For a translation of the 'letter from Ceuta', first published in the
1598 edition of the *Rimas* (the collection of Camões' lyric poetry),
see Willis, *Camões*, 229–41. Camões' early biographers (including
Correa) placed the date of his birth around 1517, but his entry into
the *Noticias das que pasarao a India* of 1550 (Hispanic Society of
America, NS5/73, fol. 102ʳ) says he was twenty-five years old at that
time, suggesting a birthdate of 1524/5, and this is now the widely
accepted birth date. Willis, *Camões*, 176–7, provides a good
overview of the speculation about his early life. An excellent
summary of the early Jesuit period in Portugal is given in Pierre-
Antoine Fabre, Jean-Claude Laborie, Carlos Zéron and Ines G.
Županov, 'L'affaire Rodrigues', in Pierre-Antoine Fabre and Bernard
Vincent (eds.), *Missions religieuses modernes. 'Notre lieu est le
monde'* (Rome: École française de Rome, 2007), 173–225; some of
the details here are taken from Francisco Rodrigues, *História da
Companhia de Jesus na Assistência da Portugal* (Porto: Apostolado

da Imprensa, 1931), I.365–75. On the affairs at Coimbra, a good summary is given in C. R. Boxer, *João de Barros: Portuguese Humanist and Historian of Asia* (New Delhi: Concept Publishing Company), 20–2. The imprisonment of the foreign professors at Coimbra took place in 1550.

9. Willis, *Camões*, 236. On the taunts, see the lyrics by Camões 'Sem olhos vi o mal claro' and 'Quem quer que viu, ou que leu'.

10. Camões uses the word *degredado* to describe himself in *Lusiadas* VII.lxxx, but it is unclear whether this is merely in a poetic sense; for examples of *degredados* in the history of Portuguese colonisation, see *CM*, for instance III, sig. B1ᵛ, for the case of João Machado, one of the *degredados* left in Malindi by Pedro Álvares Cabral, who later made his way to Diu and fought for Malik Ayaz (himself possibly a Russian slave, who served the sultans of Gujarat as a naval commander, and who is referred to as 'Miliquiaz' in Portuguese sources), before also fighting for the Adil Shahs of Bijapur, rulers of Goa.

IV. A Hole in the Wall, a Cavity in the Stairs

1. The historiography of the Torre do Tombo archive begins with João Pedro Ribeiro's *Memorias Authenticas para a Historia do Real Archivo* (Lisbon: Impressão Regia, 1819); in 1905 a series of further important documents was published in José Pessanha, 'Uma rehabilitação historica: Inventarios da Torre do Tombo no seculo XVI', *Archivo Historico Portuguez* 3, 287–303, and in D'Azevedo and Baião, *O Archivo Da Torre do Tombo*, 4–5, 9–10, 23–44. An account of the archive from 1583, made by Damião's former scribe Cristovão de Benavente for Philip II and stored in Simancas, was published by Dinis in 'Relatório', 115–59, which mentions the sturgeon on p. 153; the series of documents reproduced there gives a snapshot of the Torre in the late sixteenth century, when its staff included a clerk, two guards and a porter, with various scribes employed on an ad hoc basis. In addition to Cristovão de Benavente, Damião also mentions Amador Pinto as someone employed at the Torre (*Inéditos* II, 107–8). On the Venetian archive, see Filippo de Vivo, *Information and Communication in Venice: Rethinking early modern politics* (Oxford: Oxford University Press, 2007), and 'Ordering the archive in early modern Venice (1400–1650)', in *Archival Science*, 10/3 (2010), 235. For Damião's

description of the state in which he found the archive, see his letters to the queen and king on 15 February 1549, ANTT PT/TT/ GAV/2/11/13 and PT/TT/CC/1/82/000053. An example of the golden signature of Suleiman the Magnificent can be seen in his dispatch of 14 November 1563, ANTT PT/TT/GAV/15/14/20. The palm-leaf letter from Battak is mentioned in Stefan Halikowski-Smith, "'The Friendship of Kings was in the Ambassadors'": Portuguese Diplomatic Embassies in Asia and Africa during the Sixteenth and Seventeenth Centuries', *Portuguese Studies* 22/1 (2006), 106. On the Japanese alphabet sent to João III by Francis Xavier in his letter of 14 January 1549, see Luis Frois, *The First European Description of Japan, 1585: A critical English-language edition of striking contrasts in the customs of Europe and Japan by Luis Frois, S.J.*, trans. and ed. Richard K. Danford, Robin D. Gill and Daniel T. Reff (London: Routledge, 2014), p. 183–4, and Michael Cooper (ed.), *They Came to Japan: An anthology of European reports on Japan, 1543–1640* (London: Thames and Hudson, 1965), p. 180. On the edict of 1461, see *CM* I, sig. E1^v. On the *Leitura Nova*, see Head, *Making Archives*, ch. 4; Damião's account of the genesis of the *Leitura Nova* at *CM* I, sig. Civ^r, confirms that by his time these books were kept in the Torre do Tombo, as do his references to them elsewhere as the 'books of the Torre do Tombo' (i.e. *CM* I, sig. Ei^v). Though most of the accounts given in Dinis, 'Relatório', Head, *Making Archives*, etc., deal with the chancellery materials kept in the archive for probative purposes, Damião clearly conceived of a far wider remit for the archive, as (for example) in the case of the copper plates found in Cranganore dealing (purportedly) with St Thomas (see ch. X), the translation of which he suggested should be kept in the Torre do Tombo 'as a matter worthy of memory' (*CM* I, sig. Niii^r).

2. On Duarte Pacheco Pereira and Mondragon, see *CM* II, sig. I6^v. Duarte Pacheco Pereira, *Esmeraldo de Situ Orbis*, trans. George H. T. Kimble (London: Hakluyt Society, Second Series LXXIX, 1936), 10–11, 69, 82; Thales' belief that the earth rested on water was transmitted by Aristotle's *On the Heavens*, 294a28–b1. This idea of water underlying and existing before the land was shared in the Mexica cosmology; see Caroline Dodds Pennock, 'Aztecs Abroad? Uncovering the Early Indigenous Atlantic', *American Historical Review*, 125/3 (2020), 793. *Roteiros* (rutters) and travel accounts like

Pereira's would have been lodged at the Casa da Índia, where
Damião would have had access to them through his close friend
João de Barros, but his patterns of use (and their patterns of
survival after the destruction of the Casa da Índia) suggest that they
may also have been stored in the Torre do Tombo.

3. Damião's recommendation that those wanting to know more about
Malabar should read Duarte Barbosa is at *CM* I, sig. Ev^v; the fact
that he clarifies that it was written 'em lingoa portuguesa' is
interesting, given that the only publicly available version of Barbosa
had recently been published in Ramusio's *Primo volume delle
navigationi et viaggi* (Venice: Lucantonio I Giunta, 1550), fols. 310^r–
348^v; though it is unclear whether the copy of Barbosa he was
consulting was part of the Torre do Tombo collections, it is clear
that he was using it alongside documents from that archive while
writing his chronicles. On new evidence regarding the authorship of
the *Book of Duarte Barbosa*, see ch. XVIII n. 8 below. On Barbosa,
see Joan-Pau Rubiés, *Travel and Ethnology in the Renaissance: South
India through European Eyes, 1250–1625* (Cambridge: Cambridge
University Press, 2000), 204–6, where he clears up the longstanding
confusion between two different men named Duarte Barbosa,
stemming from Ramusio.

4. On the guarding of geographical knowledge as state secrets, often
referred to as the 'conspiracy of silence', see Donald F. Lach, *Asia in
the Making of Europe, Volume I: The Century of Discovery, Book I*
(Chicago: University of Chicago Press, 1994), 151–4, and Rubiés,
Travel and Ethnology, 3–4; the fact that Barbosa's treatise only
circulated in manuscript through acts of espionage prior to Ramusio,
as well as Ramusio's testimony regarding his difficulties acquiring
travel accounts, suggests that the 'conspiracy' was at least to some
extent a reality; see further discussion below in ch. XVIII. Damião's
account of Yahya ben Tafuf (who is variously referred to in early
modern sources as 'Iheabentafuf' or 'Jehan Bentafuf', and over the
correct version of whose name there is much disagreement) is
spread out across the chronicle, at *CM* II, sig. D4^v–D8^r; *CM* III, sig.
D4^v–[D6^v], sig. I4^v, sig. L8^r–M3^r, sig. N1^v–N2^r; and *CM* IV, sig. I8$^{r–v}$,
sig. K8^v–L1^v. His account draws in part on Leo Africanus (in whose
praise he speaks at *CM* III, sig. [D6$^{r–v}$]), whose version of the events
is found in Ramusio's *Primo volume delle navigationi et viaggi*, fols.
22^v–23^r: even Damião's idiosyncratic naming of 'Haliadux', whom

Leo calls 'Hali', appears to be a misreading of the second mention of this figure, which reads 'Hali adunque (che cosi era il suo nome) dubita[n]do davero della sua vita ...' (i.e. Damião has run together the Italian *adunque*, 'therefore', with the name). Damião was clearly using other sources as well Leo, as he adds many details to the general story, and gives an altogether more heroic account of the pair's exploits than Leo does. There are numerous references to 'Arab writers' that he is using as his sources throughout *CM*, though it is unclear how many of these are simply through Leo Africanus; he may also be drawing in some instances on Gomez Eanes de Zurara's chronicle of the taking of Ceuta; see *CM* IV, sig. F6ᵛ, and Sanjay Subrahmanyam, *Europe's India: Words, People, Empires, 1500–1800* (Cambridge, MA: Harvard University Press, 2017), 61–71. It is also clear that Damião was working alongside the author of the *Décadas da Ásia*, João de Barros – whom in his trial he termed 'one of the best friends I had in this kingdom' (*Inéditos* II, 121) – and so would have had access to the various non-European materials used by Barros. See also David Lopes, *Textos em Aljamia Portuguesa: Estudo filológico e histórico* (Lisbon: Imprensa Nacional, 1940), for further context. The Portuguese system for collecting a much wider range of documents than royal correspondence was later adopted by Philip II for Spain; see Arndt Brendecke, "'*Arca, archivillo, archivo*': the keeping, use and status of historical documents about the Spanish *Conquista*', *Archival Science*, 10/3 (2010), 268–9.

5. On struggles to date northern African affairs, see *CM* IV, sig. B1ʳ; On use of Leo Africanus, see *CM* II, sig. D4ᵛ, and *CM* III, sig. [D6] ʳ⁻ᵛ. An interesting example of this can be seen on ANTT PT/TT/ CART/891.2/67, fol. 1, where a manuscript note shows the struggle to date this Arabic document: '/27/daugsto 1517 o 1518 [???]1520'. This is followed by a description of the contents of the letter: 'fala em mexeriquos q della scriverao ...', which matches the language that Damião uses in his chronicle describing the same events – 'Dom Nuno Mascarehas por mexeriquos, & maos raportes que lhe faziam mouros, & judus de Sidihiebētafuf ... começou de desgostar d[e] sua amizade ... Sidihieabentafuf soube destas cartas, pelo que screveo a el Rei ...' (*CM* IV, sig. I8ʳ) – confirming that Damião was using these documents in writing his chronicle, and possibly that he is the author of the note on the letter. Given that the letter is not accompanied by a translation, this may suggest that Damião had an

assistant who could read Arabic working with him in the Torre do Tombo. On the *aljamia* tradition, see Lopes, *Textos em Aljamia Portuguesa*. It is possible that some of Damião's references to Arabic sources also refer to the Arabic chronicles from which Barros was working, such as the Persian chronicle of Mir Kwand. Damião was close to Nicholas Clenardus, who taught himself Arabic at Louvain, and also Frei Roque de Almeida, who at least intended to join Clenardus' Arabising project (Jean Aubin, *Le Latin et l'Astrolabe: Recherches sur le Portugal de la Renaissance, son expansion en Asie et les relations internationales*, vol. I (Lisbon: Centro Cultural Calouste Gulbenkian, 1996), 226).

6. Damião's account of the antiquities of the Azores is at *CJ* sig. B[1]^r–B2^v.

7. Patricia M. and Pierre M. Bikai, in 'Timelines: A Phoenician Fable', *Archaeology* 43/1 (1990), 20, 22–23, 84, suggest that stories of the statue derive from a Carthaginian legend about a horseman outside the Straits of Gibraltar, who pointed west, to indicate that no one could go any further, and that this was then reproduced on the 1367 Pizzigano map, though the theory relies on the notion that the power of suggestion was so strong as to make wholly natural volcanic fragments, stored in King Manuel's wardrobe, be taken for pieces of statue. Damião's source for the antiquity of Egyptian culture is Herodotus' *Histories* II.242. For a wider discussion of the mapping of classical Mediterranean cultures on to early modern cultures encountered on the Atlantic rim, see Giuseppe Marcocci, *The Globe on Paper: Writing histories of the world in Renaissance Europe and the Americas* (Oxford: OUP, 2020), ch. 1.

V. The India House

1. Recent scholarship on early modern Antwerp is usefully synthesised in Eric Mielants' article 'Early Modern Antwerp: The first "World City"?', *Journal of Historical Sociology*, 30/2 (2017), 262–83. Documents regarding the Portuguese *feitoria* (factory) are collected in Anselmo Braamcamp Freire, *Noticias da feitoria de Flandres* (Lisbon: Archivo Historico Portuguez, 1920). See also, for broader context, Simon Schama, *The Embarrassment of Riches: An Interpretation of Dutch Culture in the Golden Age* (London: Harper Perennial, 2004), and Immanuel Wallerstein, *World-Systems Analysis: An Introduction* (Durham, NC: Duke University Press, 2004).

2. For the cargoes of sugar, see ANTT PT/TT/CC/2/111/6 and PT/
   TT/CC/2/111/7; both shipments were received on 18 September
   1523, and Damião's signature is clearly visible on the former, but
   not on the latter. On the technicalities of the sugar trade from
   Madeira during this period, see the excellent study by Naidea
   Nunes, 'A terminologia de açúcar nos documentos dos séculos XV e
   XVI na ilha da Madeira', *Actas do XIII Encontro Nacional da APL*
   (Lisbon: APL/Colibri, 1997), II.155–73. For Loyola's argument with
   Juan Luis Vives over the use of spices for Lenten food, see the
   account by Loyola's secretary and biographer Juan Polanco in *Vita
   Ignatii Loiolae et rerum Societatis Jesu historia* (Madrid:
   Typographorum Societas, 1894), 43, and James Brodrick, SJ, *Saint
   Ignatius Loyola: The Pilgrim Years* (London: Burns and Oates, 1956),
   222–8. On Dutch cooking from the late fifteenth century, see
   Christianne Muusers' wonderful edition/translation of MS Gent
   University Library 1035, *Wel ende edelike spijse (Good and Noble
   Food)* (https://coquinaria.nl/kooktekst/Edelikespijse0.htm), from
   which I have taken the recipes for galantine of lamprey and spiced
   claret. For Damião's list of goods shipped to Flanders, see *Opúsculos*
   111; Manuel Severim de Faria, the seventeenth-century antiquary
   and early biographer of both Damião and Camões, mentions that
   Damião himself saved his home town of Alanquer during a shortfall
   of grain by sending a shipment from Flanders: 'Vidas de
   Portugueses Ilustres', BNP COD. 13117, fol. 73^v.
3. On Damião's activities buying manuscript and printed histories for
   the Infante Ferdinand, see *CM* II, sig. F8^{r-v}. The Book of Hours
   was acquired for Queen Catherine somewhat later, in 1544, and
   the St Sebastian probably also dates from the 1530s or 40s (see
   Inéditos II, 114–17); on Damião's presentation of a pontifical
   cloth-of-gold to the chapel of the Order of the Golden Fleece at
   'Sablona' (Notre Dame du Sablon, in Brussels) in 1524, see *CM* IV,
   sig. E8; Damião's letters to Fernando on the tapestries are ANTT
   PT/TT/CC/1/45/107 and PT/TT/CC/1/45/113. On Dürer's stay at
   the India House, see Jeffrey Ashcroft, *Albrecht Dürer: A
   Documentary Biography* (New Haven: Yale University Press, 2017),
   I.560.
4. On head-carrying African women in Portuguese art, see Gschwend
   and Lowe (eds.), *Global City*, 63–5, and fig. 54; Brandão's 1552 list of
   the African women porters of Lisbon and what they carried on their

heads is in 'Majestade e grandezas de Lisboa em 1552'. *Arquivo Histórico Português* 11 (1917), 76.

5. *Inéditos* II, 82, 107–12, 114–17. Damião mentioned in the list of pictures he owned a crucifixion for which he paid more than 100 *ducados* by 'mestre quentino', i.e. Quentin Massys (*Inéditos* II, 82); and his tutor Cornelius Graphaeus wrote of him prostrating himself in front of a painting by Massys (*Legatio*, sig. D5).

6. Rob C. Wegman, 'Who Was Josquin?', in Richard Sherr (ed.), *The Josquin Companion* (Oxford: Oxford University Press, 2000), 21–50; Patrick Macey, Jeremy Noble, Jeffrey Dean and Gustave Reese, 'Josquin (Lebloitte dit) des Prez', *Grove Music Online* (revised version, 23 February 2011).

7. Elisabeth Feist Hirsch, *Damião de Gois: The Life and Thought of a Portuguese Humanist, 1502–1574* (The Hague: Martinus Nijhoff, 1967), 5–6, 38. The poems in praise of Josquin and Ockhegem are in Damião de Góis, *Aliquot Opuscula* (Louvain: Rutgerus Rescius, 1544), sig. niii^{r-v}; both of the poems are printed under pseudonyms, and the poem in praise of Ockhegem is sometimes attributed to Erasmus. On the sending of masters to teach plainchant and polyphony in the Kongo in 1504, see *CM* I, sig. K2^v; on polyphony in India, see Luís Filipe F. R. Thomaz, *De Ceuta a Timor* (Linda-a-Velha: DIFEL, 1994), 253–4, and David Irving, 'Music in Global Jesuit Missions, 1540–1773', in Ines G. Županov (ed.), *The Oxford Handbook of the Jesuits* (New York: Oxford University Press, 2017). On the part played by Damião's music in accusations against him, see *Inéditos* II, 91–4, and ch. XVII below.

8. Damião's intelligence report on the Duke of Gelders is ANTT PT/TT/CC/1/19/12; it is erroneously dated in the catalogue to 14 October 1515, but this is corrected on the document itself to 1528. Damião's account of the naval attack on his fleet is at *CM* III, sig. F7^r. For the letters regarding the wreck of a ship belonging to Antonio Paciecho with the loss of forty men, see J. S. Brewer (ed.), *Letters and Papers, Foreign and Domestic, of the Reign of Henry VIII*, vol. IV, pt II, 1526–8 (London: Longman & Co., 1872), entries 3408, 4769 and 4770; and the documents themselves, British Library MS Cotton Nero B/I, and The National Archives SP 1/50, fol.107. On Rutgerte from Gelders, see *CM* II, sig. D2^r.

9. *CM* III, sig. O8^v–P1^r, and further discussion of this in ch. IX below. Olaus Magnus' *Carta Marina* was begun in 1527 and first printed in

Venice in 1539 (*Carta Marina Et Descriptio Septentrionalium Terrarum Ac Mirabilium Rerum In Eis Contentarum Diligentissime Elaborata Anno Dni 1539* (Veneciis/Venedig: [Thomas de Rubis], 1539). His *Historia de Gentribus Septentrionalibus* was published in Rome in 1555; references here are given to Olaus Magnus, *Description of the Northern Peoples*, trans. Peter Fischer and Humphrey Higgins, ed. Peter Foote (London: Hakluyt Society, Second Series CLXXXII, 1996), I.58–9 (decapitation by ice), I.54–5 (snowball fights and their penalties), I.51 (icicles), I.126 (Psalm 147), I.36 (Northern Lights), I.20 (reading by the midnight sun) and I.46 (eclipses). Scholars have detected signs that Olaus Magnus used Portuguese information in making his *Carta Marina*, which may have come from Damião; see John Granlund and G. R. Crone, 'The *Carta Marina* of Olaus Magnus', *Imago Mundi* 8 (1951), 36. There is a further possibility, given evidence (from Damião's friend, the historian António Galvão) that Damião himself travelled far north in Norway and Sweden, that some of Magnus' information could have come from Damião, rather than the other way around. Marcel Bataillon also suggests sugar prospecting as a reason for these voyages: 'Le Cosmopolitisme de Damião de Góis', in his *Études sur Portugal au temps de l'humanisme* (Coimbra: Por ordem da Universidade, 1952), 158–9.

10. Hirsch, *Damião de Gois*, 28–32; *CM* I, sig. N[8]^v, and *CM* III, sig. O8^v–P1^r; see also A. H. de Olivera Marques, *Damião de Góis e os Mercadores de Danzig* (Coimbra: s.n., 1959).

11. Olaus Magnus, *Description of the Northern Peoples*, I.148–54, I.77–8; Matthew of Miechów, *Tractatus de Duabus Sarmatiis Asiana et Europeana et de contentis in eis* (Augsburg: Grimm and Wirsung, 1518), II.2, sig. eiv^v. Damião de Góis, 'De Pilapiis', in his *Legatio*, sig. C4^{r-v}. On the centrality of agonistic relations to immanentist thought, see Alan Strathern, *Unearthly Powers: Religious and political change in history* (Cambridge: Cambridge University Press, 2019), 41–2, 98–9.

12. De Góis, *Legatio*, sig. A3^v, A7^r–B1^r. The English translation is *The legacye or embassate of the great emperour of Inde prester Iohn, vnto Emanuell kynge of Portyngale, in the yere of our lorde M. v.C.xiii* [*sic*], trans. John More (London: William Rastell, 1533); More states clearly in the preface that his purpose is to shame the innovators by demonstrating that the Ethiopian Church has remained loyal to

NOTES

Church tradition for 1,500 years. An earlier version of Matthew's letter offering an alliance was published in 1521, though without the wider description of Ethiopian culture, and was probably quickly withdrawn; see Aubin, 'Le Prêtre Jean Devant la Censure Portugaise', in his *Latin et l'Astrolabe*, I.184–5, and Giuseppe Marcocci, 'Prism of empire: The shifting image of Ethiopia in Renaissance Portugal (1500–1570)', in Maria Berbara and Karl A. E. Enenkel (eds.), *Portuguese Humanism and the Republic of Letters* (Leiden: Brill, 2012).

13. De Góis, *Legatio*, B6ᵛ–B8ʳ; this translation of Damião's description of Matthew is taken from More's translation, *Legacye or embassate of the great emperour*, sig. Fiʳ; *The Book of Duarte Barbosa*, xxxv; Matthew's letters complaining of his poor treatment can be found at ANTT PT/TT/CART/891.1/39–42, and in João de Sousa, *Documentos Arabicos para a Historia Portugueza* (Lisbon: Officina da Academia Real das Sciencas, 1790), 89–95. On Armenians in the Indian Ocean, see Sebouh David Aslanian, *From the Indian Ocean to the Mediterranean: The Global Trade Networks of Armenian Merchants from New Julfa* (Berkeley, CA: University of California Press, 2011), esp. 45–8; a useful comparison can be made with the Jewish agents who served as conduits between Europe and Istanbul in Noel Malcolm, *Agents of Empire: Knights, Corsairs, Jesuits and Spies in the Sixteenth-Century World* (London: Allen Lane, 2015), 226–8.

VI. The Degraded

1. Bernardo Gomes de Brito, *História Trágico-Marítima*, ed. Damião Peres (Barcelos: Companhia editora do Minho, 1942–3), 41–3; Pereira, *Esmeraldo de Situ Orbis*, 149. The departure of this fleet is documented in Francisco d'Andrade, *Cronica do muyto a dilto e muito poderoso rey destes reynos de Portugal dom Joao o III deste nome* (Lisbon: Iorge Rodrigues, 1613). sig. Mmm2ʳ⁻ᵛ. On the Libyan Berber stelae, which bear striking similarities to the *padrãos*, see Jean-Loïc Le Quellec, 'Rock Art, Scripts, and Proto-Scripts in Africa: The Lybico-Berber Example', in Adrien Delmas and Nigel Penn (eds.), *Written Culture in a Colonial Context: Africa and the Americas, 1500–1900* (Leiden: Brill, 2010), 10. Damião's friend António Galvão also emphasised that the Portuguese were preceded in their western African navigations by the Romans and others; see Marcocci, *Globe on Paper*, 71–5.

2. *Lusiadas* V.xvi–xxii. The shipwreck of Simão Vaz de Camões off Goa is first mentioned by Manuel Severim de Faria in his life of Camões, published in his *Discursos Varios Politicos* (Évora: Manoel Carvalho, 1624), fols. 88ʳ–135ᵛ; a manuscript version of the life with minor variants, also containing an early life of Damião de Góis, is found in BNP COD. 13117, Severim de Faria's 'Vidas de Portugueses Ilustres'. There is some debate over when exactly Camões arrived in India: it has generally been thought that Camões was on the flagship *São Bento*, captained by Fernão Álvares Cabral, based on Camões' reference (in the elegy 'O Poeta Simónides, falando') to taking part in an expedition supporting the king of Cochin against the 'Rei do Pimiento' (Chembe), which left from Goa in November 1553; as only Cabral's ship reached India that year (in September), it would seem that Camões had to be on his ship in order to take part in the expedition. A 1717 'Relação das Naus' in the *Brevilogio de Noticias das Couzas E dos Sujeitos da Congregacam da India Oriental Dos Ermitas Augustinhos*, Biblioteca de Ajuda, cod. 49-I-51, notes in the section for 1553 that 'Nesta moncão passou a India a celebre Poeta Luis de Camoes', which may represent independent confirmation of Camões' arrival that year from a lost document in Goa, or simply the reproduction of a tradition. See further ch. VIII, n. 12.

3. Alexander von Humboldt, *Cosmos: Sketch of a Physical Description of the Universe*, ed. Edward Sabine (London: Longman et al., 1848; repr. Cambridge: Cambridge University Press, 2010), I.57. Damião's account of da Gama's landing at Santa Helena is at *CM* I, sig. D4ʳ; Camões' rewriting of it is at *Lusiadas* V.xxvi–xxxv. The differences between Damião's version and that in Barros' *Décadas da Ásia* I.iii.3–4 demonstrates their slightly different use of the same sources; Barros, for instance, does not mention the roasted sea lion.

4. *CM* I, sig. D6ᵛ–D7ᵛ and sig. E1ʳ; *Lusiadas* V.lxxvii; Willis, *Camões*, 224; Louise Levathes, *When China Ruled the Seas: The Treasure Fleet of the Dragon Throne (1405–1433)* (Oxford: Oxford University Press, 1994), 141–2. For a far-reaching account of this world system, see Philippe Beaujard, *The Worlds of the Indian Ocean: A Global History*, trans. Philippe Beaujard, ed. Tamara Loring, Frances Meadows and Andromeda Tait, 2 vols. (Cambridge: Cambridge University Press, 2019).

5. See *CM* II, sig. B8r–C2r; *The Book of Duarte Barbosa*, 9–10; *Lusiadas* X.xciii, where Camões discusses the case of Gonçalo da Silvera, a Jesuit priest killed at Monomotapa in 1561. The claim that the circumference of Monomotapa was 800 leagues around may have been a conventional figure for a kingdom of astounding size; Garcia de Orta (*Coloquios dos simples*, sig. D[viii]$^{r-v}$) suggests that Sher Shah Suri – victor over the Mughal emperor Humayun – was known as the *Xaholam*, or 'world king', and that his realm was also 800 leagues around. Ibn Khaldun, *The Muqaddimah: An Introduction to History*, trans. Franz Rosenthal (Princeton, NJ: Princeton University Press, 2015), 66. On the ontological frameworks of divinised kingship, see Strathern, *Unearthly Powers*, 169–73.

6. The classic account of the Sousa wreck is in Gomes de Brito's *História Trágico-Marítima*, I.1–35; there is a sixteenth-century manuscript account at the Biblioteca de Ajuda, cod. 50-V-22, fols. 418^r–433^r, which may have served as Gomes de Brito's source, but which also contains a few extra details. For Camões' description of the storm near the Cape, see the elegy 'O Poeta Simónides, falando'. For a recent study of the story, and an argument for the centrality of shipwrecks in the structure of modernity, see Steve Mentz, *Shipwreck Modernity: Ecologies of Globalization, 1550–1719* (Minneapolis: University of Minnesota Press, 2015), 11–21.

7. Edwin J. Webber, 'The Shipwreck of Don Manuel de Sousa in the Spanish Theater', *PMLA* 66/6 (1951), 1114–22.

8. Gomes de Brito, *História Trágico-Marítima*, I.37–8. Orta, *Coloquios dos simples*, sig. Eviii^v. The trope of the 'coloniser worshipped by natives' was already widespread and well established (for instance, in the writings of and about Columbus); for a Portuguese example, see the account of António Fernandes, who was supposedly worshipped like a god by those he met during his expedition into Monomotapa, as described in the 1516 report of the *Alcaide-mor* of Sofala (ANTT PT/TT/CC/1/20/64).

9. *Lusiadas* IV.lxxxiii; see also the extended discussion on the Portuguese as the new constellation Argo in Manuel Faria e Sousa's commentary in the *Lusiadas de Luis de Camoes [...] comentadas por Manuel de Faria e Sousa* (Madrid: Juan Sanchez, 1639), cols. 107–8, 398–400. The constellation had become invisible as it shifted further south following the progression of the equinoxes, but this fact could

be ignored by those who wished to map the Portuguese voyages on to those of the Argonauts. Virgil, *Eclogues* IV.34–6. Apollonius follows the established tradition of placing the Fleece in the Colchian town of Aia on the eastern shore of the Black Sea, but earlier versions suggested that it was in the kingdom of the sun, in the furthest east; there were some traditions in which the return route was via the Ocean encircling the world, making it a closer match to the circumnavigation of Africa; see Apollonius of Rhodes, *Jason and the Golden Fleece*, trans. Richard Hunter (Oxford: Oxford University Press, 1993), xxi–xxvi. On Damião's presentation of a pontifical cloth to the Chapel of the Order of the Golden Fleece, see *CM* IV, sig. F[1]ᵛ; for his reading on Jason and the triton, see *Urbis Olisiponis Descriptio*, sig. [aviiiᵛ], and Ruth (trans.), *Lisbon in the Renaissance*, 11. The annotations on the *Argonautica* by George Buchanan, the Scottish humanist who was lecturing at Coimbra in the late 1540s, are in the copy he left to the Glasgow University Library (Sp Coll Bh20-a.11); see further John M. McManamon, 'Res *Nauticae*: Mediterranean Seafaring and Written Culture in the Renaissance', *Traditio* 70 (2015), 307–67, on early modern interest in accounts of the Argonauts.

10. *CM* I, sig. EIIʳ. There is a longstanding debate about the identity (and even real name) of the pilot Damião calls 'Malemocanaqua': see Sanjay Subrahmanyam, *The Career and Legend of Vasco da Gama* (Cambridge: Cambridge University Press, 1997), 121–8. On da Gama's failed attempt to sail back against the monsoon, see *CM* I, sig. Eviiᵛ. On Vincente de Sodre's fatal refusal to heed the advice of the Omanis on the winds around Khuriya Muriya in 1503, see *CM* I, sig. K1ʳ. The lines from Kampan's *Iramavataram* are from A. K. Ramanujan's translation in 'Three Hundred Ramayanas', in *The Collected Essays of A. K. Ramanujan*, ed. Stuart Blackburn (New Delhi: Oxford University Press, 2004), 152. On the initial confusions regarding religion in Asia, see Sanjay Subrahmanyam, *Empires Between Islam and Christianity, 1500–1800* (Albany, NY: SUNY Press, 2019), 27–8, and Maria Augusta Lima Cruz, 'Notes on Portuguese Relations with Vijayanagara, 1500–1565', in Sanjay Subrahmanyam (ed.), *Sinners and Saints: The Successors of Vasco da Gama* (Delhi: Oxford University Press, 1998), 13–16.

11. *CM* I, sig. Eiiiiʳ; compare *Lusiadas* VII.xlix, where Camões ended the episode by saying that they passed on after seeing the temple

'without any further events' ('Direitos vão sem outro algum desvio'),
making the omission of the episode of false worship seem even
more significant. An excellent overview of the historiography of this
episode, and of the early encounter in general, is provided in
Alexander Henn, *Hindu-Catholic Encounters in Goa: Religion,
Colonialism, and Modernity* (Bloomington: Indiana University
Press, 2014).

12. Associations between the Trimurti and the Trinity are made in (for
instance) *CM* I, sig. Ev^v; Tomé Pires, *The Suma Oriental of Tomé
Pires*, ed. and trans. Armando Cortesão (London: Hakluyt Society,
Second Series LXXXIX, 1944), 39; *The Book of Duarte Barbosa*, 115.
The idea gained wider European currency with its inclusion in
Fracanzio da Montalboddo's *Paesi Novamenti ritrovati* (Milan:
Giovanni Angelo Scinzenzeler, 1508), ch. cxxxi, which was the
earliest and most widespread report on the Portuguese voyages. For
Camões' take on this, see *Lusiadas* VII.xlvii–xlix. There is a sign in
the church of Nossa Senhora do Monte, Goa, which reads
'NOTICE: Holy Communion is not a Prasad'.

13. Samuel Purchas, *Purchas his pilgrimes In fiue bookes* (London:
William Stansby for Henrie Fetherstone, 1625), I.ii.8, sig. Cc2^v; the
note confirms that Purchas was using Osório's *De rebus Emanuelis
regis* (and so, at one remove, Damião's *CM*) as his source (see
discussion in ch. XVIII below). The aniconism that characterised
Protestant culture should be seen as a wider gesture towards the
ontological breach between the divine and the human which
underwrote the more transcendental forms of Christianity that
arose in the sixteenth century, but this in turn tended to emphasise
the iconocentrism of Catholic worship; see Strathern, *Unearthly
Powers*, 49–50, 88. The accusations of Catholic idolatry tended to
draw on the language of early Christian attacks on pagans, but the
extent to which these ideas were being reformed in the face of
encounters with 'pagans' in Asia and the Americas has perhaps
been underestimated. Here, as elsewhere, my intention is to allow
the 'form intrinsic to the matter of native discourse [...] to modify
the matter intrinsic to the form of anthropological knowledge'
(Eduardo Viveiros de Castro, *The Relative Native: Essays on
Indigenous Conceptual Worlds* (Chicago: HAU Press, 2015), 6).

VII. Between the Cup and the Lip

1. The meal is the subject of a wide number of testimonies in *Inéditos* II, from which the following account is compiled: 19–21, 23–30, 65–6, 75–7, 85–90. *A História Natural de Portugal de Leonhard Thurneysser zum Thurn*, 89.

2. On the fruit near Sintra, see *CM* I, sig. C1^r; on fruit in the Azores, see *CJ* sig. B[1]^r; on Mozambique, see *CM* I, sig. C7^v–C8^r; on Malacca, see *CM* III, sig. A2^{r-v}; on the attraction of tritons to fruit, see *Urbis Olisiponis Descriptio*, sig. [aviii^r]–bi^r, Ruth (trans.), *Lisbon in the Renaissance*, 10–12. On fast days in the sixteenth century, see Carlos Veloso, 'Os sabores da Expansão: continuidade e ruptura nos hábitos alimentares portugueses', in *Turres Veteras IX: Actas do Encontro História da Alimentação* (Lisbon: Edicões Colibri, 2007), 115–34.

3. The storeroom or pantry in Damião's apartments, and the usage of the ancillary balcony looking into the Casa do Éspirito Santo, are the subject of a separate series of testimonies in *Inéditos* II, 83, 91–9, 102–5, 117.

4. The description of the meal in Schleswig is given in *Inéditos* II, 48–9; see also Hirsch, *Damião de Gois*, 20–1, 137–8, and (for the Polish context of Damião's visits to Kraków), Franciszek Ziejka, 'Un humaniste portugaise à Cracovie', *Studia Slavica Academia Scientarum Hungaricae* 49/1–2 (2004), 99–102. On *Zutrinken*, see (for instance) *Hieronymi Emser dialogismus de origine propinandi* (Leipzig: Melchior Lotter, 1505), and B. Ann Tlusty, *Bacchus and Civic Order: The Culture of Drink in Early Modern Germany* (Charlottesville: University of Virginia Press, 2001), 91–5.

5. Erasmus, *De Esu Carnium*, in *Collected Works of Erasmus*, vol. 73, ed. and trans. Denis L. Drysdall (Toronto: University of Toronto Press, 2015), especially xxiv–xxvi, 76–7 (from which the translations are taken). The quote from St Paul is Romans 14.17. A similar event, often referred to as 'The Affair of the Sausages', happened at the same time in Zurich. Damião (*Inéditos* II, 37, 29–30) claimed that he had a licence from 'Pope Paul' (i.e., Paul III) to eat meat on feast days, which may have been inspired by Erasmus' example. For the licence to eat meat during Lent granted to Erasmus by Lorenzo Campeggi in 1525, see Er. Epist. 1542.

6. *Inéditos* II, 32–3, 49–50, 72–3; Hirsch, *Damião de Gois*, 32–3; D. *Martin Luthers Werke* (Weimar: Hermann Böhlaus Nachfolger,

1908), vol. 34.1, 181. The passages from Luther's sixteenth sermon
on St John, preached in Wittenberg on 1 April 1531, are taken from
The Works of Martin Luther (St Louis: Concordia Publishing, 1955–
86), vol. 23, *Sermons on St John, Volume Two*, ed. Jaroslav Pelikan
and Helmut T. Lehmann, 137–43.

7. Luther, *Sermons on Saint John, Volume Two*, 133–9.

8. Ulrich von Hutten, *De Morbo Gallico*, trans. Thomas Paynell
(London: Thomas Berthelet, 1533), Gii^{r-v}; the quote has been lightly
paraphrased for ease of understanding. Luther, 'On Trade and
Usury', in *The Works of Martin Luther*, vol. 45, *Christian in Society
Volume Two*, ed. Walther I. Brandt and Helmut T. Lehmann, 246.
See also Orta, *Coloquios dos simples*, sig. G[vi]^v, on the German love
of pepper. Damião's description of his visit to Luther's and
Melanchthon's houses are in *Inéditos* II, 32–3, 49–51, 72, 90–4.

9. J. S. Grewal, *The Sikhs of the Punjab* (Cambridge: Cambridge
University Press, 1990), 30–6, and (on local, detached living) 40–1.
For a compelling recent account of the ways in which periods of
instability remove the 'taken-for-granted meaningfulness' of the
status quo, and make transcendentalisms more attractive – just as
the early modern period seems to have unlocked the (suspended)
transcendental potential of Christianity and other faiths – see
Strathern, *Unearthly Powers*, esp. 23–5. Paolo Giovio has a passage
in his *Historiarum Sui Temporis* (Paris: s.n., 1533–4), where he
compares the religious divides in Asia to those in Europe; I am
grateful to Giuseppe Marcocci for drawing my attention to this.

VIII. Cooking the World

1. Camões writes about the scent-eaters both in *Lusiadas* VII.xix and
in the lyric poem 'Querendo escrever um dia'; the account is
originally from Pliny the Elder, *Historia Naturalis* VII.2. The quote
from the *Rauzat ut-Tahirin* (The Immaculate Garden, 1602–7) is in
Subrahmanyam, *Empires Between Islam and Christianity*, 251. On
the *mogory* or Arabian jasmine, and *champa* or magnolia, and on
the culture of scent in India, see Orta, *Coloquios dos simples*, sig.
Ci^v–Cii^r, and sig. Bii^r on washing habits. On drinking practices, see
M. N. Pearson, *The Portuguese in India* (Cambridge: Cambridge
University Press, 1988), 100.

2. For examples in Damião's writings of European migrants
encountered in India, see *CM* I, sig. F1^v and sig. Liii^r, *CM* II, sig.

A7^v; see also Sanjay Subrahmanyam, *Three Ways to be Alien: Travails and Encounters in the Early Modern World* (Chicago: University of Chicago Press, 2011), *Empires Between Islam and Christianity*, ch. 3, and *Europe's India*, 73, and Casale, *Ottoman Age of Exploration*, 34–7. On the 'Tiro de Diu' (Cannon of Diu), now held at the Museu Militar de Lisboa, which returned with the 1538 fleet and was kept in the Castelo de São Jorge, see Fernão Mendes Pinto, *The Travels of Mendes Pinto*, ed. and trans. Rebecca D. Catz (Chicago: University of Chicago Press, 1989), 4, and ch. 2. On the books captured during the 1509 Battle of Diu, see *CM* II, sig. I3^v; Barros also recounts this incident, and adds the detail that 'some were philosophy and others history' ('huũs de razar e outros de histórias': *Décadas da Ásia* II.iii.6), but mentions only Latin and Italian volumes and a Portuguese prayer book, and suggests that the books are evidence of how many different peoples were in the fleet. One intriguing possibility is that these books belonged to – or were destined for – Malik Ayaz, whose origins may have been 'Dalmatian, Russian, Turkish or Persian (Gilani)', even though his ships had by this point withdrawn from the battle against Francisco d'Almeida, the first governor of India (Subrahmanyam, *Empires Between Islam and Christianity*, 48–9; see also Casale, *Ottoman Age of Exploration*, 26).

3. On Brahmin delegations to protest against the treatment of Goans, led by Crisna/Krishna, including one to Lisbon, see *CM* III, sig. A8^r and sig. C7^v–C8^r; Thomaz, *De Ceuta a Timor*, 248–50; and Rui Gomes Pereira, *Goa, Vol 1: Hindu Temples and Deities*, trans. Antonio Victor Couto (Panaji: Printwell Press, 1978), 14–16. The possibility mentioned by Thomaz that transactions with Indians were based on previous state relations with Jews is given further confirmation by the fact that Nina Chetu, the Indian who was given powers over non-Christians in Malacca, is referred to interchangeably in legal documents as 'Indio' and 'Judeo' (see, for instance, the *Livro das Ilhas*, ANTT PT/TT/LN 0036, fols. cxxxviii and ccxxxi), though this might in turn have been caused by the ease with which the two words could be confused (requiring only an inversion of the 'n' and the 'u'). On Goa's need to import food, see Pearson, *The Portuguese in India*, 87–91, 112–13; on the strategic importance of its position, see Thomaz, *De Ceuta a Timor*, 247–8, and on Albuquerque's policies with regards to Goa, 248–50. Andrea

Corsali provides a wide-eyed account of the horse trade with
Vijayanagara in his letter to Giuliano Medici: Ramusio, *Primo
volume delle navigationi e viaggi*, fol. 193^v. See Rubiés' extensive
treatment of European writings on Vijayanagara in *Travel and
Ethnography*.

4. See Partha Mitter, *Much Maligned Monsters: A History of European
Reactions to Indian Art* (Chicago: University of Chicago Press,
1992), 34; this passage in the Corsali letter is Ramusio, *Primo
volume delle navigationi e viaggi*, fol. 193^v. It is possible that the
original text of Francisco Álvares' tract on Ethiopia supplied by
Damião to Ramusio, along with a copy of Corsali's letter to Giuliano
Medici (see *Primo volume delle navigationi et viaggi*, fol. 190^r),
survives as Vatican Library Ott.Lat.2202, where the two texts are
found together, starting from fol. 130^r. The Medici collection was
also soon after to contain a range of Chinese porcelain; see
Marcocci, *Globe on Paper*, 53. On the layout of Goa, see Thomaz, *De
Ceuta a Timor*, 248–9, and Pearson, *The Portuguese in India*, 94–5.

5. Subrahmanyam, 'Rethinking the Establishment of the *Estado da
Índia*, 1498–1509', in his *Empires Between Islam and Christianity*,
pp. 26–55; Pearson, *The Portuguese in India*, 94–8. Camões, 'O
Poeta Simónides, falando'.

6. R. H. Major (ed.), *India in the Fifteenth Century: being a collection of
narratives of voyages to India in the century preceding the Portuguese
discovery of the Cape of Good Hope, from Latin, Persian, Russian,
and Italian Sources* (London: Hakluyt Society, First Series XXII,
1857), 10; Camões, 'Cá neste Babilónia, donde mana', 'Super
Flumina'.

7. *The Book of Duarte Barbosa*, xliii–iv, 115; Fabre et al., 'L'affaire
Rodrigues', 194–5. On the grant of arms, see *CM* I, sig. Nv^v–Nvii^r; a
contemporary depiction with some variations can be seen in the
*Tombo das armas dos reis e titulares e de todas as famílias nobres do
reino de portugal*, ANTT PT/TT/CR/D-A/001/21, fol. 58.

8. AHEI 9529, *Provisões a favor da Cristiandade*, 1 vol. (152[?]3–
1840), especially fols. 34^r, 73^v–77^r, 90^r (orders against building/
repair of temples), 81^{r-v} (against intimidating or attempting to
persuade people against conversion), 88^v (preventing Brahmins
from holding office), 91–2 (ordering the expulsion of Brahmins
impeding conversion from the territory). Pereira, *Goa*, I.8–14; Fabre
et al., 'L'affaire Rodrigues'; Pearson, *The Portuguese in India*, 92.

Ramusio, *Primo volume delle navigationi e viaggi*, fol. 193ᵛ.
Non-Muslims in many Muslim territories were barred from office
and required to pay the *jizya*, a tax on non-believers.

9. See the account of the Italian traveller Filippo Sassetti in *Lettere da
Vari Paesi: 1570–1588*, ed. Vanni Bramanti (Milan: Longanesi,
1970), 502: 'Sono scritte le loro scienze tutte in una lingua, che
dimandano sanscruta ... e ha la lingua d'oggi molte cose comuni
con quella, nella quale sono molti de' nostri nomi, e
particularmente de' numeri el 6, 7, 8 e 9, Dio, serpe, e altri assai'
('Their sciences are all written in a language which they call Sanskrit
... and the language of today shares many things with it, in it being
many of our words, particularly the numbers 6, 7, 8 and 9, God,
snake, and plenty of others'); this observation follows on directly
from a discussion (on p. 500) of names of drugs in Garcia de Orta's
Coloquios dos simples. The fact that Sassetti may have been guided
in his knowledge of Sanskrit by access to the monumental Arabic
study of India, the *Tarikh al-Hind*, by the Persian historian
al-Biruni, has not, to my knowledge, been suggested. Sassetti's
comments on Sanskrit and other things (420–1) follow very closely
those in the introduction to al-Biruni's treatise: on vernacular–
Sanskrit distinctions, the limiting effect of verse on Sanskrit
knowledge, the vast Sanskrit vocabulary as an impediment to
learning it, the use of Muslims as bogeymen by Indian parents
wanting to scare their children, etc.; see Muhammad ibn Ahmad
Biruni, *Alberuni's India*, trans. Edward C. Sachau (London: Kegan
Paul, 1910), I.17–19.

10. *The Book of Duarte Barbosa*, I.98–108; Gaspar Correa, *Lendas da
Índia* (ANTT PT/TT/CF/040-043), II.441; Orta, *Coloquios dos
simples*, sig. Ciiiiᵛ–Cviᵛ and sig. Fiiiiᵛ. The Bahmani Sultanate, the
Muslim kingdom of the Deccan to which the Adil Shahs of Bijapur
were one of the successor states, had become a vassal of Timur the
Lame in 1398 and had retained a Persianate cultural influence ever
since; see Manu S. Pillai, *Rebel Sultans: The Deccan from Khilji to
Shivaji* (New Delhi: Juggernaut, 2018), 54, and Richard M. Eaton,
India in the Persianate Age: 1000–1765 (London: Allen Lane, 2019),
ch. 4.

11. Willis, *Camões*, 271–6; Orta, *Coloquios dos simples*, sig. D[i]ʳ;
Camões, 'Aquela Cativa'. There is a law registered in AHEI 8791, the
Livro Vermelho which records local statutes, prohibiting women

from congregating in churches for the purposes of engaging in adulterous affairs, which suggests that this habit was transplanted from Lisbon (fols. 78^v–80^r).

12. Subrahmanyam, *The Portuguese Empire in Asia*, 64–5, and *Empires Between Islam and Christianity*, 53–61, where it is pointed out that this assault on Red Sea traffic had been an aspiration of European geopolitics since the early fourteenth century. The exact itinerary of Camões' naval service in the early 1550s cannot be constructed with entire confidence (see ch. VI, n. 2): in addition to the expedition in support of Cochin that places him in India by November 1553 (described in Diogo do Couto, *Década Sexta da Ásia* (Lisbon: Pedro Craesbeeck, 1614), X.xv), see Willis, *Camões*, 209–210); the poem 'Junto de um seco, fero e estéril monte' indicates he was part of the 1555 expedition against Ottoman ships in the Red Sea, during which the fleet wintered in Hormuz.

13. *Lusiadas*, V.lxxvi, VI.xcviii; 'Junto de um seco, fero e estéril monte'. On Baraawe, see *CM* II, sig. E4; on Qalhat, see *CM* II, sig. G3^{r-v}. On water in Hormuz, see *The Book of Duarte Barbosa*, 96; on the winds in the Red Sea, see Pires, *Suma Oriental*, 9. The image of the water meal is in the *Codex Casanatense* (Biblioteca Casanatense MS.1889), 29–30; see Subrahmanyam, *Europe's India*, 34–6, and Jeremiah P. Losty, 'Identifying the Artist of *Codex Casanatense* 1889', *Anais de História de Além-Mar* 13 (2012), 13–40; and see further ch. X below. On the use of *mummia* in early modern Europe, see Louise Noble, *Medicinal Cannibalism in Early Modern English Literature and Culture* (Basingstoke: Palgrave Macmillan, 2011), and Richard Sugg, *Mummies, Cannibals and Vampires: The History of Corpse Medicine from the Renaissance to the Victorians* (London: Routledge, 2011).

14. On the western belief that *all* Mamluks were renegade Christians, see Ulrich Haarmann, 'The Mamluk System of Rule in the Eyes of Western Travelers', *Mamluk Studies Review*, 5 (2001), 1–25. For Damião's transcription of the letter 'Carta do Soldam de Babilonia aho Papo Iulio terçeiro' (from the Mamluk Sultan al-Ashraf Qansuh al-Ghuri), see *CM* I, sig. M5^v–M6^r; his source document was likely the Latin translation of the letter, ANTT PT/TT/CC/3/0026/00019. On the confrontation at Diu in Ottoman sources, see Casale, *Ottoman Age of Exploration*, 26–8. There is a long-running debate on the extent to which the Portuguese blockade of spices moving

through the Levantine routes succeeded – and, if it did, for how long – which is summarised in Subrahmanyam, 'Rethinking the Establishment of the *Estado da Índia*', 38–45; the conclusion of Jean Aubin that the decline in spices in the eastern Mediterranean was down to political instability in the Hijaz and Yemen, and not the Portuguese blockade, nevertheless it would have meant that the Portuguese sea route would have been more productive and more secure during this period. It is worth noting that, whatever the measurable effects on trade, the perception was certainly of a cataclysmic decline in spices passing to Venice through Alexandria and Beirut – on which, see the discussion of Paolo Giovio and Paulo Centurione in Ch. IX below.

15. On the project to reopen the pharaonic canal at Tor, see Casale, *Ottoman Age of Exploration*, 48–9; it was suggested by the Venetians as early as 1504 (Subrahmanyam, 'Rethinking the Establishment of the *Estado da Índia*', 45). On global empires, see Sanjay Subrahmanyam, 'Connected Histories: Notes Towards a Reconfiguration of Early Modern Eurasia', *Modern Asian Studies* 31/3 (1997), 738–9; see also Orta, *Coloquios dos simples*, sig. D[viii] $^{r-v}$, on the *Xaholam* (world king). As suggested by the conversation with the Mughal emperor recorded by the Ottoman captain Sidi Ali Reis in his *Mirat ul Memalik* (The Mirror of Countries, 1557), comparisons with Alexander the Great were a broader part of the Ottoman strategy of self-presentation, mediating their relations in the east as well as the west; see Richard Stoneman, *Alexander: A Life in Legend* (New Haven: Yale University Press, 2010), and also the recent study by Su Fang Ng, *Alexander the Great from Britain to Southeast Asia: Peripheral Empires in the Global Renaissance* (Oxford: Oxford University Press, 2019).

16. The embassy of Fernão Gomez de Lemos to Shah Ismail is described in *CM* IV, sig. B2^v–[B7^v]. See Halikowski-Smith, '"The Friendship of Kings was in the Ambassadors"', 101–34, for its context within early diplomatic relations between Portugal and eastern states.

17. The transcription of Ismail's letter is given at *CM* IV, sig. B6^v–B7^r. The Adil Shahs of Bijapur fluctuated between maintaining the Sunni faith of their nominal Bahmani overlords and declaring allegiance to the Shia faith in alignment with Persia. See Pillai, *Rebel Sultans*, 103, and Eaton, *India in the Persianate Age*, ch. 4.

IX. Summertime, 7037

1. Giovio, quoted in Sigismund von Herberstein, *Notes upon Russia: Being a translation of the earliest account of that country, entitled Rerum Muscoviticarum Commentarii*, trans. and ed. R. H. Major (London: Hakluyt Society, First Series X and XII, 1851–2), I.228–34; the original can be seen in Paolo Giovio, *Libellus de Legatione Basilii* (Basel: Johannes Froben, 1527), sig. A3ᵛ. There was another projected route for bringing spices to Europe: a sea passage north of China, of which Paolo Giovio and Matthew of Miechów both report rumours; see Granlund and Crone, 'The *Carta Marina* of Olaus Magnus', 36–7. On further doubts regarding the continuing viability of the Carreira da Índia, see Subrahmanyam, 'Rethinking the Establishment of the *Estado da Índia*', 32–5. As Noel Malcolm points out (*Agents of Empire*, 322), spices were in fact traded through Persia to Poland at this date, but this route never proved its viability as a replacement for either the Levant or Cape spice routes.

2. On the newly rediscovered copy of Giovio's map to accompany the *Libellus de Legatione Basilii*, see Giampiero Bellingeri and Marica Milanesi, 'The Reappearance of the Lost Map of Muscovy by Paolo Giovio (1525)', *Imago Mundi*, 72/1 (2020), 47–51; the public discussion of the map is suggested by the description in Ramusio of a conversation about the spice routes in which the speakers have recourse to Giovio's map of Muscovy: see R. A. Skelton and George B. Parks (eds.), *Gian Battista Ramusio: Navigationi et Viaggi* (Amsterdam: Theatrum Orbis Terrarum, 1967–70), xi. On Damião's visit to the library of Konrad Peutinger, where the medieval copy of the late-antique Roman road map was held, see his 1542 letter to Jacob Fugger, and Hirsch, *Damião de Gois*, 26n. Damião's response to Giovio was published at the end of his *Commentarii rerum gestarum in India citra Gangem a Lusitanis anno 1538* (Louvain: Rutger Rescius, 1539), sig. Eiiʳ–Eivᵛ, which was translated into Italian in the same year as *Avisi de le cose fatte da Portuesi ne l'India di qua del Gange, nel MDXXXVIII scritti in lingua latina dal signor Damiano da Goes cavalier portuese al cardinal Bembo* (Venice: Comin da Trino, 1539). Sidi Ali Reis, *Mirat ul Memalik*, details a confrontation in Gujarat with the Portuguese ambassador in which he conceded Portugal's inability to control land traffic.

3. The extent of Damião's travels in these regions has occasioned some debate, given the fragmentary nature of the evidence, which

consists of several autobiographical references in his chronicles
(Damião says he 'found himself in some of these regions', namely
the lands of the 'Muscovites, and Russians, and Lithuanians, and
Livonians': *CM* III, sig. O8^v–P1^r; see also *CM* IV, sig. B4^v); a poem
by Cornelius Graphaeus celebrating Damião's return from the
'regions of the Tatars'; and António Galvão's *Tratado ... dos diuersos
& desuayrados caminhos* (Lisbon: João de Barreira, 1563), sig. Iii^v–
Iiii^v, for which Galvão almost certainly had Damião himself as a
source, and which mentions specifically Damião's travels to the
Duchy of Muscovy as well as to Norway and Sweden, where it
claims that he travelled to 'oytenta graos daltura' (eighty degrees of
latitude) – probably an exaggeration or miscalculation, as the only
land at this latitude – the Svalbard archipelago – was supposedly
first discovered by Barentz in 1596. Hirsch (*Damião de Gois*, 21–3)
accepts that Damião travelled to Russia and the region of the Don
River, but Aubin rejects the claims that he travelled to Scandinavia
and the lands of the Tatars as 'imaginary' (*Latin et l'Astrolabe*,
253–9), owing to the hazy sense of what the 'lands of the Tatars'
were at the time. The description of the bizarre initiation rituals of
merchants in Bergen, Norway, recorded by Leonhard Thurneysser
zum Thurn during his stay with Damião in 1555–6, which must
have been recounted by his host and which appears not to derive
from Magnus (or at least from Magnus' printed works), lends
further evidence (albeit circumstantial) to the claim that Damião
travelled in Scandinavia, and perhaps in the Baltic and Russia; see
*A História Natural de Portugal de Leonhard Thurneysser zum
Thurn*, 93–5. Herberstein's mention of a pyramid of sugar
presented on a royal hunting expedition (*Notes upon Russia*, II.136)
confirms the suggestion that refined sugar was still an unusual
luxury in Moscow at the time. On Damião's involvement with
efforts to aid Hungary, see *Inéditos*, II, 57. For a discussion of the
geopolitics of this region from an Ottoman angle, see Malcolm,
Agents of Empire, 324–5.

4. Herberstein, *Notes upon Russia*, I.55–9, 61–82.
5. Marcocci, *Globe on Paper*, 92; Subrahmanyam, 'Connected
   Histories', 752–3; David Arans, 'A note on the lost library of the
   Moscow Tsars', *Journal of Library History*, 18/3 (1983), 304–16;
   Simon Franklin, review of Dimitri Obolensky, *Six Byzantine
   Portraits* (1988), *English Historical Review*, 106/419 (1991), 434–5;

Isabel de Madariaga, *Ivan the Terrible* (New Haven: Yale University Press, 2006), 17, 19.

6. De Madariaga, *Ivan the Terrible*, 24, 32–5; Herberstein, *Notes upon Russia*, I.cxxiv, I.49–50, II.49–56.

7. Herberstein, *Notes upon Russia*, II.74–5; Guillaume Postel, *Des Merveilles du Monde et principalement des admirables choses des Indes et du nouveau monde* (France: s.n., 1553), ch. XIX, sig. Iii^r–Iiii^v; Girolamo Cardano, *De Rerum Varietate Libri XVII* (Basel: Heinrich aus Basel Petri, 1557), ch. XXII. These descriptions of the vegetable lamb probably all ultimately derive from the fantastical *Travels of Sir John Mandeville* (ch. xxix). On the 'living leaves' of Borneo, see Antonio Pigafetta, *Magellan's Voyage: A Narrative Account of the First Circumnavigation*, trans. R. A Skelton (New York: Dover Books, 1994), ch. xxxiii, 105. On the bloodlessness of crabs as used by Jesuits in China, see Matteo Ricci, *The True Meaning of the Lord of Heaven*, ed. D. Lancashire and P. Hu Kuo-chen (St Louis, MO: Institute of Jesuit Studies, 1986), 265–7, and Laven, *Mission to China*, 211.

8. Nicolaus Copernicus, *Three treatises on Copernican theory*, trans. Edward Rosen (London: Dover 2018), 105. A 1566 document, first published by Oliveira Marques in *Damiao de Góis e os Mercadores de Danzig*, suggests that Damião visited Königsberg (now Kaliningrad) on one of his trips, a land voyage from Gdansk that would naturally pass through Frombork.

9. Copernicus, *Three treatises*, 57–9, 61–4. Damião probably met Johannes Dantiscus, who as Prince-Bishop of Warmia was Copernicus' superior, in 1529; he met Tiedman Giese, Copernicus' cousin and confidant in 1531, and continued to correspond with him until 1542 (Hirsch, *Damião de Gois*, 37–8).

10. The celebrations are described in great detail in a letter in *I Diarii di Marino Sanuto* (Venice: F. Visentini, 1879–1903), vol. LV, col. 414–19, where Damião is mentioned as having been one of four men waiting personally upon the Emperor during the feast.

11. The writings describing the play – a poem by the humanist André Resende, and letters from Girolamo Aleandro (who wrote the report to Rome) and Pedro Mascarenhas, are published by Esperança Cardeira, 'Jubileu', in *Cadernos Vicente* (Lisbon: Quimera, 1993) – to which the account in Sanudo can now be added; the *Guerta de Jubileu* appears in a final section of the index of prohibited books –

A HISTORY OF WATER

the *Rol dos Livros Defesos* (Lisbon: Germam Galharde, 1551). There is some confusion over the name, which is 'Jubileu damores' in the *Rol* and Aleandro's letter, but 'Guerta de Jubileu' in Sanudo.

X. Prince of Ghosts

1. Willis, *Camões*, 210; *The Travels of Mendes Pinto*, Fernão Mendes Pinto, chs 217–18.
2. On radical preachers in Goa during the late 1540s and early 1550s, see Fabre et al., 'L'affaire Rodrigues'; see also Rubiés, *Travel and Ethnography*, 8–9.
3. On reports of Latin manuscripts in Morocco, see Pereira, *Esmeraldo de Situ Orbis*, 58–9. On the copper plates from Cranganore, see *CM* I, sig. Niii^{r-v}; a retranslation made in 1604 existed in British Library Add. MS 9853, fols. 32–5, but was badly damaged by the time Boxer inspected it in 1949 (C. R. Boxer, 'More about the Marsden Manuscripts in the British Museum', *Journal of the Royal Asiatic Society of Great Britain and Ireland*, no. 1 (1949), 66); see also the discussion in Diogo do Couto, *Década Setima da Ásia* (Lisbon: Pedro Craesbeeck, 1616), X.v, fols. 217^v–223^r. On associations of certain figures in Tupinambá mythology with St Thomas, see Métraux, *La Religion des Tupinamba*, pp. 46–9; on a similar theme, see Marcocci, *Globe on Paper*, ch. 1, on Noah's descendants in New Spain (Mexico).
4. See *The Book of Duarte Barbosa*, 126–9 (on St Thomas as a peacock), and 117–18 (on the footprint on Adam's Peak). For the Chinese record of this peak on Zheng He's 1406 voyage, see Levathes, *When China Ruled the Seas*, 100.
5. Orta, *Coloquios dos simples*, sig. Ddii^{r-v}; Mitter, *Much Maligned Monsters*, 37–8 and Appendix 2, which includes a translation of João de Castro's descriptions from his *Primero Roteiro da Costa da India desde Goa até Diu* (c.1538–45). See also Filippo Sassetti's description of the temple near the Portuguese Fort at 'Bazzallir' in *Lettere da Vari Paesi*, 422.
6. Orta, *Coloquios dos simples*, sig. Ddi^v–Ddii^r. On the Indian idol taken from a captured ship by Vasco da Gama, see *CM* I, sig. I5^r. A reproduction of the Sanskrit-inscribed monument from Somnáth-Patane, near Diu, which João de Castro brought back to install at his seat near Sintra, is Inv. no. AC-012 at the Sociedade Geografica de Lisboa; see also J. Herculano de Moura, *Inscripções Indianas em*

298

Cintra de Somnáth-Patane e Elephanta (Nova Goa: Imprensa Nacional, 1906). On the movement of monuments from Divar, see Pereira, *Goa*, I.47–50. Willis, *Camões*, 209. There are many known atlases by Dourado, mostly reproduced in Armando Cortesão's six-volume *Monumenta Cartographica Portugalliae*; all of those up to 1571 show a label to the north of Goa which reads 'O pagode vam de Goa', or similar; from the 1575 one onwards there is 'O pagode queimado vam de Goa'. The Newberry Library atlas (Ayer MS Map 26), which may have drawn on Dourado, also has the 'queimado' label; the ANTT atlas (PT/TT/CRT/165) suggests that the temple in question may have been that at Chapora.

7. The portrait of Camões in prison in Goa was first identified by Maria Antonieta Soares de Azevedo in 'Uma nova e preciosa espécie iconográfica quinhentista de Camões', *Panorama*, 4th series 42/3 (1972); the dating is accepted by Willis (*Camões*, 222), but queried by Vasco Graça Moura (*Dicionário*, 850). Camões, 'Com força desusada'.

8. The story that Camões was imprisoned for slander against certain residents of Goa during the celebrations to instal Governor Rui Barreto is first recounted by Camões' early biographer Manuel Severim de Faria, and while his reference to a 'Satira do Torneio' caused some confusion for Willis (*Camões*, 219), there seems no problem in identifying it with the 'Zombaria que fez sobre algūs homēs a que não sabio mal o vinho' ('Satire made about certain men not unfamiliar with wine') that first appears in the *Rimas* of 1598 (fols. 200^r–202^r), which is reprinted in later editions as the 'Finge que em Goa, nas festas que se fizeram a successão de hum Governador' ('Performance made in Goa, at the time of the succession of a governor'). See *Dicionário*, 87, for further discussion; the poem 'Disparates da Índia' has also been suggested as a candidate for earning Camões the opprobrium of the authorities, though the case presented is less compelling than that for the 'Satira'.

9. *CM* III, sig. P3^v–P4^r. On the contested nature of Alexander's legacy, see Ng, *Alexander the Great*, and Vincent Barletta, *Death in Babylon: Alexander the Great and Iberian Empire in the Muslim Orient* (Chicago: University of Chicago Press, 2010).

10. *Lusiadas*, VII.xlvii–lvi. AHEI 9529, *Provisões a Favor da Cristandade*, fols. 34^r, 54^r, 73^v–74^v, 94^v–95^v; AHEI 8791, *Livro*

Vermelho, 41^v–42^v. On the ritual suicides, see Délio Mendonça, *Conversions and Citizenry: Goa under Portugal, 1510–1610* (New Delhi: Concept Publishing Company, 2002), 421–3, quoting from ARSI, *Indiarum Orientalum Miscellanum*, 38-II (1544–83), Rome, fol. 245. Europeans were widely shocked by ceremonies during which the zealous cast themselves under cartwheels: see *Codex Casanatense*, 78–9, and Subrahmanyam, *Europe's India*, 30. On the Cruzeiro de Margão, see Thomaz, *De Ceuta a Timor*, 272; on the Kotte ivories, including the 'Robinson Casket' at the V&A which incorporates Dürer's *Bagpipe Player*, see Gschwend and Lowe (eds.), *Global City*, ch. 9.

11. *Lusiadas*, VII.xvii; see also VII.xl, where Camões suggests that the Brahmins are Pythagoreans, and the discussion of reincarnation more generally in ch. XIV below. Orta also discusses the relationship between Brahmins/Banyans/'genosofistas' and Pythagoreans, repeating the widely reported story of their purchasing birds to free them, at *Coloquios dos simples*, sig. R[vi]$^{r–v}$, where he also discusses the widespread belief in transmigration in India. Camões' comments on the religious culture of Cambodia (discussed in ch. XIV below) can also be taken as a continuation of his discussion of Indian religion, given the dominance of Brahminism in Cambodia during this period. On taunting Indians by threatening animals, see *The Book of Duarte Barbosa*, 110–13; *CM* III, sig. P3^v. The letters of Filippo Sassetti in the 1580s (e.g. *Lettere da Vari Paesi*, 400–1) provide an example of how widely Europeans continued to rely on Barbosa for information about India; despite writing from Cochin, Sassetti repeats almost verbatim Barbosa's words (110–13) on the habits of 'Banyans' in terms of washing and of buying animals to save them from slaughter. For the episode in Cuncolim, where cows' viscera were spread on the site of a destroyed temple to prevent it from being rebuilt, see Pereira, *Goa*, I.20; for a similar act of desecration by Muslim invaders, see *Alberuni's India*, 116.

12. *CM* IV, sig. 7^v. See Descola, *Par-delà Nature et Culture*, 336, on the traditional naturalist exclusion of non-humans from economic and political activity, and 408, again on consequences of animist and naturalist ontologies; though his scheme classifies early modern European thought as heavily 'analogist', it is clear that while analogies between species may have existed in medical thought there was no spiritual analogy across the species boundary in any

major Christian philosophy. Descriptions of animals by Damião and other early Portuguese writers on the east also contradict the belief, recorded in Dante (*De Vulgari Eloquentia* I.ii) and elsewhere, that animals had no need of language because all members of a species were identical and therefore understood each other intuitively. Major (ed.), *India in the Fifteenth Century*, 13. João dos Santos, *Ethiopia Oriental* (Évora: Manuel de Lira,1609), fol. 15^r. The *Ramayana* murals in the Mattancherry Palace were painted during the 1560s, in a building which was constructed by the Portuguese for the zamorin of Cochin.

XI. Dead Men's Shoes

1. Evidence for Camões appointment as *Provedor dos Bens de Defuntos* is seen in Correa's note to *Lusiadas* X.cxxviii (*Lusiadas 1613*), Severim de Faria's 1624 life of Camões in his *Discursos Varios Politicos*, and Diogo do Couto's *Década Setima da Ásia*; see also Willis, *Camões*, 216–17. That Camões was appointed on the 1557 voyage to Macau, on which Leonel de Sousa was *capitão-mor* (captain-major), can be deduced from the fact that after this initial voyage the post of *provedor* was subsumed within the governorship of Macau (a post also held by the *capitão-mor* of the fleet), and that de Sousa had complained about the alienation of this post from him (so his complaint must have related to the first voyage); a helpful summary of the issues surrounding this part of Camões' biography is given in Willis, *Camões*, 212–16. As suggested by a document of 1580, dealing with the trade concessions to Orissa and Bengal, the major profit from these posts was attached not to the *capitão-mor's* role but rather to the *Provedor dos Bens de Defuntos*, for 'without it, they [i.e. the concessions] would be worth nothing'; see Sanjay Subrahmanyam 'Notes on the sixteenth century Bengal trade', *Indian Economic and Social History Review* 24/3 (1987), 276–7, for this passage and a useful summary of the post of the *provedor*; AHEI 4468, 'Cartas Patentes', fols. 43^v–44^v, suggests that João de Mendoza kept the post for himself when he sent his brother Simão Mendoza in his stead as *capitão-mor* in 1565–6; see also C. R. Boxer, *The Great Ship from Amacon: Annals of Macao and the Old Japan Trade, 1555–1640* (Lisbon: Centro de Estudos Históricos Ultramarinos, 1959), 31–2. *Lusiadas*, VII.lxxx, IX.xix; the latter quote has been silently changed here, as the subject in the original is female.

2. The description of Malacca is found at *CM* III, sig. A2ᵛ–A3r (the gold, slaves, durian fruit), E3ʳ (the firework and magic bracelet). The story of the oxhide trick appears and is discussed at the beginning of Subrahmanyam, *The Portuguese Empire in Asia*, 3–6.

3. *CM* III, sig. E3ʳ–E5ᵛ and sig. E8ʳ; Levathes, *When China Ruled the Seas*, 173–4.

4. Damião's account of the 1516 Pires embassy is at *CM* IV, sig. D5ᵛ–D8ʳ. Boxer (ed.), *South China in the Sixteenth Century*, xx–xxi. There was a previous voyage (in 1513) by Portuguese merchants aboard a Chinese junk to the island of Lingding, near Macau. See also Serge Gruzinski, *The Eagle and the Dragon: Globalization and European Dreams of Conquest in China and America in the Sixteenth Century*, trans. Jean Birell (Cambridge: Polity Press, 2014).

5. On the Chinese artefacts presented by Fernão Pires de Andrade to King Manuel, see *CM* IV, sig. D[7]ʳ⁻ᵛ; these included a Chinese book which Manuel sent to Pope Leo X, and which Paolo Giovio later described as concerning rituals – see Marcocci, *Globe on Paper*, 123. Leonel de Sousa's letter (15 January 1556) detailing the regularisation of trade arrangments with the Chinese is ANTT PT/TT/GAV/2/10/15; see also J. M. Braga, *The Western Pioneers and their Discovery of Macao* (Macau: Imprensa Nacional, 1949), 84–6, 202–8. A 1555 letter from Father Belchior at Macau, describing the early Japan voyages, is in *Cartas que os padres e irmãos da Compania de Iesus escreverão dos Reynos de Japão & China* (Évora: Manoel de Lyra, 1598), sig. E2ʳ. Boxer (ed.), *South China in the Sixteenth Century*, xxv. The first Portuguese ship to land in Japan was supposedly driven ashore by a storm in 1542 (Galvão, *Tratado*, sig. Liiiᵛ–Liiiiʳ), though Fernão Mendes Pinto (author of the *Travels*) also claimed that he was the first to land there. A useful summary of the China trade is found in Rui Manuel Loureiro, 'Chinese Commodities on the India Route', in Gschwend and Lowe (eds.), *Global City*, ch. 4, as well as the foundational work of C. R. Boxer in *The Great Ship from Amacon*.

6. Camões' poetic rutter from eastern India to Japan appears in *Lusiadas*, X.cxxii–cxxxviii, with the description of the Wall at cxxx. On European legends of Chiang Mai, see *The Travels of Mendes Pinto*, ch. 41. On the Chinese books and interpreter acquired by Barros, see *Décadas da Ásia*, I.ix.1–2 and III.ii.7, Boxer, *João de Barros*, 105, and Rui Manuel Loureiro, *Fidalgos, missionários e*

mandarins: Portugal e China no Século XVI (Lisbon: Fundação Oriente, 2000); Mendes Pinto also mentions some books he brought back from the east in ch. 164 of the *Travels*. One of these Chinese books later made its way to the Vatican, via the papal nuncio Giovanni Ricci, who passed it on to Paulo Giovio (see Marcocci, *Globe on Paper*, 122–3); Damião may have been involved in this transaction, as Ricci was at this time attempting to acquire his Bosch paintings (*Inéditos*, II, 114–17).

7. Frois, *The First European Description of Japan*, 17, 18, 52, 63, 67–8, 76, 132, 138, 183–5, 194; *Cartas que os padres*, sig. F8^r. Markus Friedrich, 'Archives as networks: The geography of record-keeping in the Society of Jesus (1540–1773)', *Archival Science* 10/3 (2010), 285–98; Head, *Making Archives*, 41.

8. For an analysis of moves from immanent to transcendental modes of thought, see Strathern, *Unearthly Powers*, ch. 3.

9. Magnus, *Description of the Northern Peoples*, I.70–2; Magnus' source on the origin of the twelve-hour division is Niccolò Perroti's *Cornucopiae sive comentarii linguae latinae* (Milan: Ferrarius, 1506), col. 779, though see also Polydore Vergil, *De Inventoribus Rerum*, II.5 (Venice: de Pensis, 1499), sig. fiii^r. On the commissioning of a mechanical clock in China in 1583 from a Portuguese-trained Indian, see Luís Filipe Bareto, 'Macao: An Intercultural Frontier in the Ming Period', in Luís Saraiva (ed.), *History of Mathematical Sciences: Portugal and East Asia II. Scientific Practices and the Portuguese Expansion in Asia, 1498–1759* (Lisbon: EMAF-UL, 2001), 7.

10. On Christian and Muslim agreement on the nearness of the apocalypse see Subrahmanyam, 'Connected Histories', 747–51. As A. Azfar Moin points out in *The Millennial Sovereign: Sacred Kingship and Sainthood in Islam* (New York: Columbia University Press, 2014), Mughal interest in Christian culture was often focussed on millenarianism, as the first Islamic millennium approached. On dates and dating systems, see *The Travels of Mendes Pinto*, ch. 126; *The Boxer Codex: Translation and transcription of a late sixteenth-century Spanish manuscript concerning the geography, ethnography, and history of the Pacific, South-East Asia, and East Asia*, ed. George Bryan Souza and Jeffrey S. Turley, trans. Jeffrey S. Turley (Leiden: Brill, 2015), 574; Johannes Oranus, *Japonica, Sinensia, Mogorana* (Liège: Art de

Coerswarem, 1601), sig. G2ᵛ–G3ᵛ; these estimates of the age of the world gained a wider circulation in travel compendia such as Samuel Purchas' *Purchas his pilgrimage* (London: William Stansby for Henrie Fetherstone, 1613), 406–7. On Firishta, see Subrahmanyam, *Europe's India*, 82. Al-Biruni's extensive discussions of Indian calculations of time take up chs. XXXII–XLIX of his history of India (*Alberuni's India*), but see especially the discussion in ch. XLIX. The quote from the Japanese converts comes from *The Travels of Mendes Pinto*, ch. 39, and while of course Mendes Pinto's claims always need to be treated cautiously, this nevertheless suggests recognition of timescales as an important confessional and cultural distinction.

11. *Cartas que os padres*, sig. E2ᵛ–E4ᵛ. Gaspar da Cruz, *Tractado em que se cõtam*, ch. xvii (on God and natural philosophy). Boxer, *The Great Ship from Amacon*, 5–6.

12. *Cartas que os padres*, sig. F7ᵛ; *CM* IV, sig. D7ʳ. On early Macau, see Boxer (ed.), *South China in the Sixteenth Century*, xxiii and 224; for instances of the association of Mazu with the Virgin Mary, see Giovanni Botero, *Discorso di vestigii, et argomenti delle fede Catholica, ritrovati nell'India da Portoghesi, e nel mondo nuovo da' Castigliani* (Venice: Giovanni Martinelli, 1588); 14, Gaspar da Cruz, *Tractado em que se cõtam*, ch. xxvii; and Boxer (ed.), *South China in the Sixteenth Century*, 213. The confusion seems also to have arisen during the later Jesuit mission to China; see Laven, *Mission to China*, 80. For the description of Tian Fei's appearance over Zheng He's fleet see Levathes, *When China Ruled the Seas*, 103–4; J. J. L. Duyvendak, 'The True Dates of the Chinese Maritime Expeditions in the Early Fifteenth Century', *T'oung Pao*, 34/1 (1938), 345–6. See also *The Boxer Codex*, 598–9, for Fr. Martin de Rada's account of Mazu, whom he calls 'Niangma'.

13. Willis (*Camões*, 221–2) makes a convincing case that it was not de Sousa, founder of the Macau factory, who ejected Camões, but rather his successor, Rui Barreto. *Lusiadas* I.cii.

XII. Our Dying Gods

1. Cornelis Augustijn, *Erasmus: His Life, Works, and Influence* (Toronto: University of Toronto Press, 1991), 123, 125; Aubin, 'Damião de Góis dans une Europe Évangélique', in *Latin et l'Astrolabe*, I. 211–12; Hirsch, *Damião de Gois*, 23.

2. Andreas Vesalius, *On the Fabric of the Human Body*, trans. William Frank Richardson (San Francisco: Norman, 1998–9), I.382–3.

3. The *Vetālapañcaviṁśatikā*, or *Twenty-Five Stories of the Vampire*, exists in many versions, perhaps the most famous being that by the eleventh-century Kashmiri poet Somadeva.

4. Erasmus, *De Delectu Ciborum Scholia*, in *Collected Works of Erasmus*, vol. 73, 106; Augustijn, *Erasmus*, 125 (quoting a letter to Richard Pace), 159, 163; Hirsch, *Damião de Gois*, 69–71; Aubin, *Latin et l'Astrolabe*, I.216–17.

5. *Inéditos* II, 42; Hirsh, 45, 79, 87. On the portrait of Erasmus, see *As Cartas Latinas de Damião de Góis*, ed. and trans. Amadeu Torres (Paris: Fundacão Calouste Gulbenkian, 1982), 214/373. The passage on Sophocles is at *De Senectute* VII.22–3; Damião's translation of the text was published as *Livro de Marco Tullio Ciçeram chamado Catam maior, ou da velhiçe, dedicado a Tito Pomponio Attico* (Venice: Stevão Sabio, 1538).

6. Er. Epist. 3043; Hirsch, *Damião de Gois*, 80–1; Erasmus, *Ciceronianus* (1528). I have largely followed Hirsch's translations of Erasmus' letters to Damião, with some minor variations.

7. Er. Epist. 2987, 3079, 3085; Hirsch, *Damião de Gois*, 76, 83–4. On Erasmus' public curation of his letters, see Lisa Jardine, *Erasmus, Man of Letters: The Construction of Charisma in Print* (Princeton, NJ: Princeton University Press, 1993).

8. The sole surviving copy of Damião's translation – *Ecclesiastes de Salamam, con algunas annotações neçessarias* (Venice: Stevão Sabio, 1538) – survives in Oxford as All Souls, Codrington Library, 12:SR.70.b.24(1), where it was discovered by Thomas Earle in April 2000 and subsequently published by him with an extensive introduction as *O Livro de Ecclesiastes* (Lisbon: Fundaçao Calouste Gulbenkian, 2002). On *hevel*, see Damião's note at sig. biiii[r]. The translation may have been prompted by the fact that Erasmus was even then preparing a commentary on Ecclesiastes, published by Froben in Basel in 1535.

9. Er. Epist. 2846; *CM* III, sig. O[7][v]; Hirsch, *Damião de Gois*, 73; Aubin, *Latin et l'Astrolabe*, I.183–210, 273–5.

10. *CM* III, sig. O4[v]–O6[r]; Hirsch, *Damião de Gois*, 146–7; Marcocci, *Globe on Paper*, 96–8.

11. *Ineditos*, II, 33; Aubin, *Latin et l'Astrolabe*, I.222; Er. Epist. 2963; Hirsch, *Damião de Gois*, 75.

12. The first Portuguese index of prohibited books was produced only in manuscript form in 1547, and was first published by António Baião in 'A Censura literária inquisitorial', in *Boletim da Segunda Classe da Academia das Ciências de Lisboa*, 12 (1918), 474–83. The 1551 index, to which Damião's attention was drawn in his trial (*Inéditos* II, 51–2), was published as *Este he o rol dos libros defesos por o Cardeal Iffante* ... (Lisbon: Germam Galharde, 1551). Neither of Damião's works were included on these published lists, but his translation of Ecclesiastes was included in a general prohibition against vernacular translations of scripture (and his was the only one in Portuguese), which in 1571 was extended across Catholic territories (Archive of the Congregation for the Doctrine of the Faith, Index, Diari 01 (1571–1606), fol. 3^v, 5 September 1571), and his translation of Zagazabo's treatise was subject to a specific injunction by the Cardinal-Infante Henrique, whose letter laying out his reasons is reproduced in *Inéditos*, II, 46–8, and is discussed in ch. XVII below. Hirsch, *Damião de Gois*, 175, quoting Diogo de Teive. On the history of censorship in early modern Europe, see Simona Munari, 'Translation, Re-Writing, and Censorship during the Counter-Reformation', in José María Pérez Fernandez and Edward Wilson-Lee (eds.), *Translation and the Book Trade in Early Modern Europe* (Cambridge: Cambridge University Press, 2014), 185–200.

XIII. Inside a Dog

1. *Inéditos*, II, 7–10, 12–13, 16–17, 50–1. The relevant verse is 1 Corinthians 7.9. There is some difficulty reconciling the exact date of these events within the years 1536–7, given the different estimates provided over the course of four decades by those involved, and other evidence about the activities of Loyola and his companions in and around Venice; Damião himself estimated that it was a year and a half or two after he had arrived in Padua (in October 1534). See Aubin, *Latin et l'Astrolabe*, I.220, for discussion. St Ignatius of Loyola, *Personal Writings*, ed. and trans. Joseph A. Munitz and Philip Endean (London: Penguin, 2004), 22.

2. See the excellent account of the University of Padua's history in Jonathan Woolfson, *Padua and the Tudors: English Students in Italy, 1485–1603* (Toronto: University of Toronto Press, 1998); though the students' powers over appointments had been greatly reduced by the time of Damião's arrival in 1534, they still retained rights over

appointments to certain lectureships (p. 13). For Damião's description of attending lectures at Padua, see *CM* II, sig. G5^r. On Damião and Pole, see Marcel Bataillon, 'Damião de Góis et Reginald Pole', in his *Études sur le Portugal au temps de l'humanisme*, pp. 141–7; on Erasmus and Bembo, see Er. Epist. 3043 and Hirsch, *Damião de Gois*, 80–1.

3. Sarah Blake McHam, 'Renaissance Monuments to Favourite Sons', *Renaissance Studies*, 19/4 (2005), 458–86. On the public lectures at Hormuz, see *CM* II, sig. G5^r; on Ksar el-Kebir, see *CM* I, sig. I5^v.

4. *Ineditos*, II, 8. On Marot, see Damião de Góis to Boniface Amerbach, 24 September 1536.

5. Ines G. Županov, 'The First Fathers of the Society of Jesus', in Županov (ed.), *The Oxford Handbook of the Jesuits*; 'L'affaire Rodrigues', 174–6.

6. John W. O'Malley, *Trent: What Happened at the Council* (Cambridge, MA: Belknap Press, 2013), 67–8; *Inéditos*, II, 6, 72–3; Hirsch, *Damião de Gois*, 80, 96.

7. Aubin, *Latin et L'Astrolabe* I.227-230; Hirsch, *Damião de Gois*, 152.

8. See *Inéditos*, II, 42, for Damião keeping Erasmus' letters in his 'boeta' (coffer) with his most important documents. On Damião's abandonment of the plan to edit Erasmus' works, see Damião's letter from Padua to Amerbach on 31 August 1536, transcribed in Bataillon, 'Le Cosmopolitisme de Damião de Góis', 160–1. Erasmus omitted the 'Johannine Comma' (from 1 John 5.7–8) from the first two editions of his *Novum Instrumentum* (1516 & 1519). On Anti-Trinitarian thought and Islam, see Alexander Bevilacqua, *The Republic of Arabic Letters: Islam and the European Enlightenment* (Cambridge, MA: Belknap Press, 2018), 10; on association between Islam and Protestantism through iconophobia, see Subrahmanyam, *Europe's India*, 28–9; on Protestant attempts to find common ground with the Ottomans over hatred of Catholic idolatry, see Matthew Dimmock, *New Turkes: Dramatizing Islam and the Ottomans in Early Modern England* (Aldershot: Ashgate, 2005), 56–7; Malcolm, *Agents of Empire*, 353.

9. Vesalius, *On the Fabric of the Human Body*, I.xlix, xiii–xiv (quoting Aristotle, *Historia Animalium*, I.16). The testimony in the Inquisition trial makes clear that Damião was living with Flemings at Padua (see *Inéditos*, II, 8), so it was likely that he was associated with the Fleming 'nation' at the university, as Vesalius was.

10. Vesalius, *On the Fabric of the Human Body*, I.xl, xlix, liii–liv; Maurice Merleau-Ponty, *La Nature* (Paris: Éditions du Seuil, 1994), 25; see also Descola, *Par-delà Nature et Culture*, 132–3.

XIV. História Trágico-Marítíma

1. Gaspar da Cruz, *Tractado em que se côtam*, ch. xviii; Boxer (ed.), *South China in the Sixteenth Century*, 158; Wenxian Zhang, 'Dang An: A Brief History of the Chinese Imperial Archives and its Administration', *Journal of Archival Organization*, 2/1–2 (2004), 17–38. For Sun Wukong's *ledger-de-main*, see Wu Cheng'en, *Monkey King: Journey to the West*, trans. Julia Lovell (London: Penguin, 2021), ch. 3. For an excellent overview of the bureaucratic structure of the Chinese afterlife, see Noga Ganany, 'Baogong as King Yama in the Literature and Religious Worship of Late-Imperial China', *Asia Major*, 28/2 (Fall 2015), 39–75.

2. Barros, *Décadas da Ásia*, I.ix.1; Boxer (ed.), *South China in the Sixteenth Century*, lxxxiv–lxxxv, which gives the list of books translated by the Sangleys in the words of the Elizabethan translation of Mendoza's history of China; Subrahmanyam, *Europe's India*, 26; Marcocci, *Globe on Paper*, 53–8. The 'Chinese slave' whom Barros used to translate the materials may well have been among those 'escravas blancas' Damião mentions in the Casa do Cível at *CM* III, sig. K2ᵛ; see also ch. II n. 8.

3. *Lusiadas*, VI.lxxi–lxxvi. The sources regarding Camões shipwreck are helpfully summarised and discussed in Gerald M. Moser, 'Camões' Shipwreck', *Hispania*, 57/2 (1974), 213–19. See Boxer, *The Great Ship from Amacon*, 24–32, for various shipwrecks of the period which offer candidates for it.

4. *Lusiadas*, VII.lxxx; Isaiah 38.10, 40.3. The quotation from the *Reamker*, the sixteenth–seventeenth-century Rama epic, is taken from *Reamker (Rāmakerti): The Cambodian version of the Rāmāyana*, trans. Judith M. Jacob (London: The Royal Asiatic Society, 1986), 7.42. Fernão Mendes Pinto, *Perigrinaçam* (Lisbon: Pedro Crasbeeck, 1614), sig. E3 (Ch. 37). Though Diogo do Couto suggests that the wreck was on the coast of Siam, this is clearly a mistake, as that version aligns neither with the shipping route between Macau and Goa nor with Camões' own version of events in the *Lusiads*.

5. *Lusiadas*, X.cxxviii. Babur, *The Baburnama: Memoirs of Babur, Prince and Emperor*, trans. Wheeler M. Thackston (New York:

Modern Library, 2002), 453; Thackston suggests in his introduction (xix) that this storm likely accounts for the loss of significant portions of the text.

6. 'Histoire du Procès au Palais des Dragons', in Nguyên Du, *Vaste Recueil de Légendes Merveilleuses*, trans. Nguyên-Tran-Huan (Paris: Gallimard/Unesco, 1962).The poems thought to refer to the drowning of Camões' Chinese mistress are 'Alma minha gentil que te partiste' and 'Ah, minha Dinamene! Assi deixaste', which is quoted and translated here. Camões continued this theme even after finishing the *Lusiads*, in (for example) the sonnet 'Vos Ninfas da Gangética espressura', which was written for the 1576 publication of Magalhães Gândavo's *História da Província de Sta Cruz*.

7. *The Boxer Codex*, 545, from which the translation is taken; Gaspar da Cruz, *Tractado em que se cōtam*, ch. i; Boxer, *South China*, 59–65.

8. *Lusiadas*, X.cxxvii, VII.xl. Gaspar da Cruz, *Tractado em que se cōtam*, sig. A[vi]ᵛ; translation taken from Boxer (ed.), *South China in the Sixteenth Century*, 61. See also Filippo Sassetti's letter to Ferdinando de' Medici (January 1584) on the same subject, which confirms the widespread use of Pythagoreanism to think through eastern religion: *Lettere da Vari Paesi*, 399–400. The Buddhist doctrine of reincarnation was seen as a central stumbling block to conversion in China, and Matteo Ricci's catechism *The True Meaning of the Lord of Heaven* shows his struggle to confront the idea; see Ricci, *True Meaning*, ch. 5; Laven, *Mission to China*, 209–10. For an example of shapeshifting narrative in sixteenth-century Viet literature, see the fifteenth story in Nguyên Du's *Vaste Recueil de Légendes Merveilleuses*, 'Histoire d'une Beuverie sur la Rivière Dà', which features a fox and a monkey who decide to become human students; see also Descola's discussion of animism and perspectivism, *Par-delà Nature et Culture*, 235–253, and Viveiros de Castro, *A Inconstancia da Alma Selvagem* (São Paulo, SP: Cosac & Naify, 2002).

9. *Monkey King: Journey to the West*, 31–2. For an excellent discussion on the theories of how the story of Sun Wukong might relate to the Hanuman of the *Ramayana*, see *The Journey to the West*, trans. Anthony Yu (Chicago: University of Chicago Press, 2012), I.10–11; as Yu points out, the continuity of spirit between human and animal was not shared by the Confucians, who saw ritual as what separated man from beast, a belief that perhaps helps further explain the

alignment of the Jesuits with the Confucians against the Buddhists in China.

10. *The Travels of Mendes Pinto*, ch. 73; *Alberuni's India*, 306–7; Nils Bubandt, 'Of wildmen and white men: cryptozoology and inappropriate/d monsters at the cusp of the Anthropocene', *Journal of the Royal Anthropological Institute*, 25/2 (2019), 223–40.

XV. The Land Behind the Wind

1. Damião published an account of the siege of Louvain as *Damiani Gois Equitis Lusitani Louaniensis Obsidio* (Lisbon: Luis Rodrigues, 1546); see also his letter to the king at ANTT PT/TT/CC/1/78/37. In another letter, from December 1571 and reproduced at *Inéditos*, II, 69–71, Damião mentions that he was passed over for the post of Master of the Wardrobe to Infante João in 1545. The story of the poor wise man is given at Ecclesiastes 9.14–16.

2. *The Book of Duarte Barbosa*, II.18. Dinis, 'Relatório', 127, for the prohibition against the scribes accessing the secret part of the archive and for the swearing-in ceremony. Zhang, 'Dang An', 31–2. On the birth of modern English record collections, mostly driven by Reformist zeal, see Nicholas Popper, 'From abbey to archive: managing texts and records in Early Modern England', in *Archival Science*, 10/3 (2010), 249–66. On the information published elsewhere in Europe, see Subrahmanyam, *Europe's India*, 49–52. On similar secrecy regarding documents at the Consejo de Indias in Spain, see Brendecke, *Arca, archivillo, archivo*, 271–2. On documents and the state, see Ernest Gellner, *Nations and Nationalism*, 2nd edn (Ithaca: Cornell University Press, 2006), especially p. 30. For further discussion of the 'conspiracy of silence', see ch. XVIII.

3. Damião wrote to the king on 20 July 1569 to report that there was no place in the Torre for sixty cases of documents sent to him by the king's secretary Pero de Alcaçova Carneiro, and the king wrote back on 27 December ordering the documents to be stored in the Camara do Rei Fernando in the Paço de Alcaçova; see ANTT PT/TT/CC/1/108/134. The document also commands Damião to sort and catalogue the documents, making clear that this was the common practice by that point: 'E aquela p[ar]te deles q ainda não temdes visto poreys em maços apartadas seg[undo] forem as materias de q tratarem e serão vistos p[ara]vos some[n]te pera

separardes os papeis e cartas q forem de segredo dos outros de menos calidade Dos quoaes papeis (depois deos verdes e co[n] tardes) fareis outra folha como a q ora me emvyastes e a declyvereis [*sic*]. A miguel de moura perase saber que papeis são pera quoando cu[m]prir a meu servyco verlhe algu[m] deles, e peraq[ue] lhe possão achar mais facylme[n]te quoando se buscarem numerareys os maços e em cada arca cofre e escrytoryo estara a folha dos papeis q tyves co[n] declaracão dos q estyveren em cada maço' ('And those parts of the documents which you have not yet reviewed you shall [now] put in separate packets according to the materials they treat and they will be seen by you alone in order that you can separate out the papers that are private from those of a lesser quality. For the which papers (after you have seen and checked them) you shall make another document like the one you are now sending me and deliver it to Miguel de Moura so that he may know what papers they are when he needs one of them for my service, and so that he can find them more easily when he is looking for them you should number the packets and in each chest, coffer and cabinet there will be a list of the papers in it with a declaration of what is in each packet.'). A letter of 14 April 1570, renewing a demand (apparently made several times before) for the inventory of these documents, makes clear that it was not completed by this point; see ANTT PT/ TT/GAV/22/3/6. Dinis, 'Relatório', 138, makes clear that by 1583 the documents had been sorted and locked away into 'armarios' and 'gavetas'. On early modern efforts to read tattoos, see Juliet Fleming, 'The Renaissance Tattoo', *Res* 31 (1997), 34–52, and Sebastian Kroupa, 'Reading Beneath the Skin: Indigenous Tattooing in the Early Modern Philippines, *c.*1520–1720', *American Historical Review*, 27 September 2021.

4. Damião's transcriptions of the letters of King Afonso of Kongo occupy *CM* III, sig. I5^r–K1^v; the source document for the 'Carta de obediência de D. Afonso, rei de Manicongo' is ANTT PT/TT/ CC/2/30/1, with a date and note of contents in what may be Damião's hand on the verso. On the king of Cochin, see *CM* I, sig. I7^r. On António Galvão's manuscript history of the Moluccas, bequeathed to Damião, see *A Treatise on the Moluccas (c.1544): Probably the preliminary version of António Galvao's lost 'História das Moluccas'*, ed. and trans. Hubert Jacobs (Rome: Jesuit Historical Institute, 1971).

5. On Monomotapa, see *CM* II, sig. B7ʳ–C1ᵛ; on Gujarat (Cambaya), *CM* III, sig. P3ʳ–[P5ʳ]; on Eleni, *CM* III, sig. O[7]ᵛ; on the king of Kongo's sister, *CM* IV, sig. A4ʳ⁻ᵛ. As well as using the documents in the Torre do Tombo and travel accounts like those of Barbosa and Pires, Damião may also have had access to certain Asian sources, either directly or through his friend João de Barros; Barros consistently refers to the Chinese, Arab and Persian documents which he used as things which 'we' have had translated, suggesting that these sources were not exclusively translated for or used by him. See Subrahmanyam, *Europe's India*, 73–8. The erosion of royal centrality by focus on other things bears relation to a similar process studied in Richard Helgerson's *Forms of Nationhood: The Elizabethan Writing of England* (Chicago: University of Chicago Press, 1992); the openness to other cultures had been modelled by previous works, such as the *Omnium gentium mores* (1520) of Hans Böhm (on which see Marcocci, *Globe on Paper*, 86–98, where he points out the obvious influence of Böhm on Damião's 1545 Ethiopian tract), but its integration into a project of national history was relatively new.

6. *CM* I, sig. C1ʳ and sig. O[1]ᵛ–O3ᵛ; see Marcocci, 'Remembering the Forced Baptism of the Jews', for the relation of Damião's account to broader debates about the legitimacy of the forced conversion of the Jews in 1497; as Marcocci points out, Damião may even have drawn on a Jewish account of these events in the form of Samuel Usque's *Consolations for the Tribulations of Israel* (Ferrara, 1553). The second part of Damião's *CM* ends with the death of Francisco d'Almeida, the first governor of India, in a confrontation at Saldanha near the Cape of Good Hope (*CM* II, sig. I7ʳ–K3ᵛ), which death Damião blamed on d'Almeida's 'irrational violence' during previous victories, most notably the atrocities during the campaigns against Dabul and Diu (*CM* II, sig. H6ʳ–I4ᵛ); the third part ends with the abandonment of Albuquerque by the king, despite Damião's feeling that he deserved better from the king for his service in India (*CM* III, sig. R8ʳ–[S2]ʳ).

7. On hosting foreigners, see *Inéditos*, I, 99–101. Damião's setting of 'Surge, propera amica mea' was published in Sigmund Salminger's *Cantiones Septem, sex et quinque vocum* (Augsburg: Melchior Kriegstein, 1545); his motet 'Nec laeteris inimica mea' was included in Henricus Glaureanus' *Dodecachordon* (Basel: Heinrich Petri,

1547). Petrus Nannius, *Orationes Tres* (Louvain: Rutger Rescius, 1541), sig. Biv^{r-v}. Damião may have been inspired in this line of thought by the ancient Greek word *kelados*, which can mean a rushing of water, a musical sound, a birdsong or a clamour. On Hans Pelque (Johannes von Pelken), see also Damião's letter to the Senate of Gdansk promising to represent their interests in Portugal (*Cartas Latinas*, 220/378).

8. For an example of Leonardo's writings on water, see *Leonardo da Vinci's Codex Leicester: A New Edition*, ed. Domenico Laurenza and Martin Kemp (Oxford: Oxford University Press, 2019), vol. 3, fols. 4^v–6^v.

9. The comparison of history to a river is inspired in part by the *Kathāsaritsāgara* (Confluence of the Rivers of History), an eleventh-century Kashmiri work by Somadeva.

XVI. The Tale of the Tribe

1. Diogo do Couto, *Decadas da India*, VIII, ch. xxviii; Camões is also said to have written the poem 'Amado Couto meo' at this period, though the poem is excluded from many modern collections on grounds of inauthenticity (see *Dicionário*, 90). The fort on the island of Mozambique had been built in 1558, replacing Sofala as the main centre of operations in the region. See João dos Santos, *Ethiopia Oriental*, fol. 78^{r-v}, and (on the building of the fort in Mozambique) ANTT PT/TT/CC/1/100/1. *Lusiadas*, X.viii–ix.

2. *Lusiadas*, I.xxvii, liii, xlix. For a recent comparative account of the *Lusiads* in the context of early modern epic and globalisation, see Ayesha Ramachandran, *The Worldmakers: Global Imagining in Early Modern Europe* (Chicago: University of Chicago Press, 2015), ch. 3.

3. *Lusiadas*, I.i, V.iv.

4. *Lusiadas*, II.xxxi, VII.lxvii.

5. *Lusiadas*, I.xxxiii, xxxv.

6. *Lusiadas*, V.xxxix, II.xviii, VI.lxxxvi.

7. *Lusiadas*, IX.lxxv. The classic account of the sexual psychology of colonisation is given in Edward Said's *Orientalism* (London: Routledge & Kegan Paul, 1978), especially ch. 2, pt IV.

8. *Lusiadas*, IX.xxv.

9. *Lusiadas*, VII.xl–xli. J. H. Cunha Rivara (ed.), *Archivo Portuguez-Oriental* (New Delhi: Asian Educational Services, 1992), 6.725–6; quoted in Mendonça, *Conversions and Citizenry*, 421–3. *The Book of*

Duarte Barbosa, 104 (on the punishment of sodomy in Hormuz);
Pires, *Suma Oriental*, 23 (on same-sex relations in Persia); Laven,
Mission to China, 180-2.

10. *Dicionário*, 90.

XVII. When I Sit in Darkness

1. *Inéditos*, II, 31. The question as to what extent Damião's testimony
   in his Inquisition process should be seen as evidence that he had
   Protestant sympathies or not has been discussed at length in
   Bataillon, *Études sur le Portugal au temps de l'humanisme*; Aubin,
   Latin et l'Astrolabe, I.211–35; Hirsch, *Damião de Gois*.

2. *Inéditos*, II, 31–5.

3. *Inéditos*, II, 35–71.

4. *Inéditos*, II, 42, 46–8, 101. Edgar Prestage, *Critica contemporanea á
   Chronica de D. Manuel de Damião de Goes. (Itemis comtra os eros da
   Chronica.) MS. do Museu Britanico publicado e anotado por Edgar
   Prestage* (Lisbon: s.n., 1914). On the political stakes of chronicling
   in early modern Spain, see Brendecke, *Arca, archivillo, archivo*,
   273–8.

5. *Inéditos*, II, 38.

6. *Inéditos*, II, 39.

7. *Inéditos*, II, 52–5.

8. *Inéditos*, II, 5–10, 69–71.

9. *Inéditos*, II, 12–13. Simão Rodrigues to Loyola, 18 March 1546,
   ARSI, Antica Compagnia, Epp.NN.58, fol. 358r.

10. *Inéditos*, II, 15–18.

11. The formula, repeated throughout the trial, asks witnesses 'se hera
    lembrada ver ou ouvir dizer ou fazer a algūa pessoa algūa cousa que
    lhe parecesse contra notra sacta fee catholica e contra o que tem e
    ensina a sancta madre igreja, ou de qu se escandalizasse …'; see, for
    instance, *Inéditos*, II, 23. The manuscript documents of the trial are
    not in chronological order, although most are dated, and so a
    chronological order can be followed; the first set of accusations of
    various witnesses come before Damião's testimony and the
    publication of charges in the manuscripts of the trial (*Inéditos*, II,
    17–31), but date from 5 May to 1 July 1571, after the publication of
    charges on 2 May.

12. *Inéditos*, II, 23–5.

13. *Inéditos*, II, 29–30.

14. *Inéditos*, II, 56–71.
15. *Inéditos*, II, 91–9.
16. *Inéditos*, II, 103–17. Damião had in fact complained about this drain as early 1549; see his letter to the king of 15 February 1549, ANTT PT/TT/CC/1/82/000053.
17. *Inéditos*, II, 114–17, 123–5. The quotation is from Psalm 119.51–5.
18. *Inéditos*, II, 126–9.

XVIII. All Our Scattered Leaves

1. The evidence for any patronage and rewards that Camões received between his return in 1570 and his death is mixed. An *alvará* of 28 July 1572 shows that the king gave him a pension of 15,000 *reais* in return for the book he wrote 'on India' (presumably the *Lusiads*) and other services; this document, the renewals and disbursements of the pension throughout the 1570s, and the document mentioning his death on 10 June 1580, are usefully transcribed alongside facsimiles of the originals in José Perreira da Costa, 'Luís de Camões … e Outros', in *Luís de Camões no seu tempo e na actualidade* (Lisbon: Academia Portuguesa da História, 2005), 181–225. There are other suggestions of patronage – including the commissioning of a portrait, perhaps by the Conde de Vimioso, and the dedication of a sonnet to Dom Manuel, in which Camões refers to him as a 'mecenas' or patron – yet these suggestions are contradicted by reports that he died impoverished and in obscurity. On Camões' later influence, see George Monteiro, *The Presence of Camões* (Louisville, KY: University of Kentucky Press, 1966); Catarina Caldeira Martins, 'Friedrich Schlegel e Camões', in *Actas da VI Reunião Internacional de Camonistas* (Coimbra: University of Coimbra Press, 2012).
2. The idea of neoclassicism as a form of play-acting has a long critical history (see Mario Praz, *Gusto Neoclassico* (Firenze: s.n., 1940/*On Neoclassicism*, trans. Angus Davidson (Thames & Hudson, 1969)),though the solemnity with which it was undertaken is perhaps best understood in the context of the imperialism it accompanied and underwrote. Though the awareness of Arabic culture – to take one example – was far wider than has often been recognised, it nevertheless was not (is not) the case that Arabic materials were integrated into environments (school curricula, histories, etc.) where they could be read alongside European ones,

and that this was even more the case for other non-European languages suggests that it was not wholly anti-Islamic sentiment that was to blame; see John-Paul Ghobrial, 'The Archive of Orientalism and its Keepers: Re-imagining the Histories of Arabic Manuscripts in Early Modern Europe' (*Past and Present* supplementary issue 2016), and Bevilacqua's *Republic of Arabic Letters*. For the wider history of attempts to counteract this in the early modern period, see Marcocci, *Globe on Paper*, where this is discussed in the introduction; the course of turning from an openness to other cultures to antagonism is charted throughout the book. Non-European contributions to European thought tended to be anonymised when they were integrated; the desire to maintain this separation is amply demonstrated by the manoeuvres to isolate parts of Greek culture from the east. This has begun to be remedied by projects like Donald F. Lach's monumental *Asia in the Making of Europe* series; see Viveiros de Castro, *The Relative Native*, 75–94, on anthropology and decolonisation. See also Strathern, *Unearthly Powers*, 37 and 49, on the alignment between immanentist ritual and modern secular values, and on the positioning of transcendentalism against the relativism of the world.

3. Xavier da Cunha, *Uma carta inedita de Camões* (Coimbra: Imprensa da Universidade, 1904). Introduction, 7–8, followed by da Cunha's transcription of the letter in BNP COD. 8571, on 9–23. The translations here are lightly adapted from those in Willis, *Camões*, 267.

4. See, for instance, Isabel dos Guimarães Sá and Máximo García Fernández (eds.), *Portas Adentro: Comer, vestir e habitar na Península Iberica (ss. xvi–xix)* (Coimbra: Imprensa da Universidade, 2010), 76, and Sheila Moura Hue, *Delícias do descobrimento: a gastronomia brasileira no século XVI* (Rio de Janeiro: Zahar, 2009), 82, discussing the 'marmeladas' being sent to Brazil by the Lisbon Jesuits.

5. Friedrich, 'Archives as networks', 291; Bento Rodrigues, *Tractado historico, critico e apologetico da vida de V. P. Mestre Simão Rodrigues* (ANTT PT/TT/AC/M021.01-00006), 295–9. The account given there suggests that Simão was in Coimbra in September and after that undertook a visitation of all the Jesuit foundations in Portugal (299). As pointed out by Eduardo Javier Alonso Romo, the letter printed in the Jesuit *Monumenta* dated 18 January 1574

cannot be by Simão, as he can be placed in Portugal at that time; see 'El legado escrito de Simão Rodrigues', in *A Companhia de Jesus na Península Ibérica nos sécs. XVI e XVII: Espirualidade e Cultura*, Actas do Colóquio Internacional, Maio 2004 (Porto: Universidade de Porto, 2004), 79.

6. The most likely source for the information in Mylius' biography was Jerónimo Osório, the translator of Damião's chronicle of the reign of Manuel into Latin; the second and subsequent editions of the translation were printed in Cologne by Birckmann (starting in 1574), who seems with Mylius to have written the life of Damião. However, the information may also have come from the correspondence network of Christophe Plantin, who was in regular contact both with numerous sources in Lisbon and also with the publisher of the life, Mylius (see, for instance, Christophe Plantin to Arnold Mylius, 20 January 1575, *Correspondance de Christophe Plantin*, ed. M. Rooses and J. Denucé (Antwerp: J. E. Buschmann, 1883–1918) IV.235–6). Birckmann may also have had a direct link to Damião, as the seventeenth-century antiquarian Manuel Severim de Faria reports another book printed in Cologne in 1562 with an early biography of Damião, which may have been by Birckmann; see de Faria, 'Vidas de Portugueses Ilustres', fol. 74^{r-v}. The anecdotal account of Damião's death in Biblioteca de Ajuda 51-IX-22, fol. 130^{r-v}, is intended to illustrate the idea that 'death by fire awaits those to whom fate has allotted it'; the anecdote also recounts how he was discovered burned by his servants, and so suggests that the account discovered by Vieira da Sousa was already circulating before the mid-seventeenth century.

7. The quotation is from the 'Apology for Raymond Sebond'. See also Descola on Montaigne's treatment of animals as an important dissenting voice to European naturalism: *Par-delà Nature et Culture*, 306–8. On the relationship between the writings of Damião and Jerónimo Osório, see António Guimarães Pinto, 'Damião de Góis e D. Jerónimo Osório: A *Crónica de D. Manuel e o De rebus Emmanuelis gestis*', in *Damião de Góis na Europa do Renascimento* (Braga: Universidade Católica Portuguesa, 2003), 307–48. On historiographical changes in the seventeenth century which led to a centring of Europe, see Marcocci, *Globe on Paper*, ch. 5. Examples of Montaigne's use of Damião's writing (through the medium of Osório and of Simon Goulart, the French translator of Osório)

include his discussion of the treatment of the Jews in 'The Taste of Good and Evil Things Depends on Our Opinion', which corresponds to *CM* I, sig. B[1]^r; the description of the Tupinambá people in 'On the Cannibals', which draws on *CM* I, sig. Giiii^v–Gvii^v; of the Dioscorides (i.e. Socotra) in 'On Prayer', which draws on *CM* II, sig. E6^r; the account of the Indian caste system in 'On Some Lines of Virgil', which is based on *CM* I, sig. E6^v; his discussion of the self-immolation of Ninachetu, the local agent of the Portuguese in Malacca, in 'On a Custom of the Isle of Cea', which draws on *CM* III, sig. P3^r; etc.

8. Damião also supplied maps on parchment and a globe to Lazaro Buonamico (see the 1539 letter to him in Damião's *Opuscula* of 1544), which may have entered the orbit of Ramusio as well. Ramusio recounts his acquisition of the manuscript of Francisco Álvares' description of Ethiopia in the third edition of the first volume of the *Navigazzione e Viaggi* (Venice: Giunti, 1563), fol. 176^r, where he says that his printer, Giunti, sought Damião out 'nell'estreme parti di Holanda', which means that they were in contact at least before Damião's return to Portugal in 1545. Skelton and Parks (*Gian Battista Ramusio*, introduction, viii), suggest that Damião was the source of some of the Portuguese documents related to the navigations to India, and that these were supplied to Ramusio late in the printing process; and indeed the curious mention of Damião's account of the siege of Diu as 'una minima particella rispetto a quello che l'huomo desidereria di leggere' ('a tiny part of what men might want to read [about the Indies]': *Primo Volume delle navigationi et viaggi*, fol. 129^r) makes little sense unless it is an instance of authorial modesty carried over from Damião's own correspondence with Ramusio. Ramusio also says that he was having the manuscript of Barbosa copied in Lisbon (*Primo volume delle navigationi et viaggi*, fol. 310^r) but does not mention by whom; we know, however, that he was in contact with Damião, and that Damião had a copy of the Barbosa, making this perhaps the most likely source for Ramusio's Lisbon copy; Ramusio's complaint that the power of princes was to blame for the difficulty of securing the texts makes most sense in the context of documents in the archive, which could be released only with the written permission of the king (Dinis, 'Relatório', 156). It is possible that it was also Damião who formed the conduit between João de Barros and Ramusio,

allowing Ramusio to republish selections of the *Primeira Década* only two years after its initial publication. Aubin (*Latin et l'Astrolabe*, I.192) downplays the differences between the printed Lisbon edition of Álvares and the manuscript supplied by Damião to Ramusio, though his willingness to supply it still attests to his desire to promulgate information about the world. The manuscript of Barbosa from the Hernandine Library in Seville – which seems to have been Ramusio's control text and is, to my knowledge, hitherto unknown – survives today as Biblioteca Colombina 7-5-11, *Declaración y relación de la India y de sus reinos y señoríos*, though the manuscript there is attributed to one Juan de Acosta, which may cast doubt on the attribution to Barbosa (even if it is more likely that the Portuguese manuscript was copied for Hernando's use at the Junta de Badajoz, which would explain its influence on the world maps of Diego Ribeiro, who worked under Hernando's direction at the Casa de Contratación); Dames sees the presence of Barbosa in Ribeiro's 1529 world map (*Book of Duarte Barbosa*, liii). For the later history of this openness to the wider world, see M. C. Jacob, *Strangers Nowhere in the World: The Rise of Cosmopolitanism in Early Modern Europe* (Philadelphia: University of Pennsylvania Press, 2006); for a comparative global perspective, see Sanjay Subrahmanyam, 'The Hidden Face of Surat: Reflections on a Cosmopolitan Indian Ocean Centre, 1540–1750', *Journal of the Economic and Social History of the Orient*, 61/1–2 (2018), 207–57. Marcocci, 'Remembering the Forced Baptism of the Jews', 333–4. A good example of Montaigne's relativist legacy can be seen in Stefan Zweig's *Montaigne* (1942).

9. Levathes, *When China Ruled the Seas*, 179–80. On Spanish plans to create a secret archive containing matters related to the Indies, see Brendecke, *Arca, archivillo, archivo*, 269; also Laura Fernandez-Gonzalez, 'The Architecture of the Treasure-Archive: The Archive at Simancas Fortress, 1540–1569', in Bernardo J. García García and Vanessa de Cruz Medina (eds.), *FELIX AUSTRIA: Lazos Familiares, cultura politica, y mecenazgo artistico entre las Cortes de los Habsburgo* (Madrid: Fundación Carlos de Amberes, 2013). On oral history in the Moluccas, see Barros, *Décadas da Ásia* III.v.5; Jacobs (ed. and trans.), *A Treatise on the Moluccas*, 85; and Marcocci, *Globe on Paper*, 59–61.

LIST OF ILLUSTRATIONS

Maps

A map of the principal locations visited by Damião de Góis.

A map showing the route of Vasco da Gama's first voyage to India, as well as sites associated with Luís Vaz de Camões.

In-text images

Map of Lisbon by Braun and Hogenberg, from *Civitates Orbis Terrarum*, possibly based on Damião's description (Cologne, 1612–18). (Album/Alamy Stock Photo)

'Rhinoceros', by Albrecht Dürer, a posthumous portrait of the rhinoceros Damião saw in Lisbon in 1515. (Courtesy of the National Gallery of Art, Washington)

Portrait of Luís de Camões later in life, likely by Fernão Gomes, c.1573–5. (The Picture Art Collection/Alamy Stock Photo)

Working with documents at the end of the fifteenth century: an image of the translator Jean Miélot, secretary to the Duke of Burgundy. (Album/Alamy Stock Photo)

Illuminated title page from the *Livro das Ilhas*. (Arquivo Nacional Torre do Tombo, Lisbon, Leitura Nova, liv. 36)

Portrait of Katherina, by Albrecht Dürer, 1521, Uffizi Gallery, Florence. (The Picture Art Collection/Alamy Stock Photo)

Portrait of Damião de Góis, by Albrecht Dürer or follower, Vienna, Albertine Museum. (© Purix Verlag Volker Christen/Bridgeman Images)

Plates from the *Carta Marina et Descriptio Septentrionalium Terrarum Ac Mirabilium Rerum In Eis Contentarum Diligentissime Elaborata*

Anno Dni 1539, by Olaus Magnus. (© NPL – DeA Picture Library/
M. Seemuller/Bridgeman Images)

Jason Returning with the Golden Fleece by Ugo da Carpi (1480–1532).
(Library of Congress, Prints and Photographs Division, LC-DIG-
ppmsca-18714)

Evangelium Lucae am XVI cap by Hanns Lautensack, c.1556. (© The
Trustees of the British Museum)

A Portuguese man and unmarried Indian Christian women, from the
Codex Casanatense, Biblioteca Casanatense Ms. 1889 (*Album di
disegni, illustranti usi e costumi dei popoli d'Asia e d'Africa con brevi
dichiarazioni in lingua portoghese*), c. 94.

Section of the *Tabula Peutingeriana*, the only surviving copy of the
Roman road map, showing India and the area east of the Caspian
Sea.

Image of a Tatar couple from the *Boxer Codex* (c.1590).

Image of Indian Gods from the *Codex Casanatense* (*Album di disegni,
illustranti usi e costumi dei popoli d'Asia e d'Africa con brevi
dichiarazioni in lingua portoghese*) (Su concessione della Biblioteca
Casanatense, Roma, MiC)

Camões in Prison, Museu Nacional de Arte Antiga, Lisbon.
(Christophel Fine Art/Universal Images Group via Getty Images)

Map showing Guangzhou, from an Atlas of the Ming Empire (c.1547–
1559). (Library of Congress, Geography and Map Division, G2305.
D3 1559)

Bird on Tree (Haha-chō), attributed to Shūkō (active 1504–20).
(Metropolitan Museum of Art, The Howard Mansfield Collection,
Purchase, Rogers Fund, 1936)

Mazu saving the Chinese fleet during a storm, from a seventeenth-
century compilation of the Miracles of Mazu.

Portrait of Erasmus by Hans Holbein, produced as a print by Johannes
Froben, 1538. (AlFA Visuals/Alamy Stock Photo)

The portrait of Erasmus by Dürer that Damião kept in a locked coffer
until the end of his life. (Artefact/Alamy Stock Photo)

Frontispiece to Andreas Vesalius', *De Humani Corporis Fabrica*, by John
of Calcar (Basel: Johannes Oporinus, 1543). (Classic Image/Alamy
Stock Photo)

Plate section

Adoration of the Magi (1501–6) by the Portuguese painter Grão Vasco. (Bridgeman Images)

A sixteenth century painting of one of Lisbon's busiest streets, the Rua Nova dos Mercadores (Merchants' New Street)

The Battle of Mohács (1526), between Hungary and the Ottomans, as depicted in the Ottoman visual epic, the *Süleymanname*, from 1558. (CPA Media Pte Ltd/Alamy Stock Photo)

The 'Robinson Casket', produced in Kotte, Ceylon, c.1557. (Marie-Lan Nguyen)

A sixteenth-century ivory salt cellar produced in Benin for the Portuguese market. (Bridgeman Images)

Screen, c.1600, by Kano Naizen showing the arrival of the Namban (Southern Barbarians, i.e. the Portuguese) into a Japanese port. (Kobe City Museum/DNPartcom)

Triptych of the Temptation of Saint Anthony by Hieronymus Bosch. (Bridgeman Images)

INDEX

Abrahamic faiths, 136, 146, 162,
208–9, 224, 230, 247 *see
also* entries for individual
faiths
Aden, 68, 112
Afonso, King of Kongo, 216
Africa: the Banu Saadi in, 32;
Butua kingdom, 73–4; the
Cape, 4, 69, 71, 72, 74, 227–8;
culture as still unfamiliar to
most Europeans, 5; de Sousa
episode, 74–7; goods from in
Lisbon, 15, 16, 17; kingdom of
the Monomotapa, 73, 217; the
Maghreb, 4, 31–2, 44, 45, 216;
in Pereira's *Esmeraldo de Situ
Orbis*, 40; Portuguese arrival in
south-east/east, 72–80;
Portuguese presence in North
Africa, 4, 9, 31–2, 35, 134;
Portuguese ships move down
west coast, 9, 32, 69–71; Sao
Jorge da Mina fortress, 40;
slaves from, 18–20, 52–5;
sub-Saharan, 40; Tafuf and Hali
in Safi, 43–5, 216; Wattasid

sultans of Fez, 32; western
African art, 17
alcohol, 88–9, 91–2, 116–17, 122,
125–6, 131, 151, 157–8
Alexander the Great, 114, 115,
124, 143, 144, 202
Alexandria, 15, 78, 102, 112, 114,
119, 120, 204
Álvares, Francisco, 255
Amsterdam, 15, 46
anatomy, 170–1, 193–7, *195*
Angola, 69
animals: animist beliefs in east,
82–3, 146–8, 207–9, 230; and
anthropocentrism, 146, 207–9,
254; arrival at Lisbon's docks,
17; and Galen's anatomy, 196–7;
goshawks (*acores*), 46; Indian
relationship with, 146, 147–8,
208, 230; in Japanese art, *159*,
161; rhinoceros and elephant
contest, 17–18, 147
Antenor, 185
anthropocentrism, assumptions of,
146, 208–9, 254
anthropology, 248

Magnus, 60, *62–3*; map of Piri
Reis, 115; maps of Fernao Vaz
Dourado, 139–40; in Ming
China, *154–5*; Ottoman, 115;
Renaissance maps, 139–40;
Tabula Peutingeriana, 120, *121*
Caspian Sea, 119, 120, 126
Catarina (daughter of Damião),
85, 239–40
Catholic Church: catalogues of
forbidden books (Library of the
Damned), 132, 181–2, 220, 234,
235; Council of Trent, 198, 242;
Cristaos Velhos (Old
Christians), 29–30, 218; and
Damião in Padua, 98, 171, 180,
183–4, 186, 188; dietary laws/
calendar, 50–1, 86, 87–8,
89–91, 94, 98–9, 128, 171, 184,
234–5, 239–40; and Eastern
Church, 124; and Erasmus,
90–1, 169–70, 171–2, 179, 188;
exiled heads of Swedish
Church, 60–1; growing
intolerance in Louvain, 169–70;
irenic party in Rome, 188–90,
192–3; language of crusade
against the Reformers, 192; and
Lisbon's demi-monde, 27, 28,
30–1; and luxuriant global
marketplace, 32; Moors and
Jews as Christian converts,
29–31, 108, 218; pilgrims' route
to Santiago de Compostela, 49;
Portuguese use of polyphony,
58, 179; Prester John legend,
66, 115–16, 134; proposed
papal council at Mantua,
188–92, 198; and Vicente's

Guerta de Jubileu, 131–2, 181
see also Jesuits
cave writings, 204–5
Centurione, Paolo, 119–20, 122
Ceuta, northern Africa, 9, 31–2,
35
Ceylon, 104, 136
Champa, kingdom of, 156, 206
Charles V, Emperor, 49, 78, 130–1
China: archivists in legends, 3;
cartography, *154–5*; civil
servants in, 199–200; closed
doors to Europeans, 256;
colonial ambitions, 115;
culture, 153, 164–7, *166*,
199–201, 209, 253, 256; feelings
of cultural superiority, 256;
geography of, 152, 156–7;
goods from in Lisbon, 16–17;
Great Wall, 156–7; imperial
archive, 213–14, 215; Jesuits in,
128, 153, 164, 213, 250;
merchants from, 151–2;
meritocratic nature of state,
199–200; and notions of time,
162; Pires in, 42, 152; porcelain,
16–17, 20, 72; Portugal's first
expedition to, 152–3; same-sex
relations in, 231; ships visit East
Africa, 72–3; silk robes in, 126;
temple of A-Ma, 164–5, 206,
253; trade with Japan, 153, 157,
163; Xavier's mission to, 134,
153
Christianity: Adam's footprint in
Ceylon, 136; and animist
beliefs, 82–3, 146–8, 207–9,
230; Armenian Church, 135,
177; and Copernicus' theory,

vast river estuary, 15; visitors from beyond Christian Europe, 20–2, 65–8, 176–8 *see also* Torre do Tombo, Lisbon

Lithuania, 59–60, 64, 122, 128

Livonia, 122

Livy (Roman historian), 185

Llull, Ramon, 205

London, 59, 214

Lores (in Armenia), 114

Louvain, University of, 88, 98, 169–71, 186, 193, 211

Lovati, Lovato, 185

Loyola, Ignatius, 33, 50, 133–4, 183, 184, 186–7, 192, 238, 251; and Damião in Padua, 186, 188, 240

Luis, Tibaldo, 219

Lusiads ('Song of the Portuguese,' Luis Vaz de Camões): Adamastor (Untamed Man) in, 227–8; as archetype for the colonial fantasy, 227–30, 247, 254; and attitudes to animals in the east, 146, 208, 230; autobiographical sections, 70–1; captivity described in, 25; claim of as cave writing, 204–5; de Sousa episode in, 74–7; drowned Chinese lover in, 205–6; eastern sexuality in, 230, 231; in elect library of drowned books, 203–5; encounters with established trade world, 72–4; as epic of forgetting, 224–7; erasure of eastern culture in, 143, 144–5, 226–8; finishing off of at Mozambique, 223, 224; Great Wall described in, 156–7;

introduction and notes to 1613 edition, 248–9; Island of Love in, 228–9, 231; and lack of heroism in seafaring life, 71–2; Mekong delta in, 207; Herman Melville on, 71; pagan classical deities in, 226–7, 228, 253; plea for a place of safety in, 167–8; portrayal of Muslims in, 225–6, 228, 247; publishing of, 246; and route to Macau, 156; scene in the temple at Calicut, 82–3; Schlegel admires, 117, 246; sea disasters in, 201–2, 203–4; vision of heroic nationalism in, 77, 143, 224–8, 247, 254

Lusus, mythical figure, 25

Luther, Martin, 92–5, 96–7, 129, 180, 183, 233, 235, 241; Erasmus criticised by, 171; writing on Ecclesiastes, 184, 237, 239; writings in catalogue of forbidden books, 181

Macau, 153, 156, 157, 163–8, 199, 201, 204–6, 225, 249

Machiavelli, Niccolò, 124

Madagascar, 72

Madeira, 50

the Maghreb, 4, 31–2, 44, 45, 216

magnolia trees, 101

Magnus, Johannes, Bishop of Uppsala, 48, 60, 64, 65–6, 89, 190

Magnus, Olaus, 60, 64, 65–6, 89, 107, 123, 161–2, 256; *Carta Marina* of, 60, *62–3*; *Description of the Northern Peoples*, 60–1

Pomponius Mela, 48
porcelain and chinaware, 16–17,
20, 72
Pori, island of, Maharashtra
('Elephanta'), 136–7, 144, 145
Portugal: capture of Ceuta (1415),
9, 31; capture of Safi in
Morocco, 43–5, 216;
foundation of (1139), 4, 9;
'golden age,' 9; goods from the
east, 15, 16–17; and hatred of
the Muslim enemy, 31; Mughal
view of Europeans as dirty, 102;
posthumous fame of Camoes,
245–7, 248–9; Spain's
annexation of (1580–1640),
246, 256–7; war in the Maghreb
(from 1415), 4, 31–2 see also
Lisbon
Portugal's exploration/overseas
ventures: Camões' vision of
heroic nationalism, 77, 143,
224–8, 247, 254; Carreira da
India (Route to the Indies), 43,
69–80, 102; China-Japan trade,
153, 157, 163; and Chinese
merchants, 151–2; the
'conspiracy of silence,' 43, 214,
255; degredados in fleet, 35–6;
eastern view of the Portuguese,
102, 112–13, 117, 150–1,
209–10; Estado (domain in
India), 107–8, 149–50; faithless
treatment of local allies, 43–5,
102–3, 112, 151, 225–6; first
expedition to mainland China,
152–3; forts along rim of
western Indian Ocean, 112–14;
Italian attack on control of

spice trade, 119–20, 122; Livro
das Ilhas (Book of the Islands),
39, 41; Malacca as centre in
southeast Asia, 42; move east to
Malacca, 150–2; opening of
trade/travel routes, 5, 9, 43; and
the Ottoman Turks, 114–16;
playing off of local powers
against each other, 43–5, 103,
112, 216; Portugal as Europe's
conduit with wider world, 4–5,
9; Portugal's weakness in east,
72–3, 102–3, 143; Portuguese
brutality, 112–13; and religion
in India, 80–3, 106–8, 145, 225;
and Shah Ismail of Persia,
116–17, 119 see also Goa
Portuguese royal archive: archivist
writes official chronicles, 9–10,
42–6, 212, 214, 215–18, 220–1,
236, 255; classified material in,
214; the 'conspiracy of silence,'
43, 214, 255; Damião becomes
Guarda-mor of, 211, 212; death
of Damião (1574), 1–2; and
dependence on the written
record, 212–13; diverse
purposes of, 6–7; holdings
protected from Napoleon, 6;
holdings taken to Brazil, 6;
pilfered by the Spanish, 6 see
also Torre do Tombo, Lisbon
Postel, Guillaume, 128, 192
Prester John, 66, 115–16, 134
printing in China, 200
Protestant Reformation, 60, 64,
89–90, 91, 92–5, 96–7, 183–4;
'Affaire des Placards,' 180, 186;
allegiance to the local over the